Oh My Goddess!

ああっ女神さまっ　Mara Strikes Back!

PUBLISHER
Mike Richardson

SERIES EDITOR
Dave Chipps

COLLECTION EDITOR
Chris Warner

COLLECTION DESIGNERS
Amy Arendts & Julie Eggers Gassaway

ART DIRECTOR
Mark Cox

English-language version produced by Studio Proteus
for Dark Horse Comics, Inc.

OH MY GODDESS! Volume VI: Mara Strikes Back

This book collects issues six through eight of the Dark Horse comic-book series *Oh My Goddess!
Part IV* and issues one and two of the Dark Horse comic-book series *Oh My Goddess! Part V*.

Published by
Dark Horse Comics, Inc.
10956 SE Main Street
Milwaukie, OR 97222

www.darkhorse.com

First edition: April 2000
ISBN: 1-56971-449-5

1 3 5 7 9 10 8 6 4 2
Printed in Canada

Oh My Goddess!

ああっ女神さま　Mara Strikes Back!

STORY AND ART BY

Kosuke Fujishima

TRANSLATION BY

Dana Lewis & Toren Smith

LETTERING AND TOUCH-UP BY

Susie Lee & PC Orz

DARK HORSE COMICS®

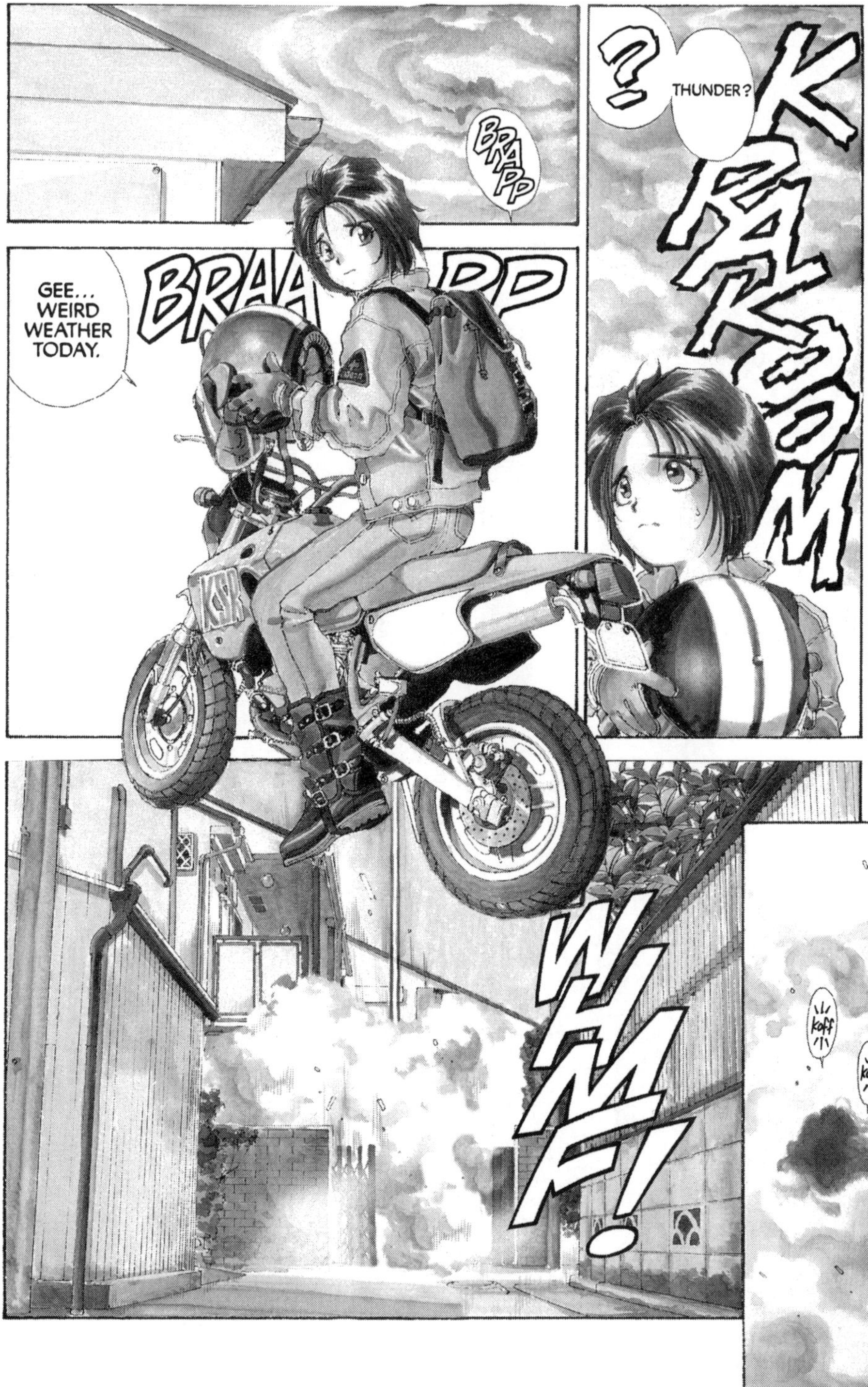
BRAPP
GEE... WEIRD WEATHER TODAY.
BRAA PP
?
THUNDER?
KRAKOOM
WHMF!
koff
koff

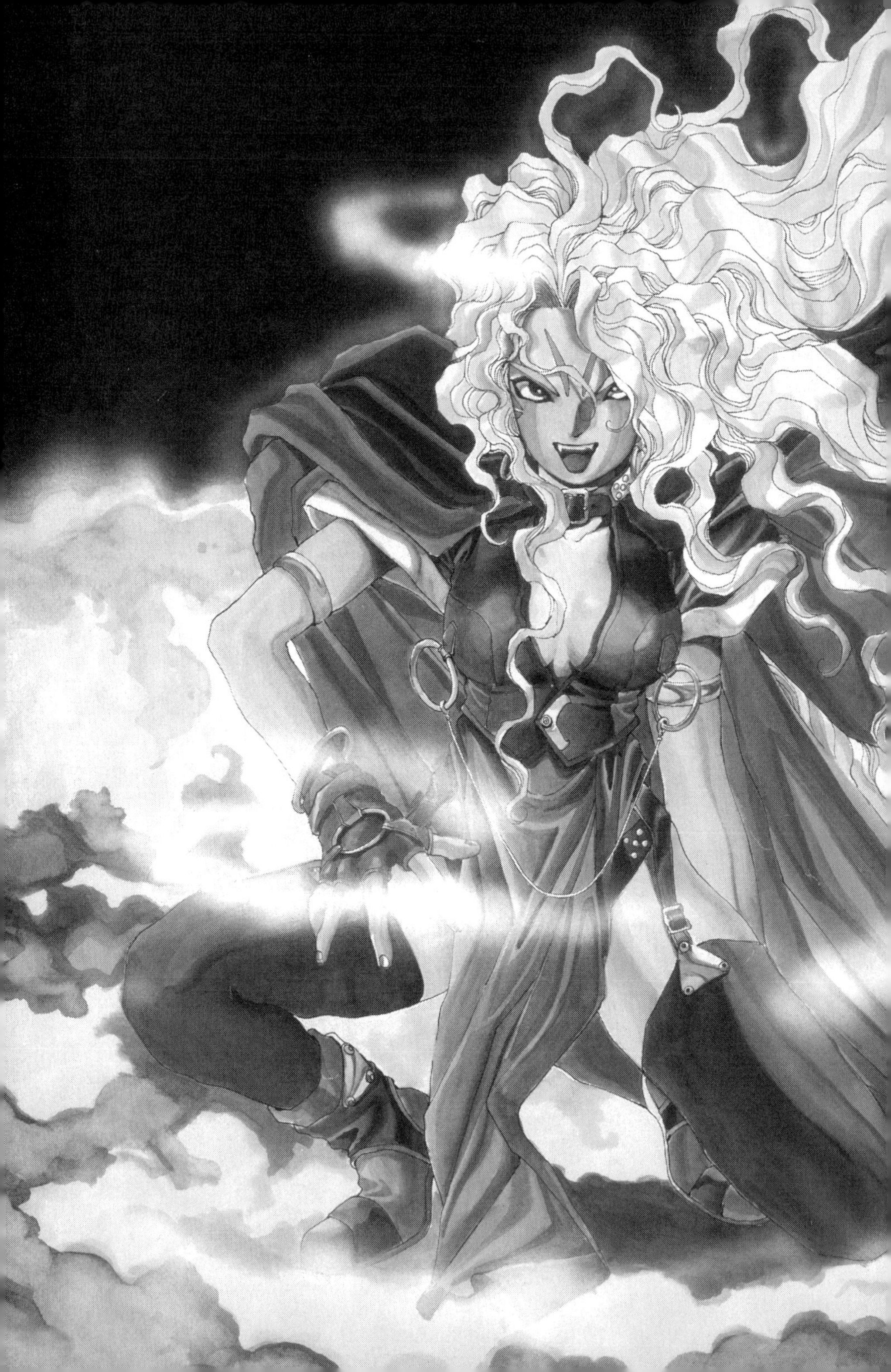

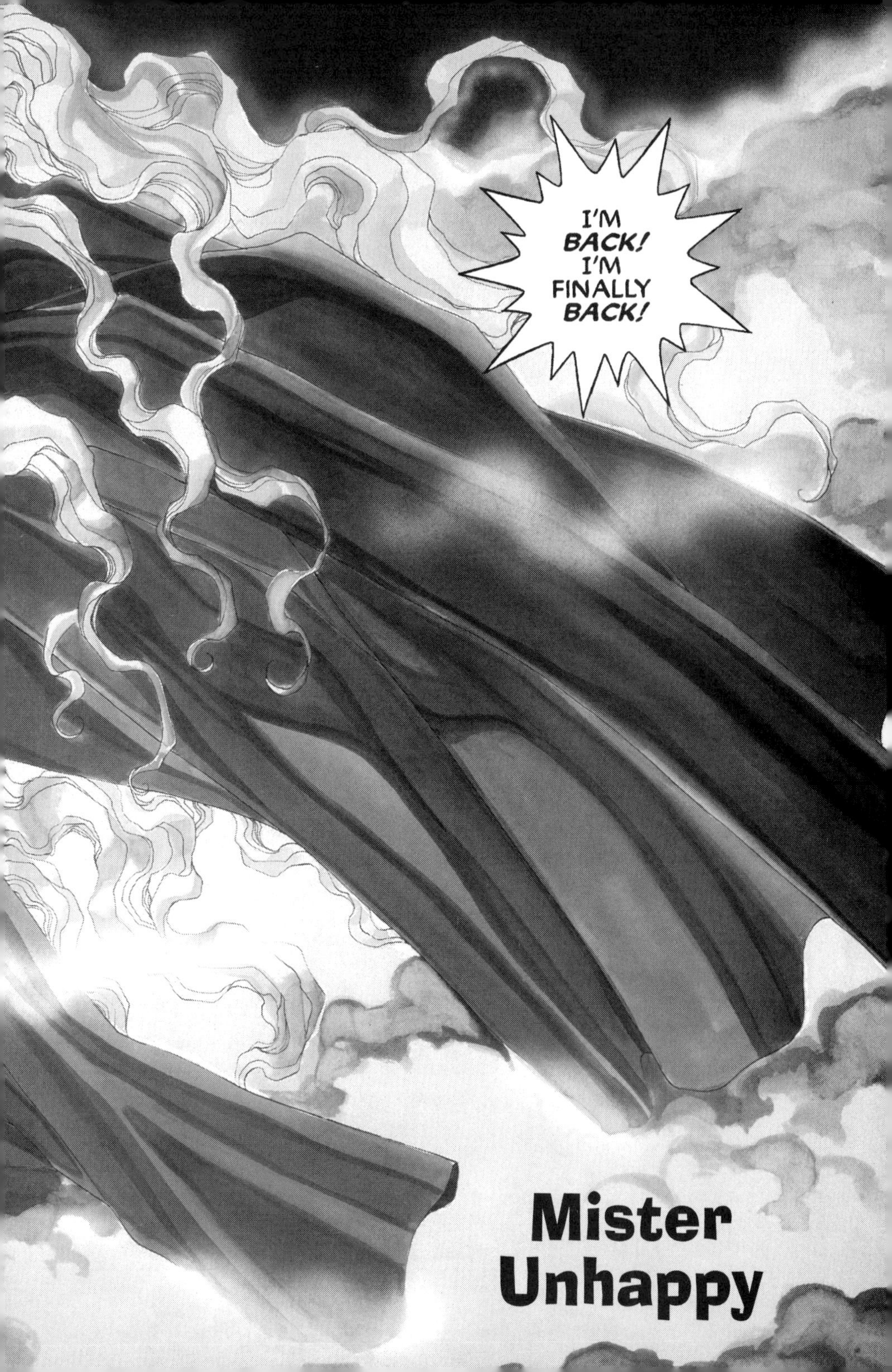
I'M BACK! I'M FINALLY BACK!
Mister Unhappy

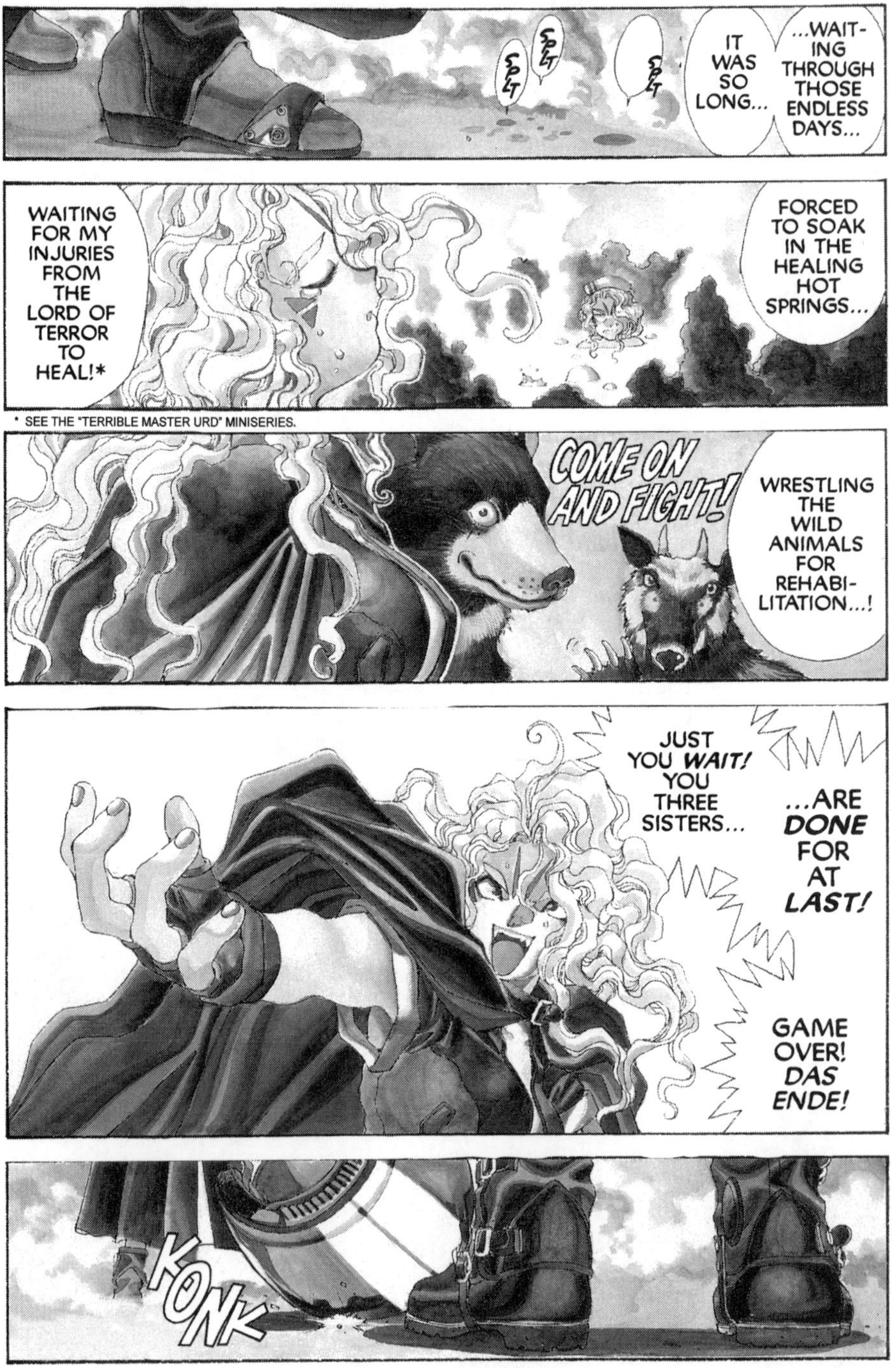
SPLT
SPLT
SPLT
IT WAS SO LONG...
...WAITING THROUGH THOSE ENDLESS DAYS...
WAITING FOR MY INJURIES FROM THE LORD OF TERROR TO HEAL!*
FORCED TO SOAK IN THE HEALING HOT SPRINGS...
COME ON AND FIGHT!
WRESTLING THE WILD ANIMALS FOR REHABILITATION...!
JUST YOU *WAIT!* YOU THREE SISTERS...
...ARE *DONE* FOR AT *LAST!*
GAME OVER! *DAS ENDE!*
KONK

* SEE THE "TERRIBLE MASTER URD" MINISERIES.

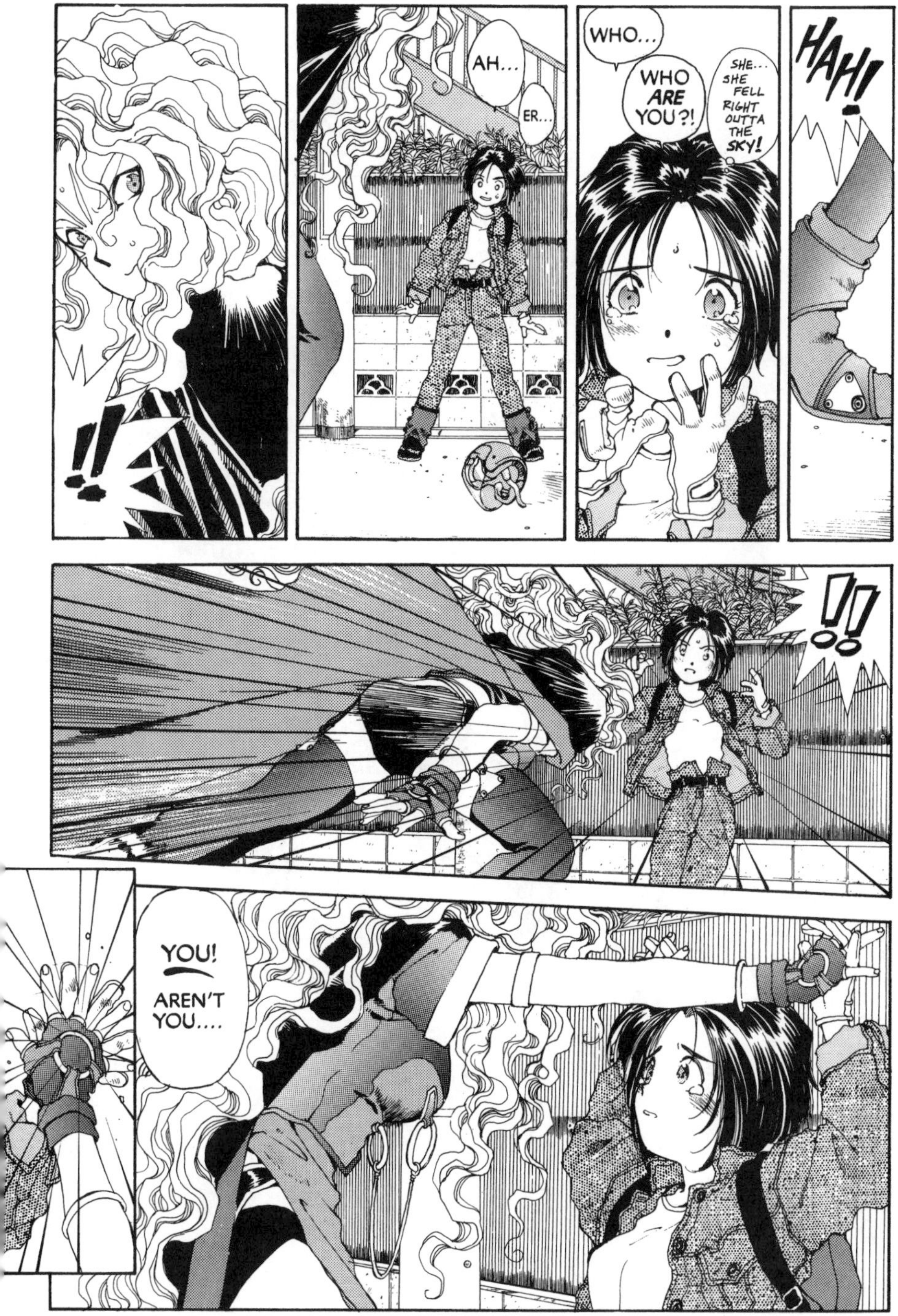
!!
AH...
ER...
WHO...
WHO ARE YOU?!
SHE... SHE FELL RIGHT OUTTA THE SKY!
HAH!
!!
YOU! AREN'T YOU....

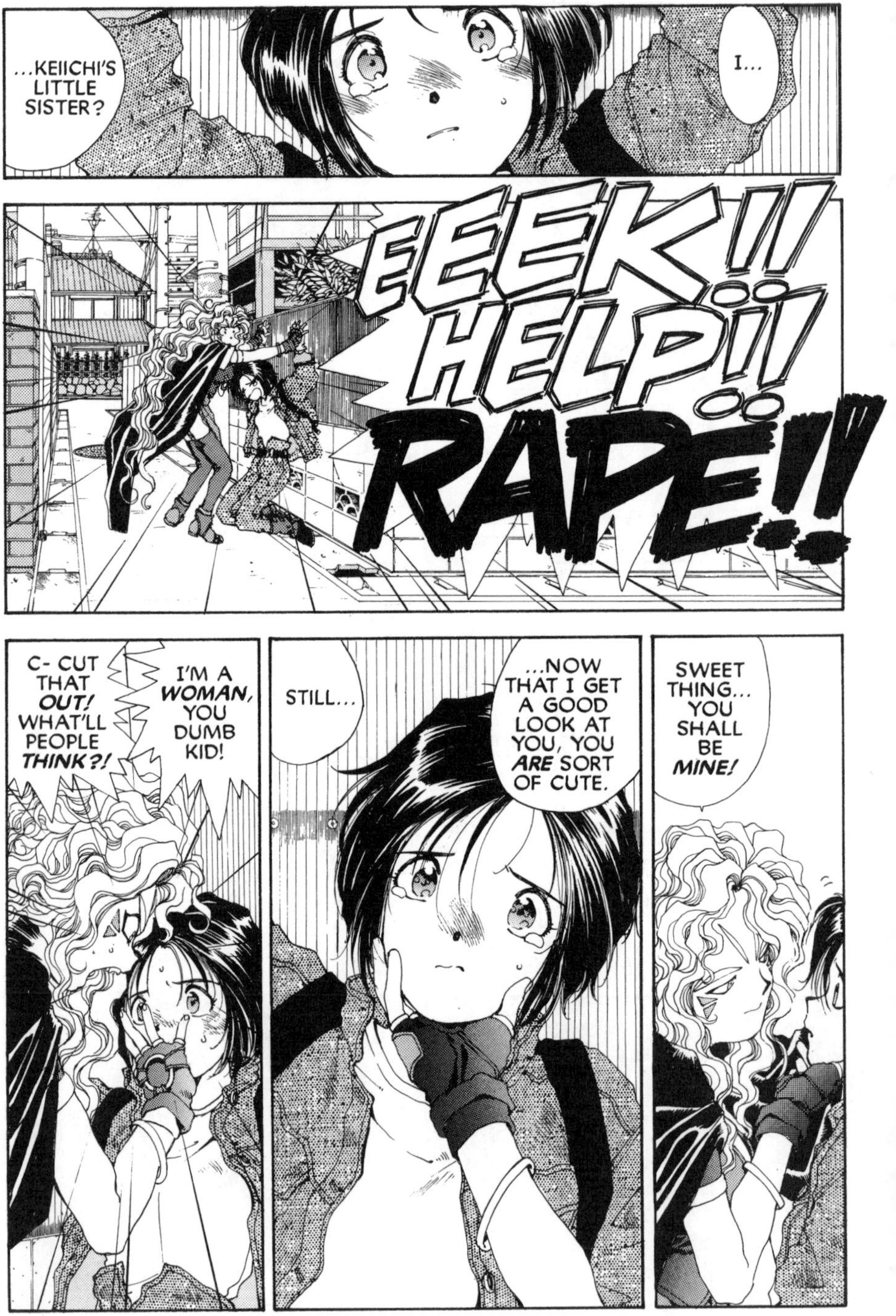
...KEIICHI'S LITTLE SISTER?
I...
EEEK!! HELP!! RAPE!!
C- CUT THAT OUT! WHAT'LL PEOPLE THINK?!
I'M A WOMAN, YOU DUMB KID!
STILL...
...NOW THAT I GET A GOOD LOOK AT YOU, YOU ARE SORT OF CUTE.
SWEET THING... YOU SHALL BE MINE!

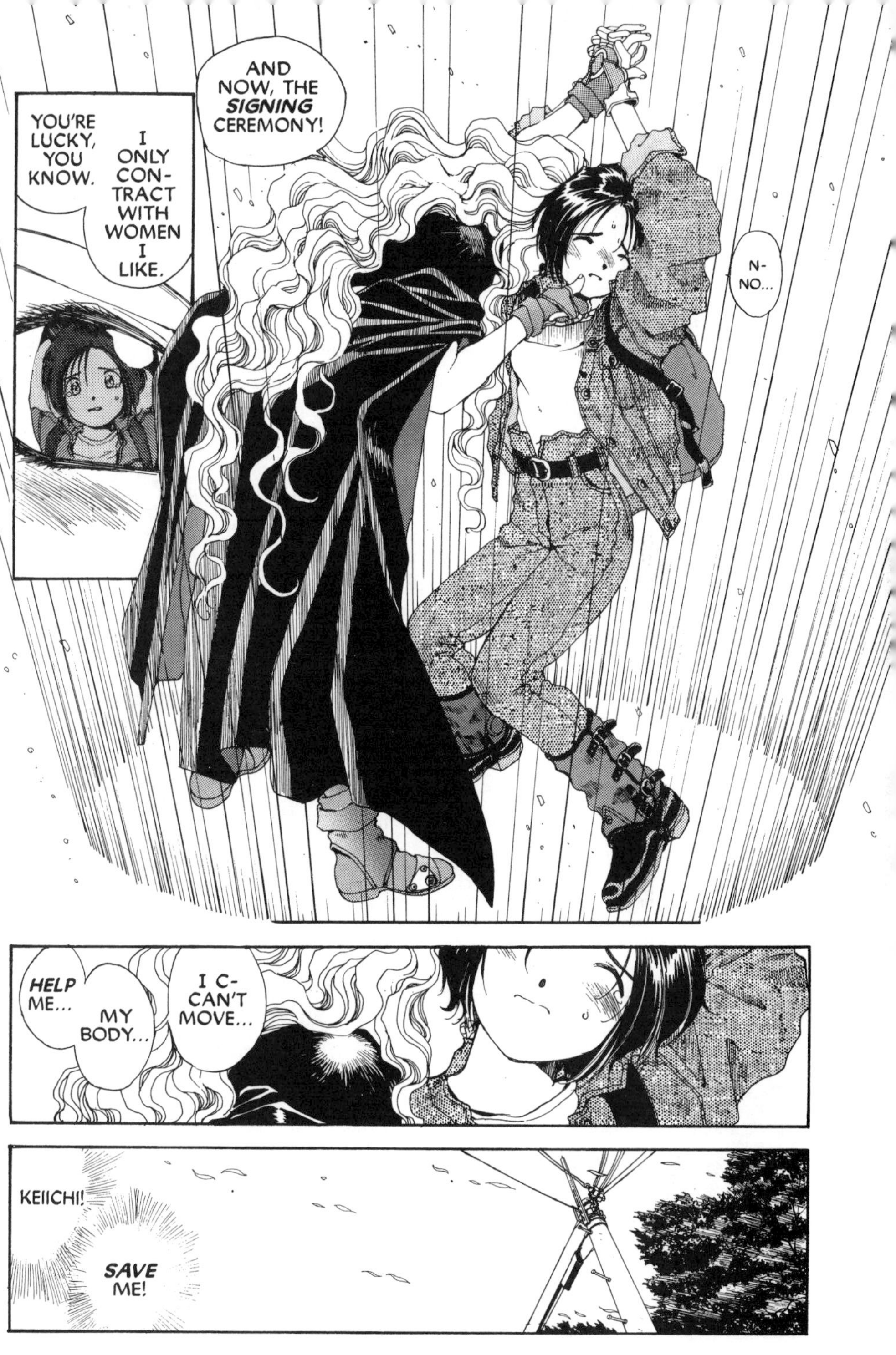
YOU'RE LUCKY, YOU KNOW.
I ONLY CONTRACT WITH WOMEN I LIKE.
AND NOW, THE **SIGNING** CEREMONY!
N-NO...
HELP ME...
MY BODY...
I C-CAN'T MOVE...
KEIICHI!
SAVE ME!

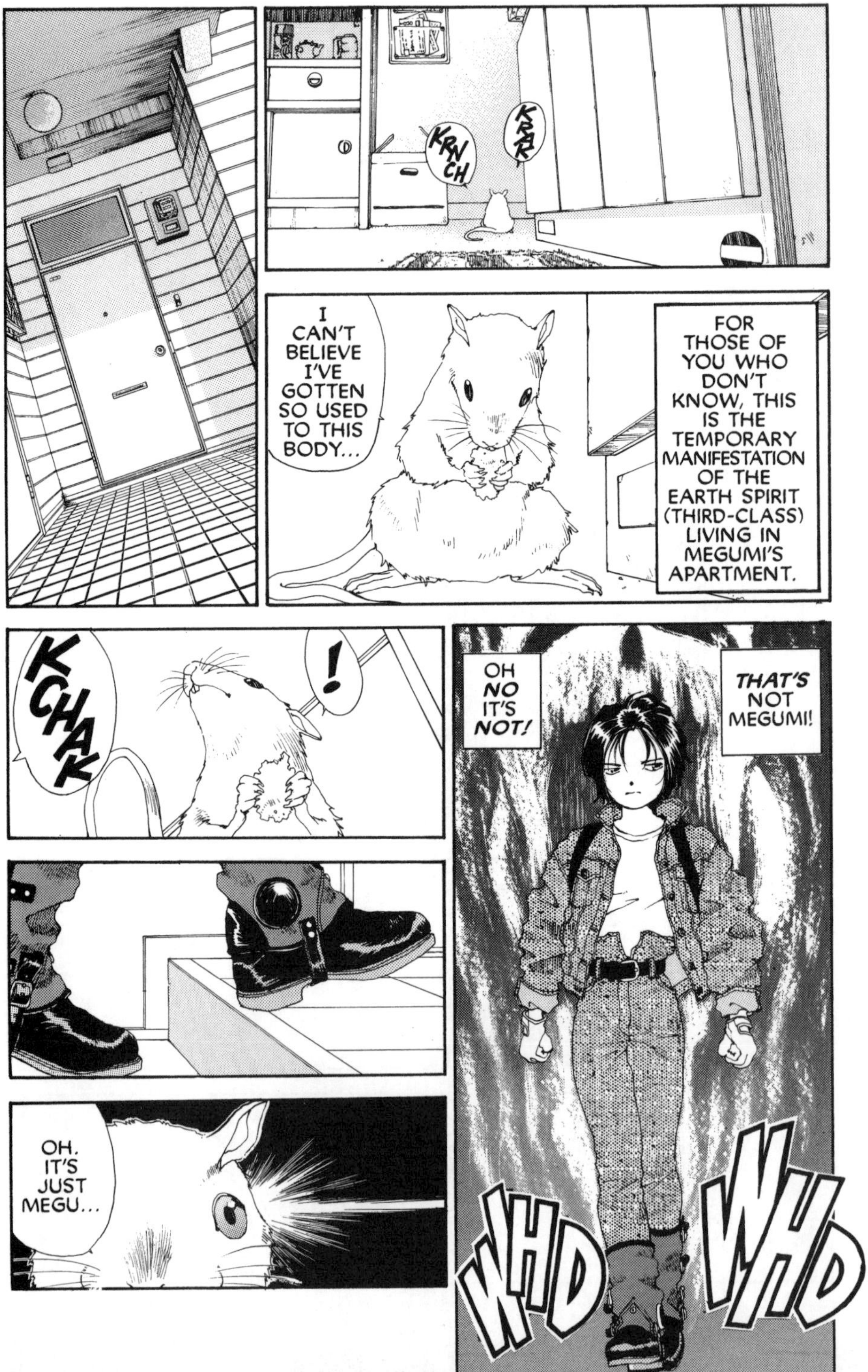
KRNCH
KRAK
I CAN'T BELIEVE I'VE GOTTEN SO USED TO THIS BODY...
FOR THOSE OF YOU WHO DON'T KNOW, THIS IS THE TEMPORARY MANIFESTATION OF THE EARTH SPIRIT (THIRD-CLASS) LIVING IN MEGUMI'S APARTMENT.
KCHAK
!
OH. IT'S JUST MEGU...
OH *NO* IT'S *NOT!*
THAT'S NOT MEGUMI!
WHD
WHD

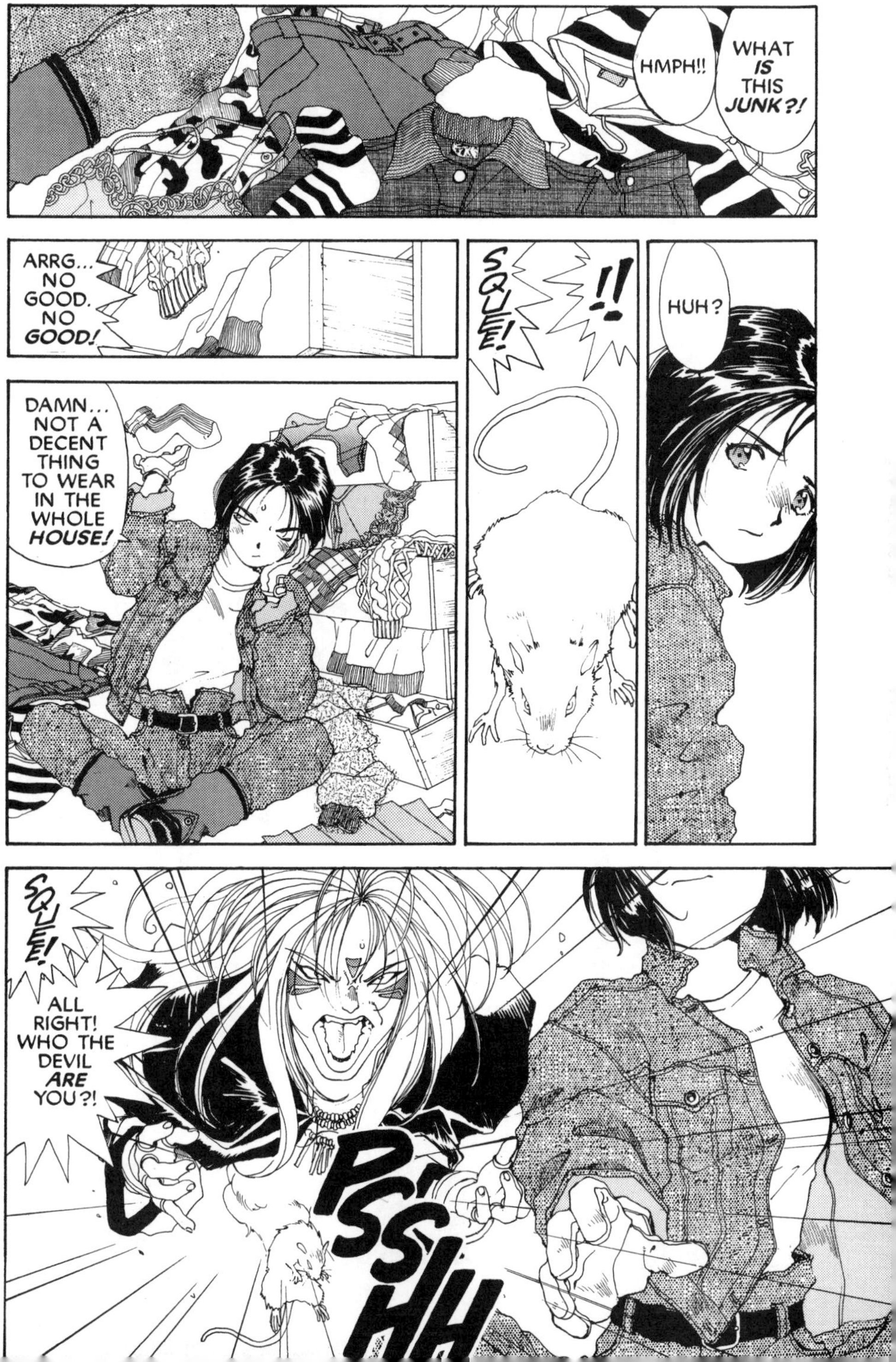
HMPH!!
WHAT IS THIS JUNK?!
ARRG... NO GOOD. NO GOOD!
DAMN... NOT A DECENT THING TO WEAR IN THE WHOLE HOUSE!
SQUEE!
!!
HUH?
SQUEE!
ALL RIGHT! WHO THE DEVIL ARE YOU?!
PSSHH

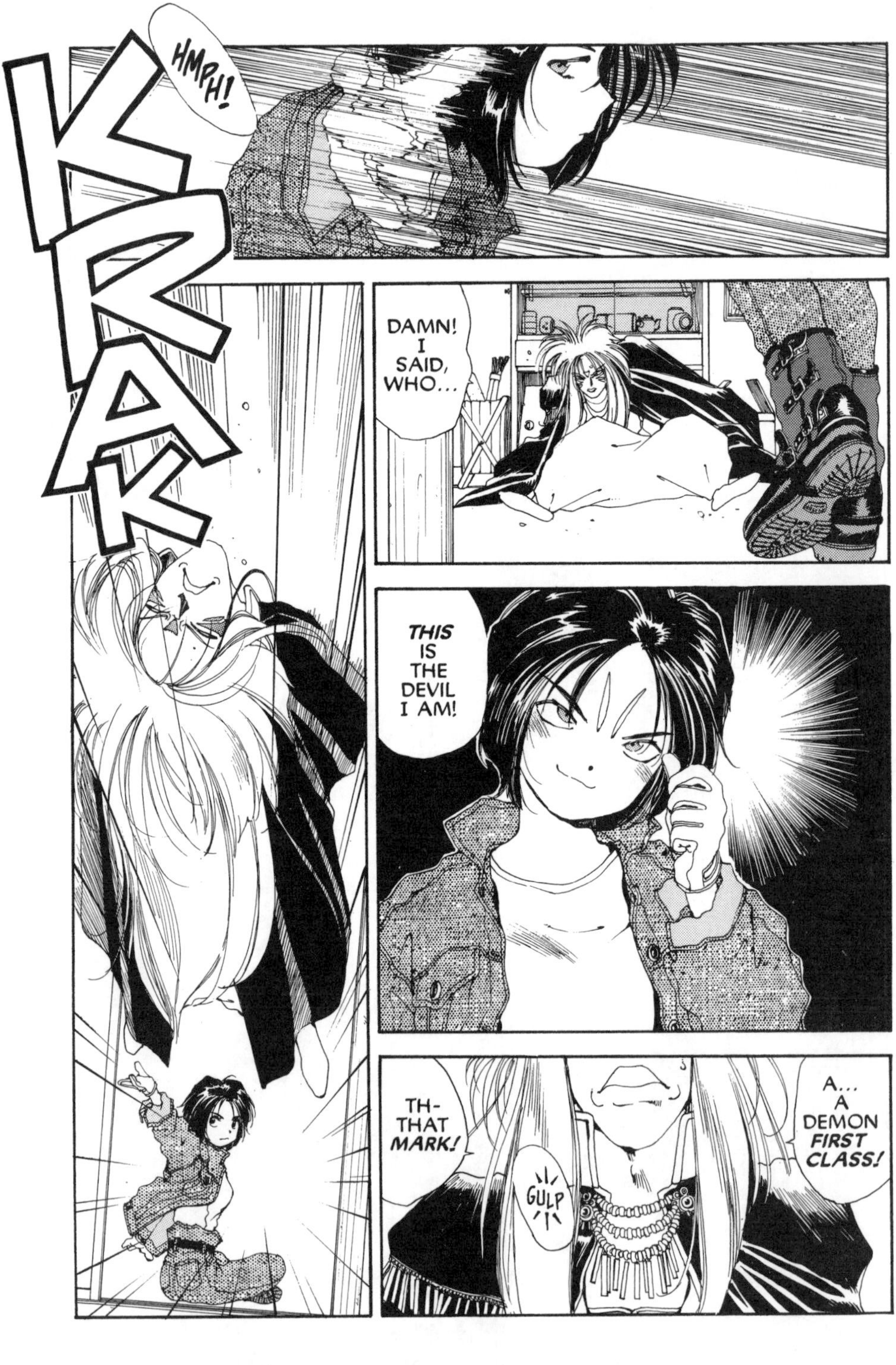
KRAK
HMPH!
DAMN! I SAID, WHO...
THIS IS THE DEVIL I AM!
TH-THAT MARK!
GULP
A... A DEMON FIRST CLASS!

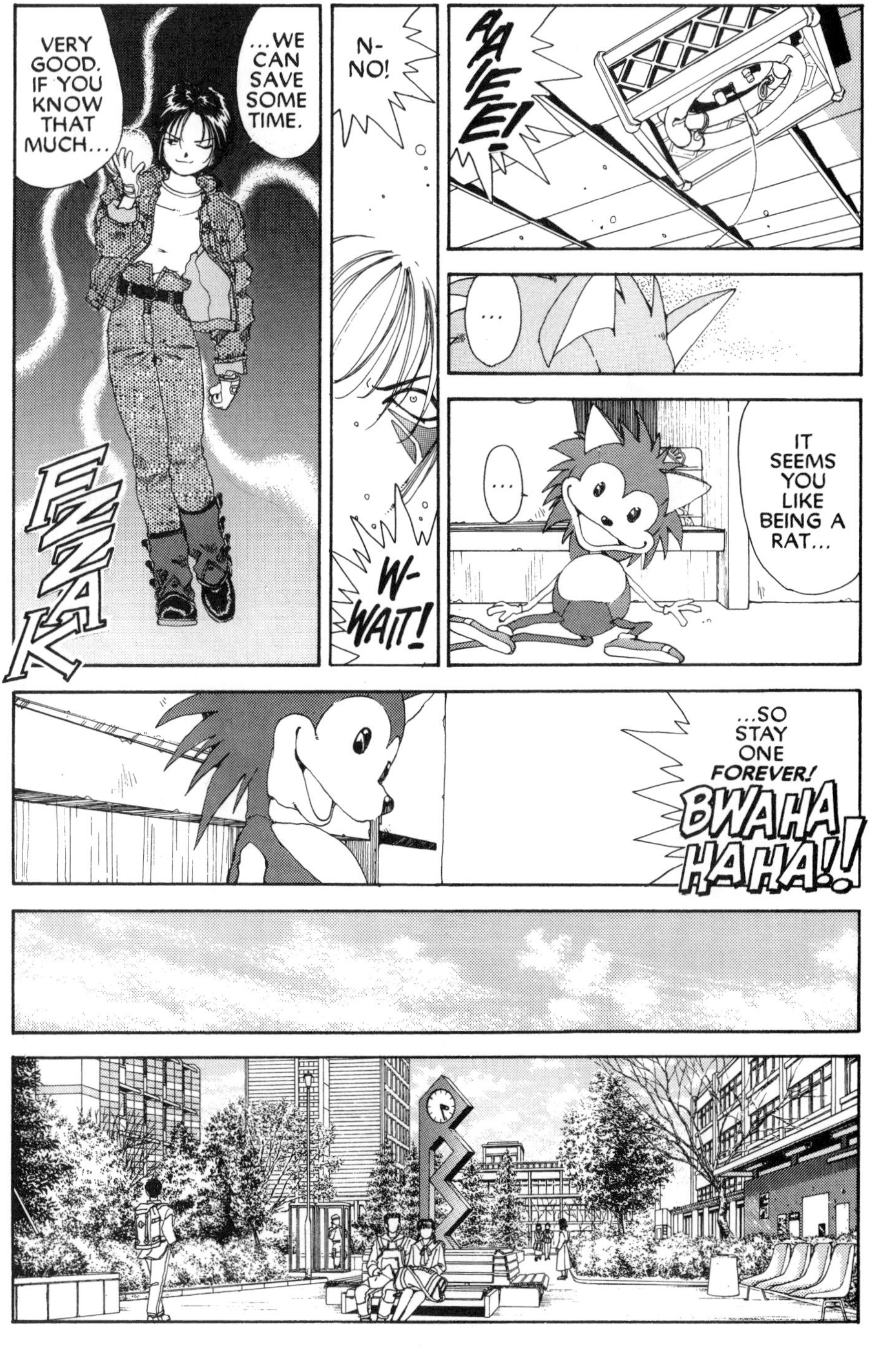
VERY GOOD. IF YOU KNOW THAT MUCH...
...WE CAN SAVE SOME TIME.
FZZAK
N-NO!
W-WAIT!
AAIEEE!
...
...
IT SEEMS YOU LIKE BEING A RAT...
...SO STAY ONE FOREVER!
BWAHA HAHA!!

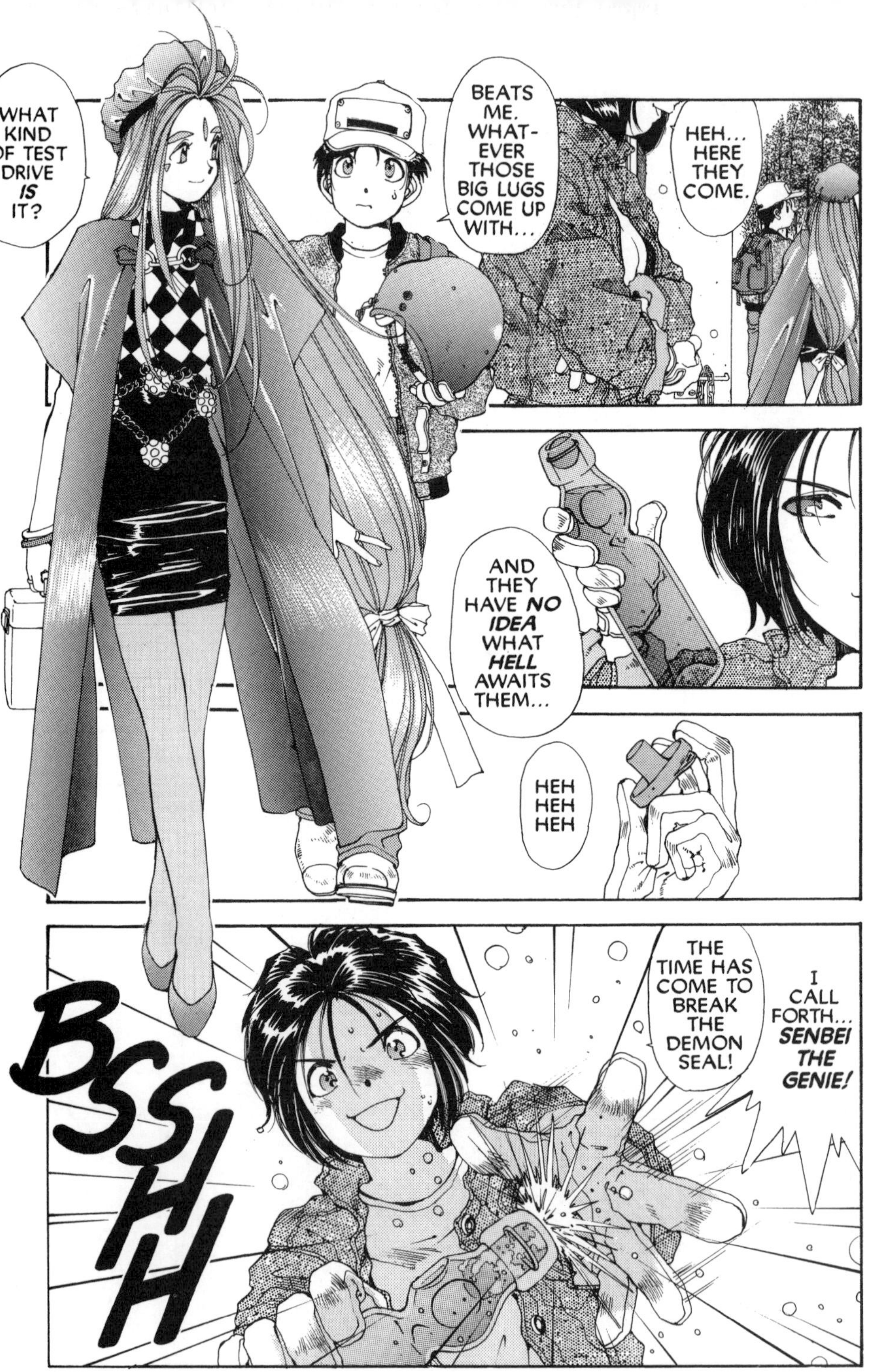
WHAT KIND OF TEST DRIVE *IS* IT?
BEATS ME. WHATEVER THOSE BIG LUGS COME UP WITH...
HEH... HERE THEY COME.
AND THEY HAVE ***NO IDEA*** WHAT ***HELL*** AWAITS THEM...
HEH HEH HEH
BSSHH
THE TIME HAS COME TO BREAK THE DEMON SEAL!
I CALL FORTH... ***SENBEI THE GENIE!***

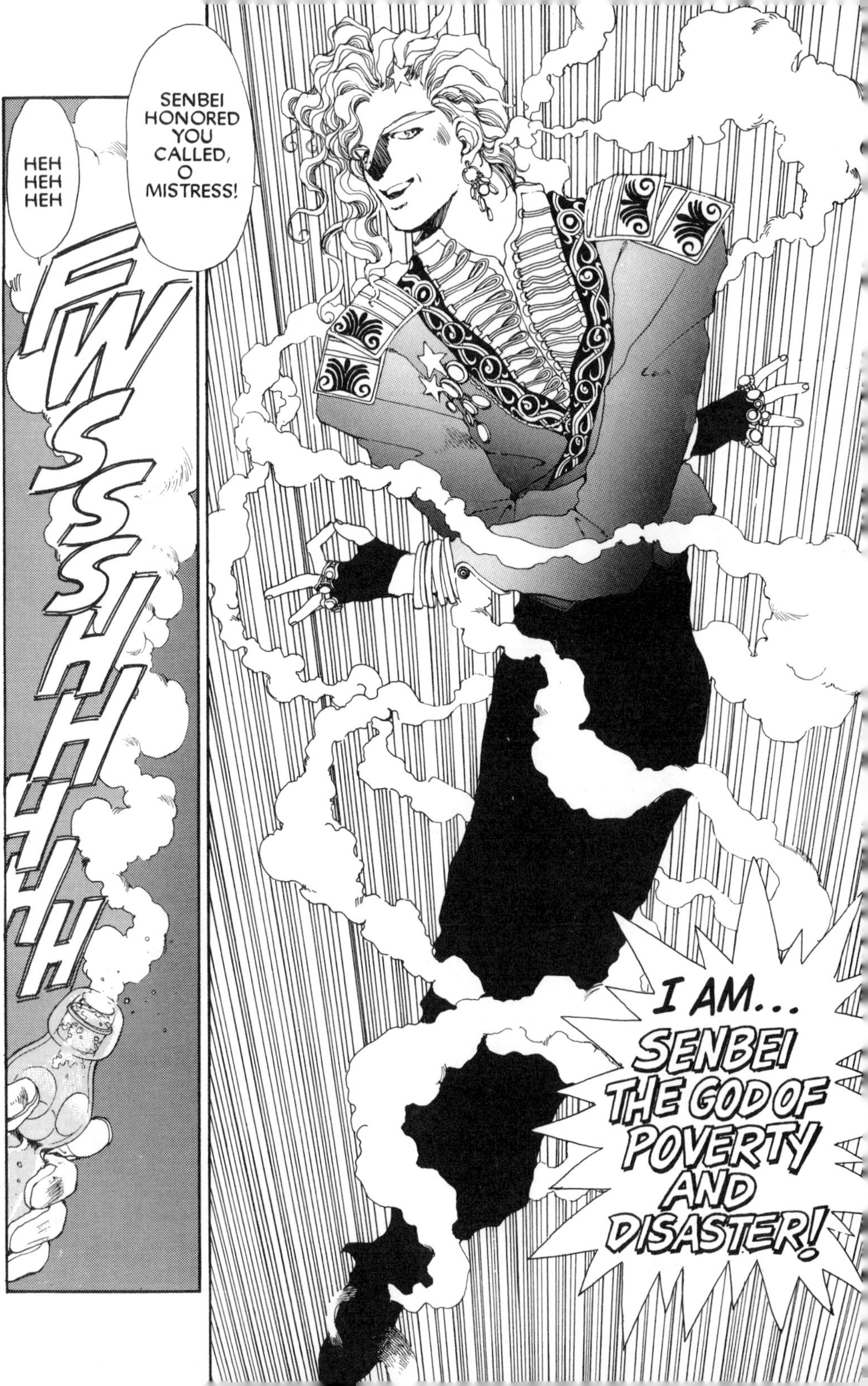
HEH HEH HEH
SENBEI HONORED YOU CALLED, O MISTRESS!
FWSSSHHHHHH
I AM... SENBEI THE GOD OF POVERTY AND DISASTER!

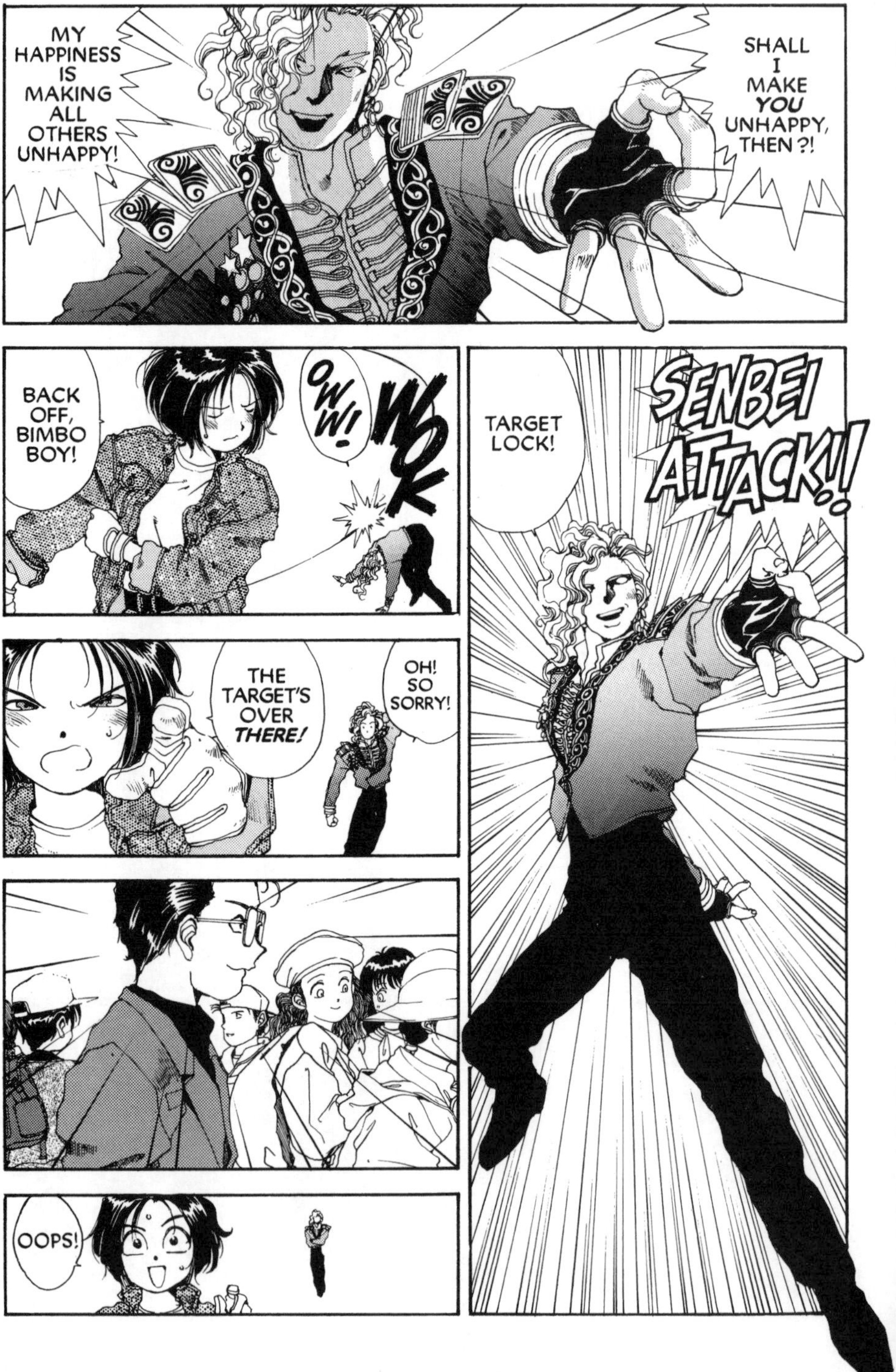
MY HAPPINESS IS MAKING ALL OTHERS UNHAPPY!
SHALL I MAKE YOU UNHAPPY, THEN?!
BACK OFF, BIMBO BOY!
OWW!
WOK
THE TARGET'S OVER THERE!
OH! SO SORRY!
OOPS!
TARGET LOCK!
SENBEI ATTACK!!

SHSS

!!

WHAT WAS THAT? THAT SUDDEN CHILL...?

ATTACK!!

FWIP

A IEE!

I'M NOT *FOOL* ENOUGH TO FALL FOR *THAT!*

FIRE

THOK

OH, COME *ON!* A FORTY-YEAR-OLD GAG LIKE *THIS?!*

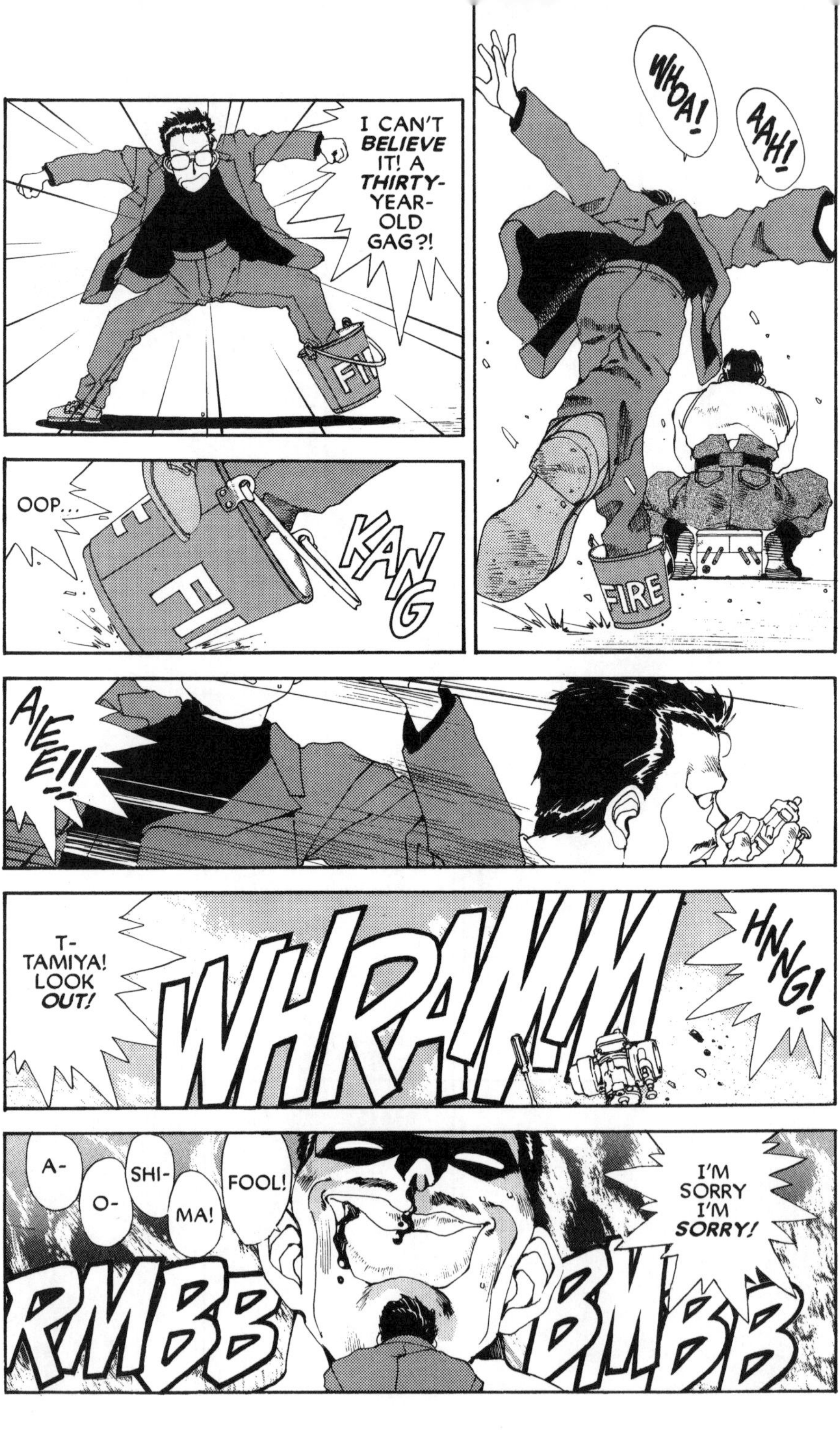
I CAN'T BELIEVE IT! A THIRTY-YEAR-OLD GAG?!
OOP...
KANG
WHOA!
AAH!
FIRE
AIEE!!
T-TAMIYA! LOOK OUT!
WHRAMM
HNNG!
A-
O-
SHI-
MA!
FOOL!
RMBB
I'M SORRY I'M SORRY!
BMBB

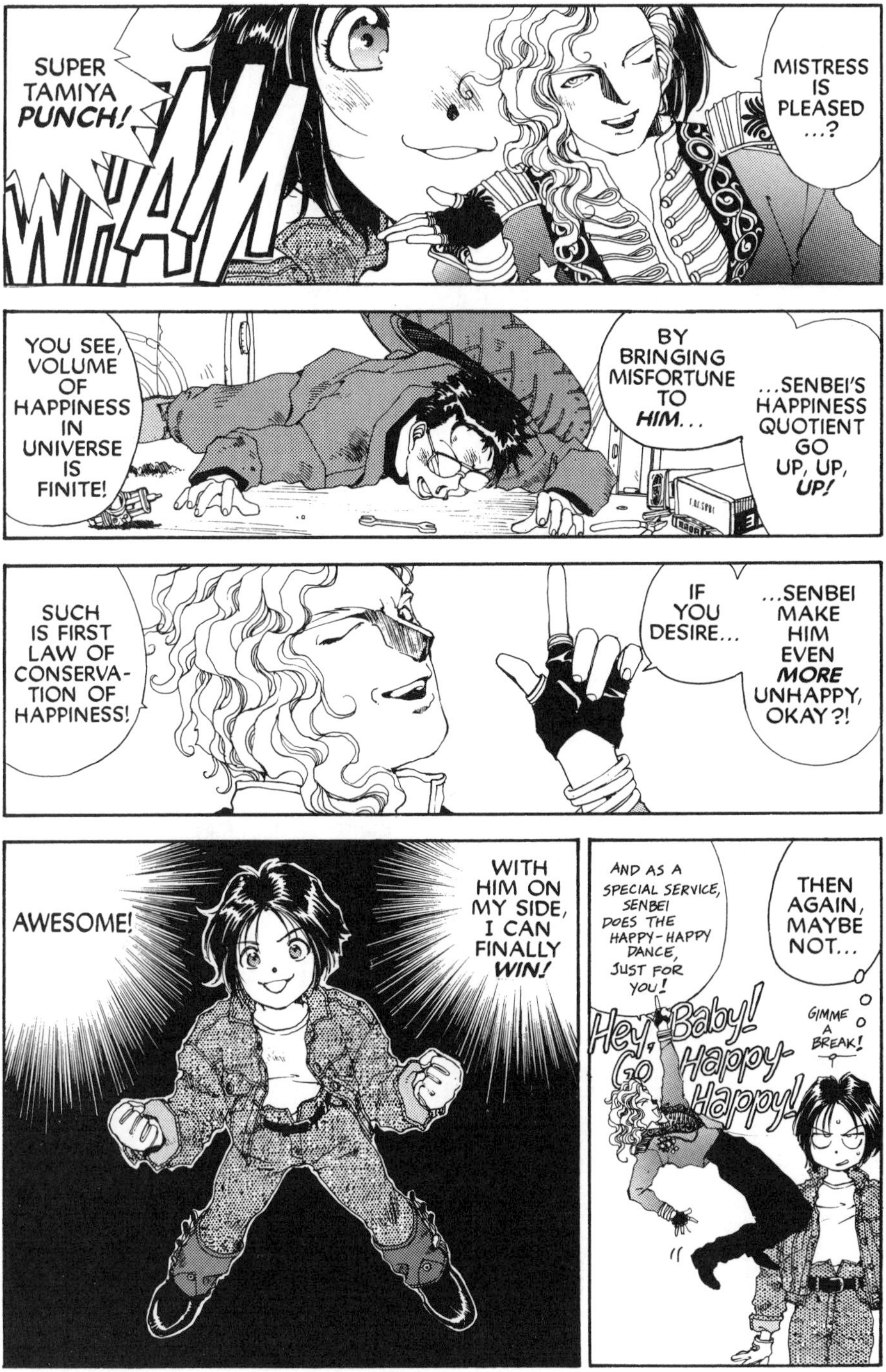
SUPER TAMIYA PUNCH!
WHAM
MISTRESS IS PLEASED ...?
YOU SEE, VOLUME OF HAPPINESS IN UNIVERSE IS FINITE!
BY BRINGING MISFORTUNE TO HIM...
...SENBEI'S HAPPINESS QUOTIENT GO UP, UP, UP!
SUCH IS FIRST LAW OF CONSERVATION OF HAPPINESS!
IF YOU DESIRE...
...SENBEI MAKE HIM EVEN MORE UNHAPPY, OKAY?!
AWESOME!
WITH HIM ON MY SIDE, I CAN FINALLY WIN!
AND AS A SPECIAL SERVICE, SENBEI DOES THE HAPPY-HAPPY DANCE, JUST FOR YOU!
THEN AGAIN, MAYBE NOT...
Hey, Baby! Go Happy-Happy!
GIMME A BREAK!

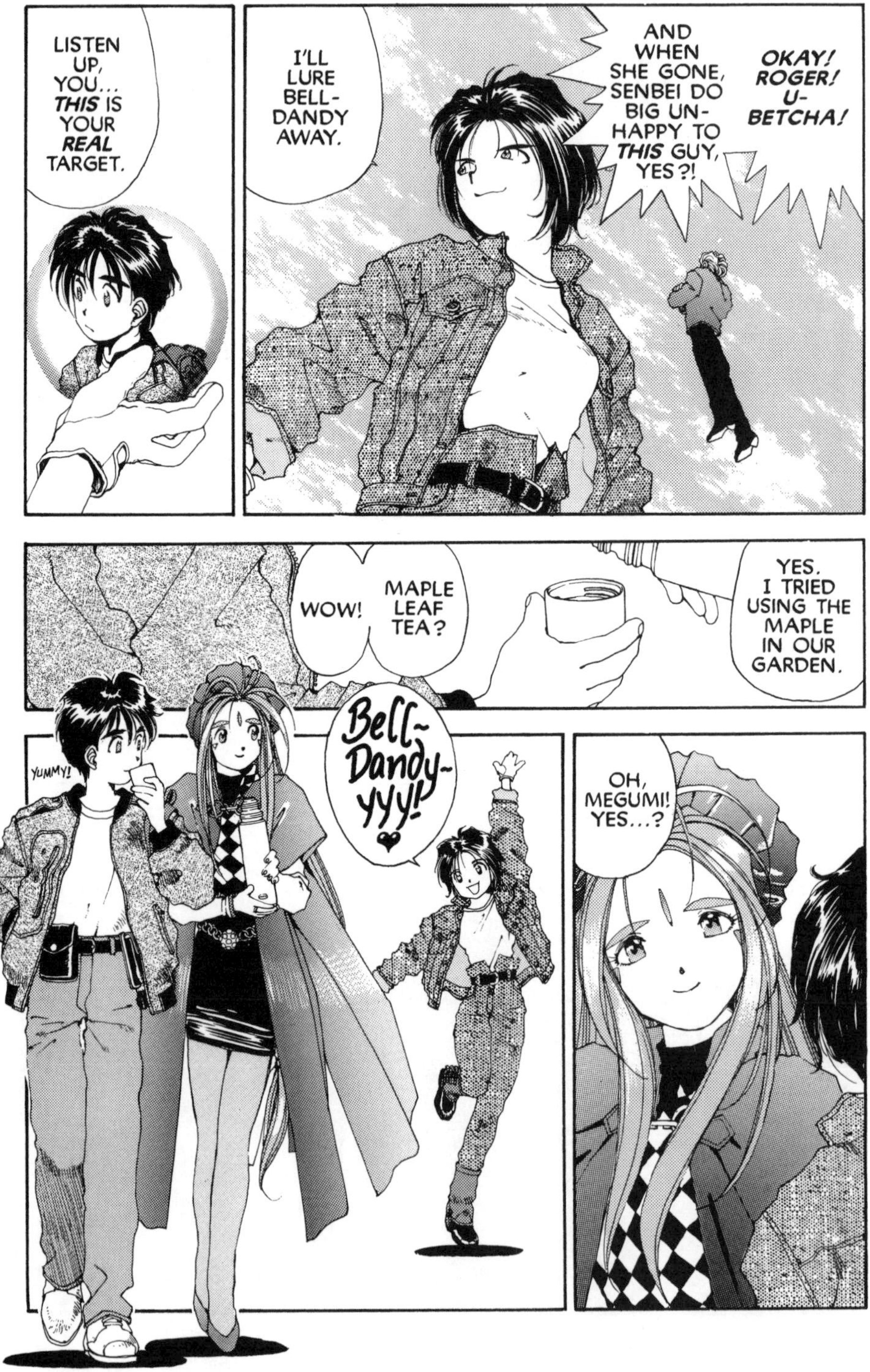
LISTEN UP, YOU... *THIS* IS YOUR *REAL* TARGET.
I'LL LURE BELL-DANDY AWAY.
AND WHEN SHE GONE, SENBEI DO BIG UN-HAPPY TO *THIS* GUY, YES?!
OKAY! ROGER! U-BETCHA!
WOW!
MAPLE LEAF TEA?
YES. I TRIED USING THE MAPLE IN OUR GARDEN.
YUMMY!
Bell-Dandy-yyy!
OH, MEGUMI! YES...?

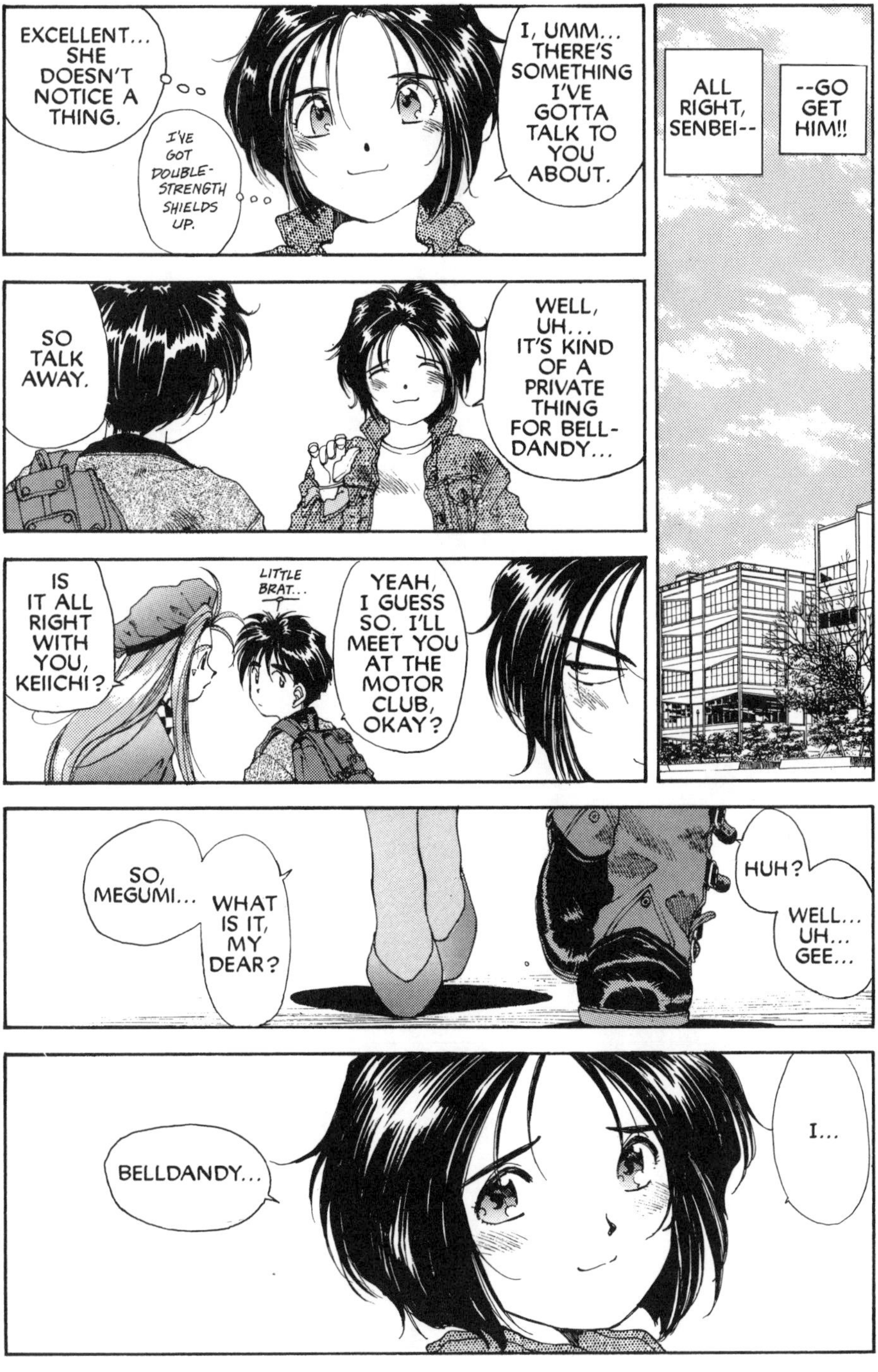
EXCELLENT... SHE DOESN'T NOTICE A THING.
I'VE GOT DOUBLE-STRENGTH SHIELDS UP.
I, UMM... THERE'S SOMETHING I'VE GOTTA TALK TO YOU ABOUT.
SO TALK AWAY.
WELL, UH... IT'S KIND OF A PRIVATE THING FOR BELL-DANDY...
IS IT ALL RIGHT WITH YOU, KEIICHI?
LITTLE BRAT...
YEAH, I GUESS SO. I'LL MEET YOU AT THE MOTOR CLUB, OKAY?
ALL RIGHT, SENBEI--
--GO GET HIM!!
SO, MEGUMI...
WHAT IS IT, MY DEAR?
HUH?
WELL... UH... GEE...
BELLDANDY...
I...

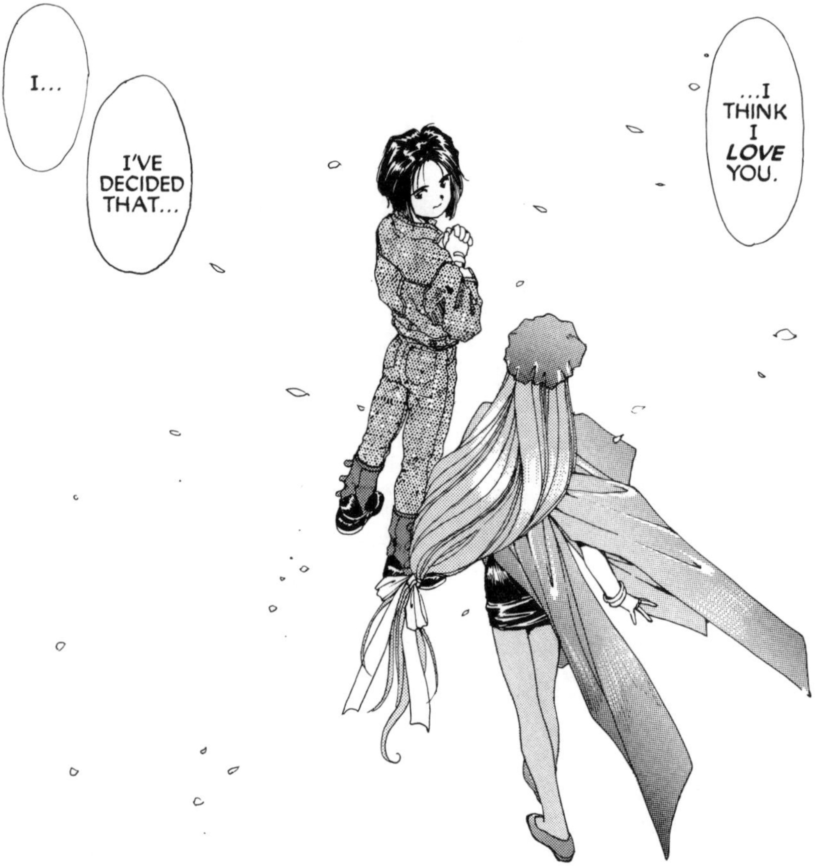
I...
I'VE DECIDED THAT...
...I THINK I *LOVE* YOU.

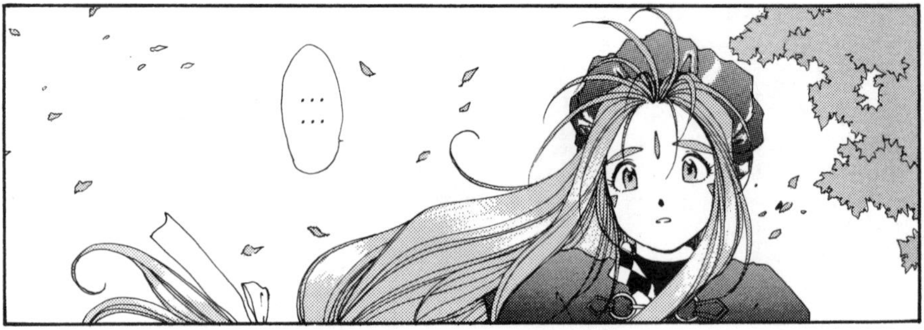
... ...

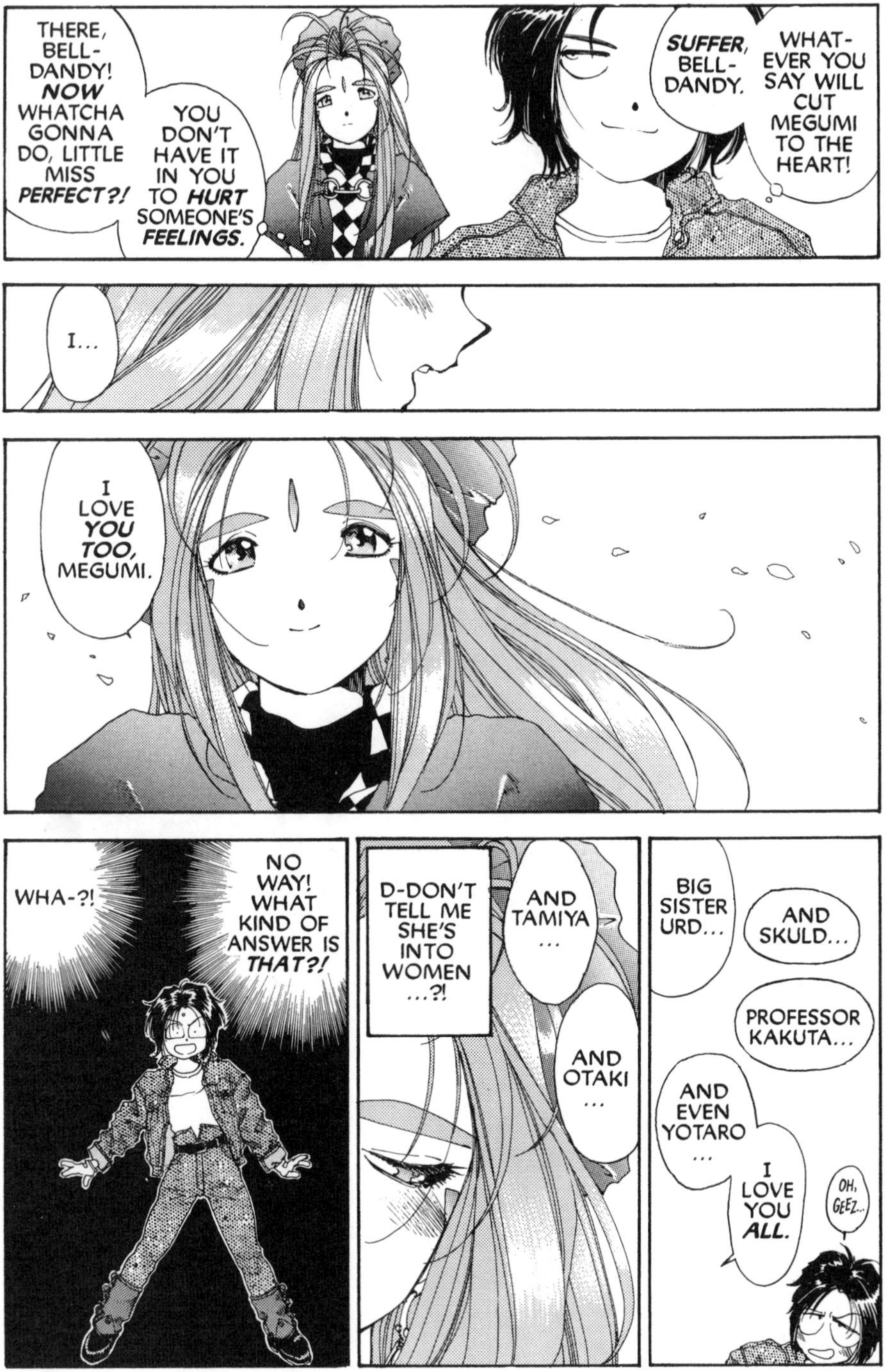
THERE, BELL-DANDY! NOW WHATCHA GONNA DO, LITTLE MISS PERFECT?!
YOU DON'T HAVE IT IN YOU TO HURT SOMEONE'S FEELINGS.
SUFFER, BELL-DANDY.
WHAT-EVER YOU SAY WILL CUT MEGUMI TO THE HEART!
I...
I LOVE YOU TOO, MEGUMI.
WHA-?!
NO WAY! WHAT KIND OF ANSWER IS THAT?!
D-DON'T TELL ME SHE'S INTO WOMEN ...?!
AND TAMIYA ...
AND OTAKI ...
BIG SISTER URD...
AND SKULD...
PROFESSOR KAKUTA...
AND EVEN YOTARO ...
I LOVE YOU ALL.
OH, GEEZ...

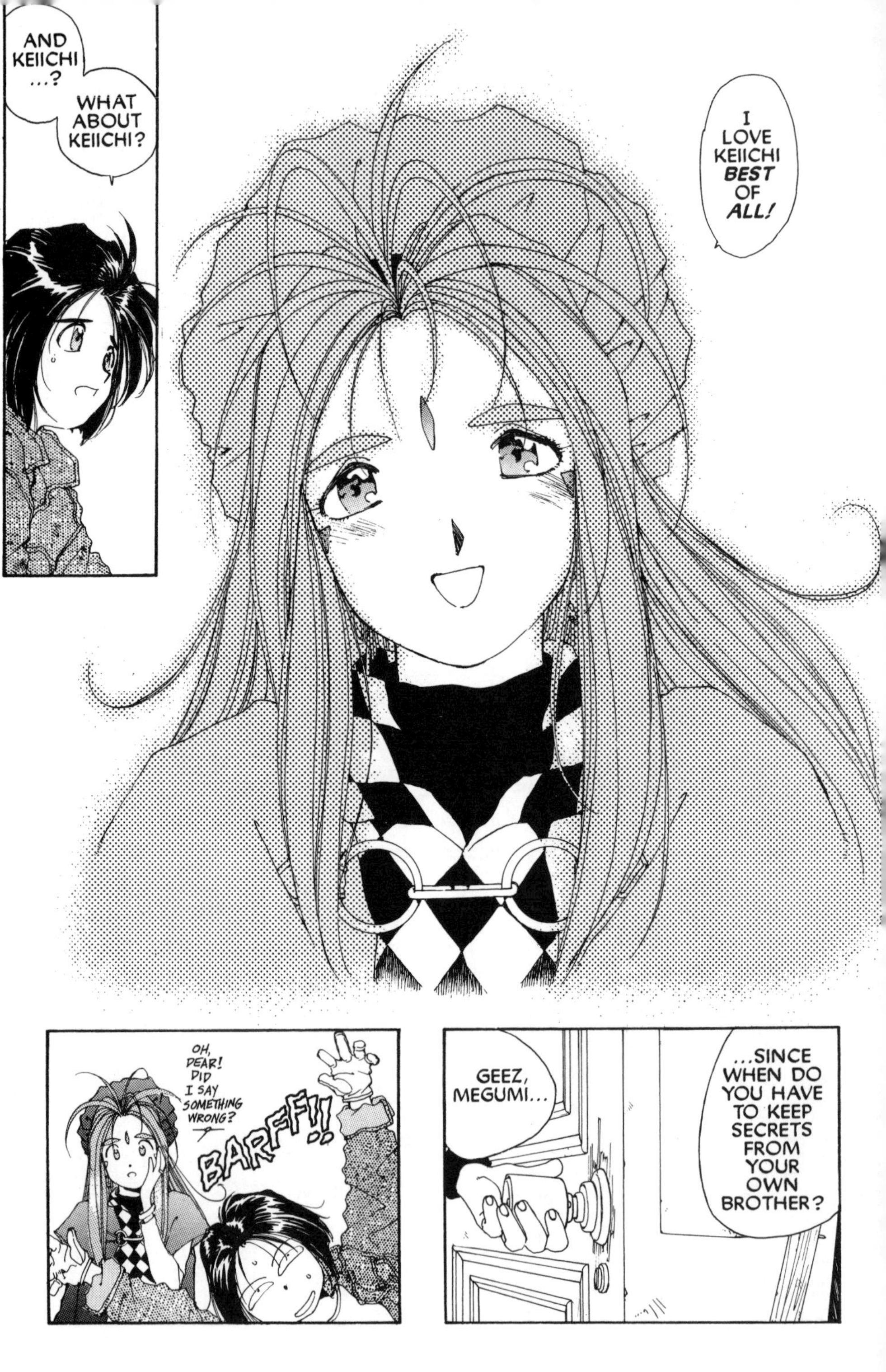
AND KEIICHI ...?
WHAT ABOUT KEIICHI?
I LOVE KEIICHI BEST OF ALL!
OH, DEAR! DID I SAY SOMETHING WRONG?
BARFF!!
GEEZ, MEGUMI...
...SINCE WHEN DO YOU HAVE TO KEEP SECRETS FROM YOUR OWN BROTHER?

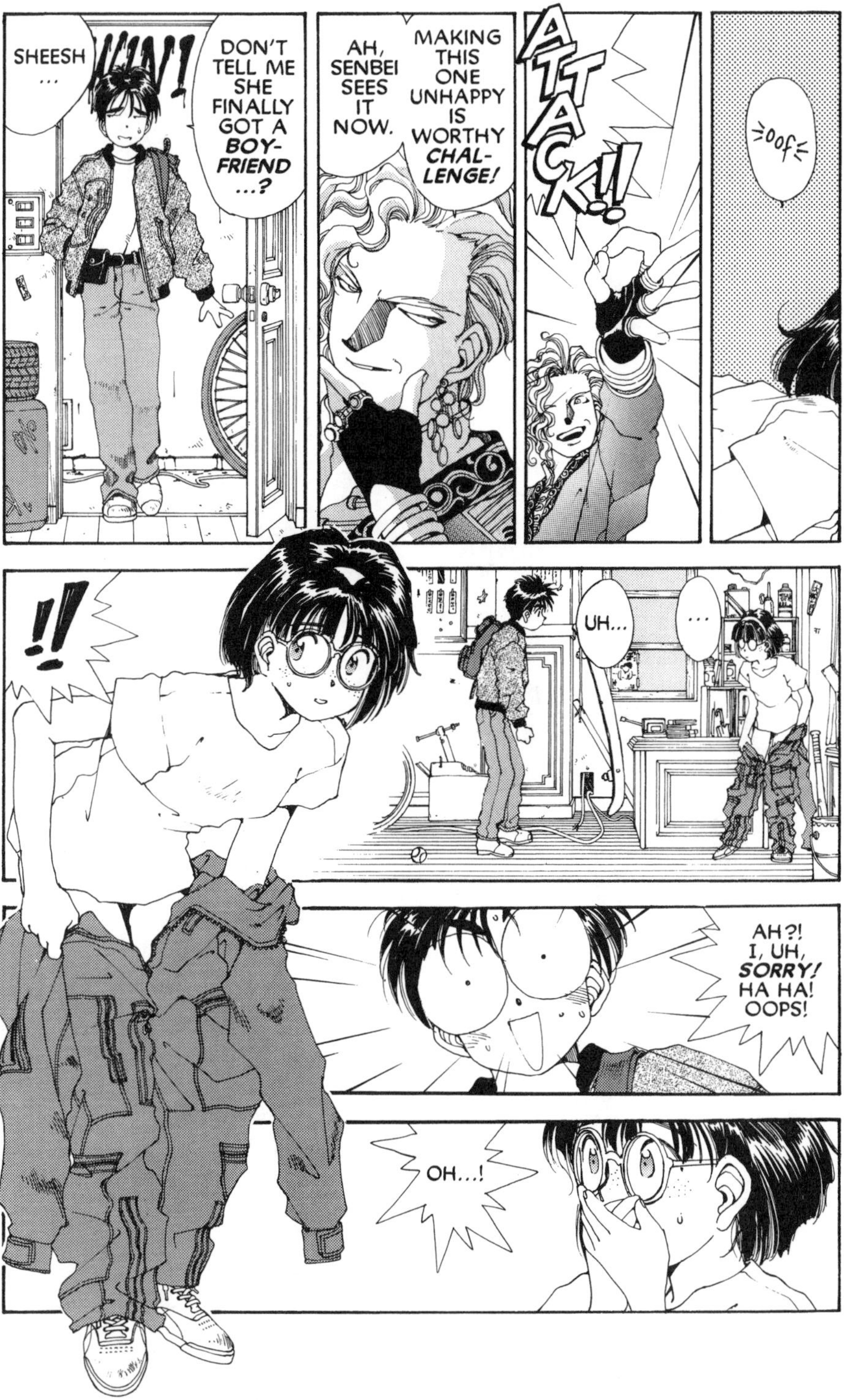
SHEESH ...
DON'T TELL ME SHE FINALLY GOT A ***BOY-FRIEND*** ...?
AH, SENBEI SEES IT NOW.
MAKING THIS ONE UNHAPPY IS WORTHY ***CHAL-LENGE!***
ATTACK!!
oof
!!
UH...
...
AH?! I, UH, ***SORRY!*** HA HA! OOPS!
OH...!

CLUB MEMBER SORA HASEGAWA ↓

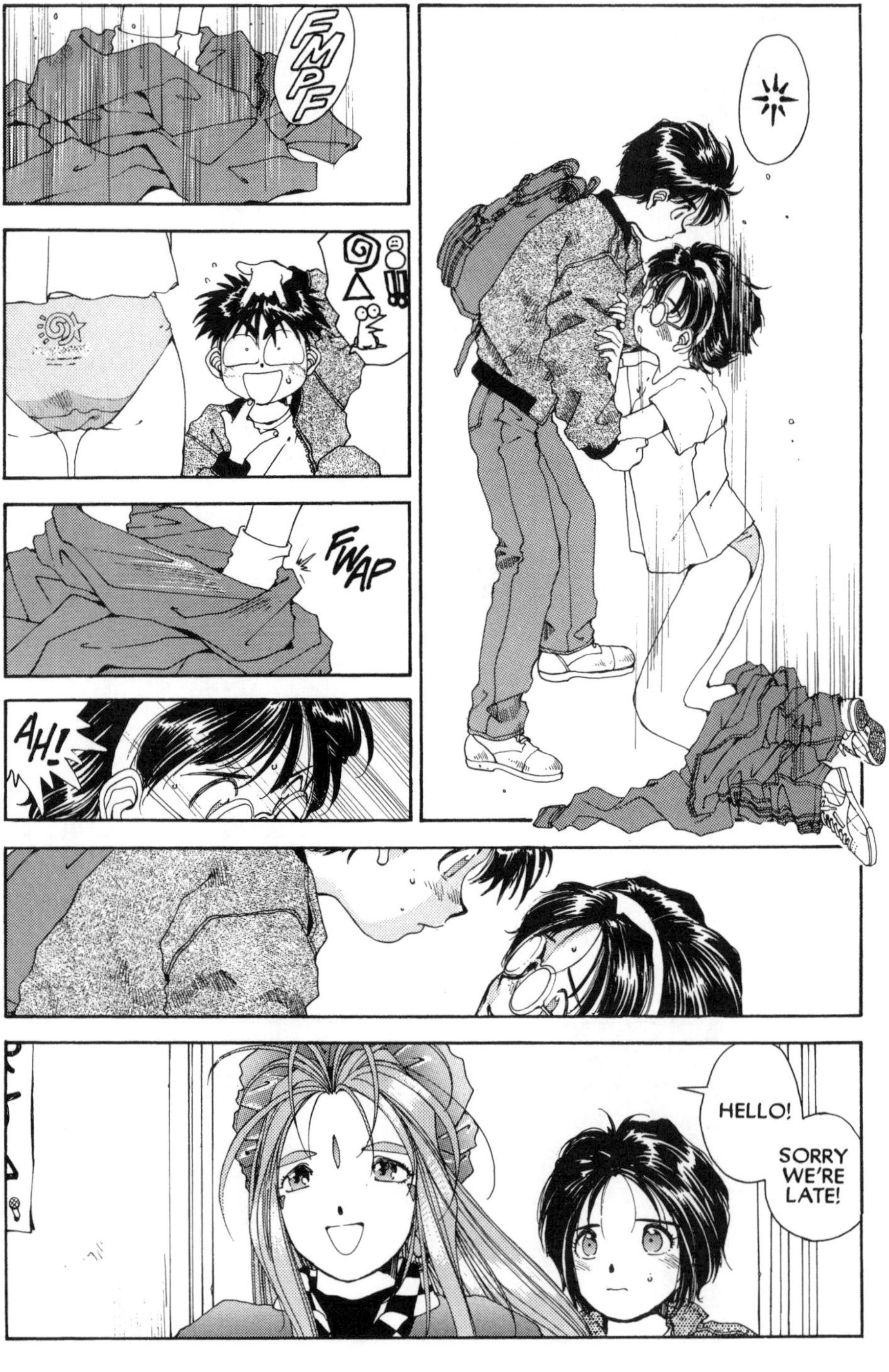
FMPF
FWAP
AH!
HELLO!
SORRY WE'RE LATE!

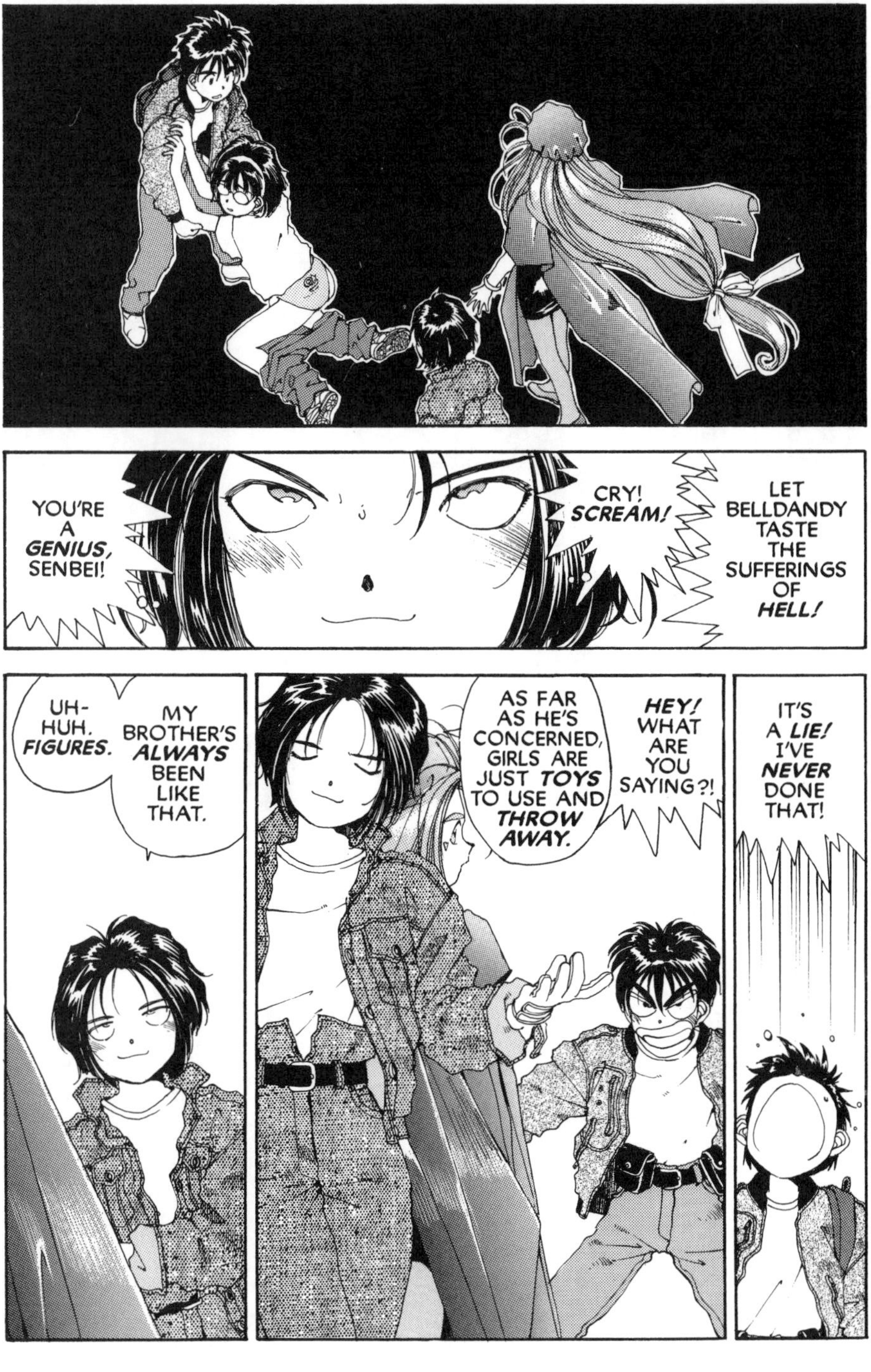
YOU'RE A GENIUS, SENBEI!
CRY! SCREAM!
LET BELLDANDY TASTE THE SUFFERINGS OF HELL!
UH-HUH. FIGURES.
MY BROTHER'S ALWAYS BEEN LIKE THAT.
AS FAR AS HE'S CONCERNED, GIRLS ARE JUST TOYS TO USE AND THROW AWAY.
HEY! WHAT ARE YOU SAYING?!
IT'S A LIE! I'VE NEVER DONE THAT!

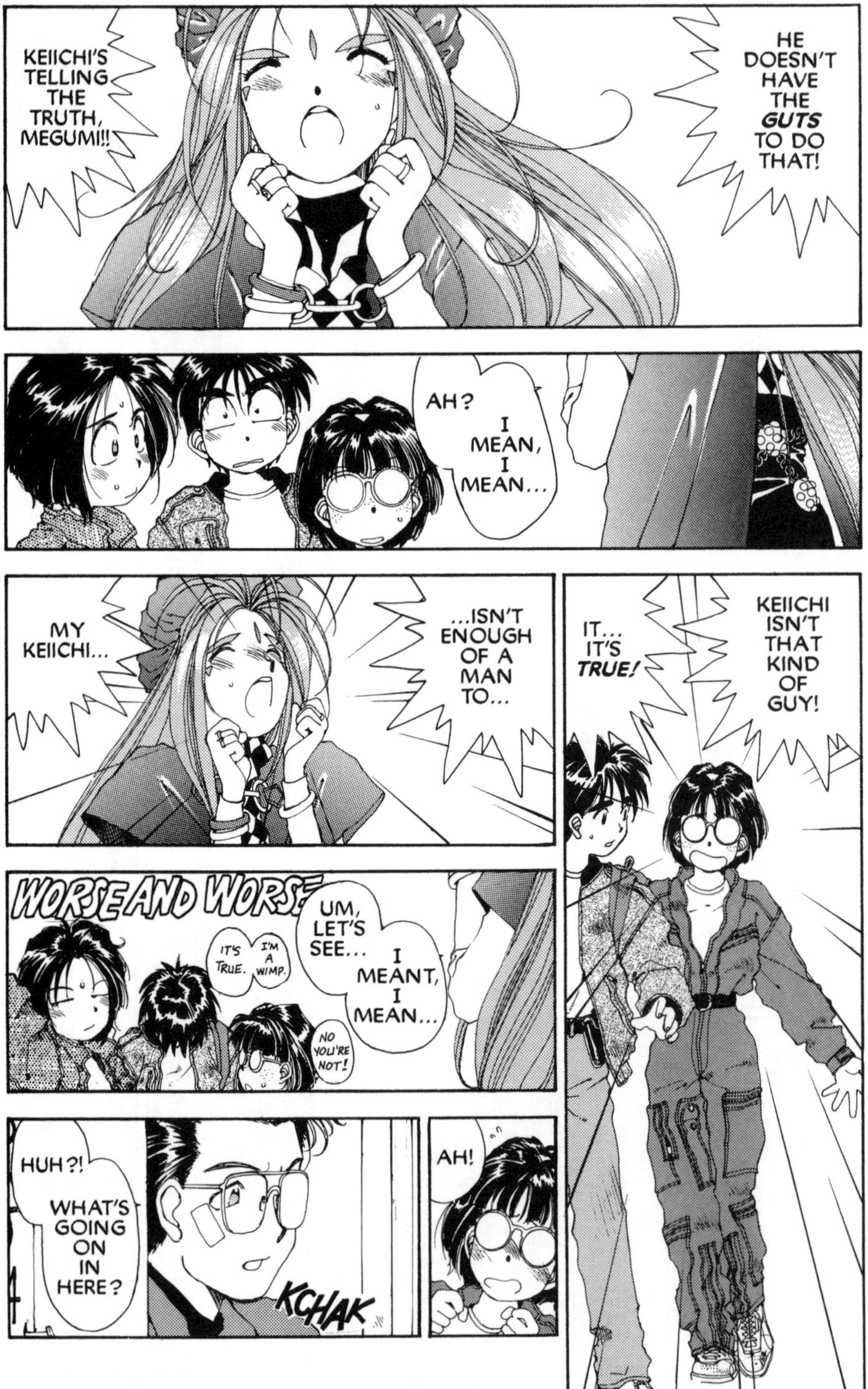
KEIICHI'S TELLING THE TRUTH, MEGUMI!!
HE DOESN'T HAVE THE GUTS TO DO THAT!
AH? I MEAN, I MEAN...
MY KEIICHI...
...ISN'T ENOUGH OF A MAN TO...
WORSE AND WORSE
IT'S TRUE.
I'M A WIMP.
UM, LET'S SEE... I MEANT, I MEAN...
NO YOU'RE NOT!
HUH?! WHAT'S GOING ON IN HERE?
KCHAK
AH!
IT... IT'S TRUE!
KEIICHI ISN'T THAT KIND OF GUY!

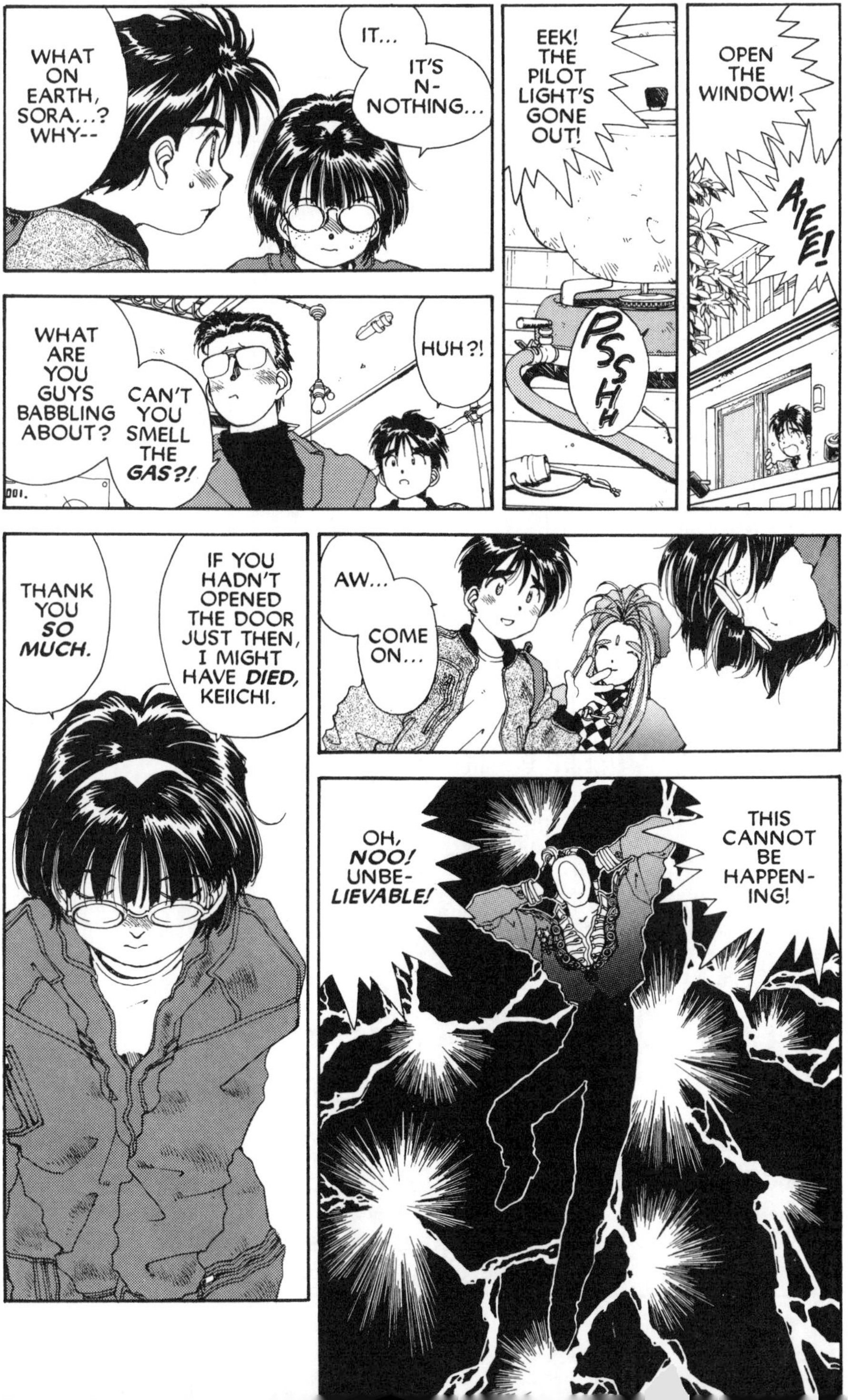
WHAT ON EARTH, SORA...? WHY--
IT...
IT'S N-NOTHING...
WHAT ARE YOU GUYS BABBLING ABOUT?
CAN'T YOU SMELL THE *GAS?!*
HUH?!
EEK! THE PILOT LIGHT'S GONE OUT!
PSSHH
OPEN THE WINDOW!
AIEE!
THANK YOU *SO MUCH.*
IF YOU HADN'T OPENED THE DOOR JUST THEN, I MIGHT HAVE *DIED,* KEIICHI.
AW...
COME ON...
OH, *NOO!* UNBE-*LIEVABLE!*
THIS CANNOT BE HAPPEN-ING!

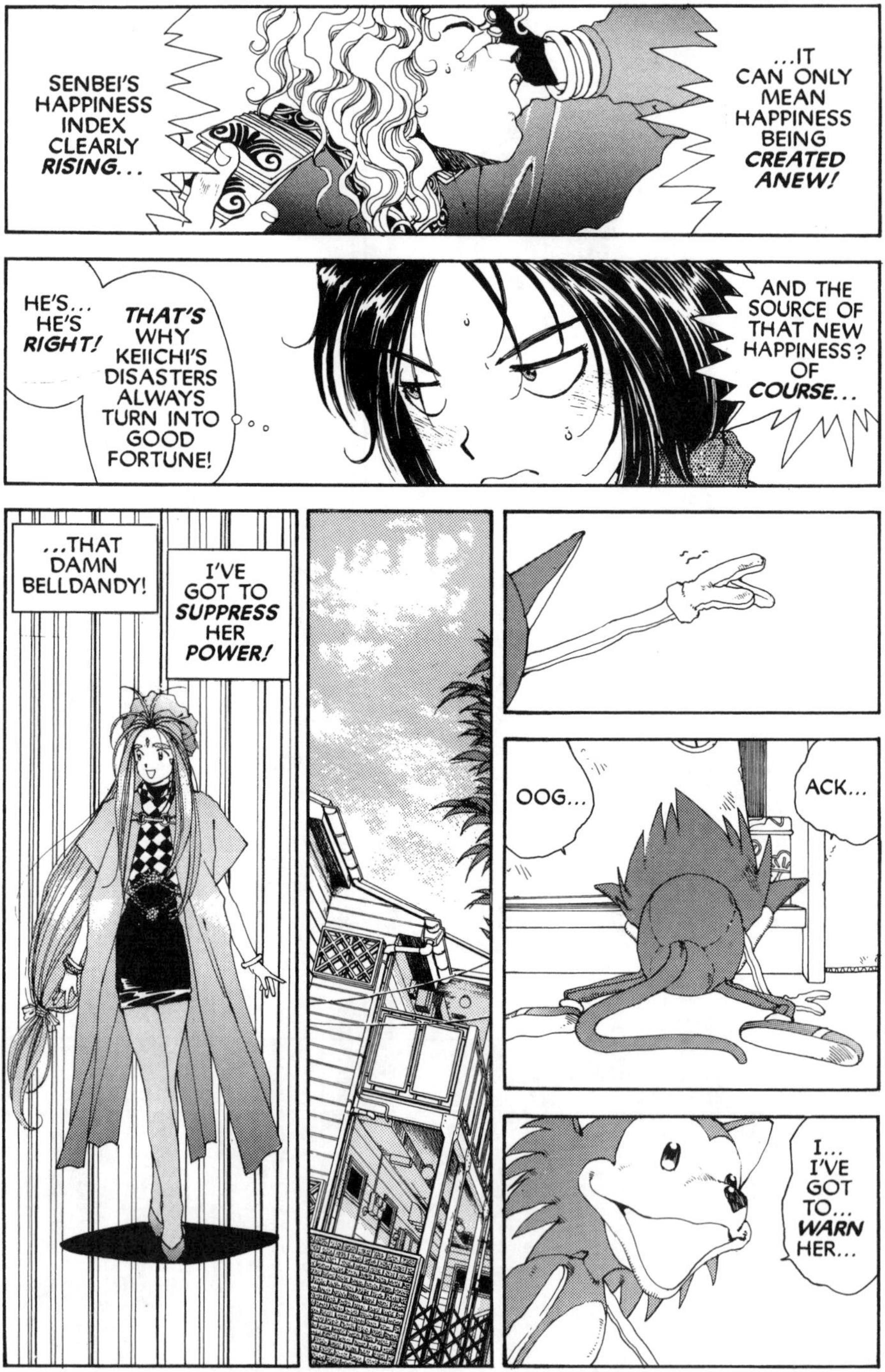
SENBEI'S HAPPINESS INDEX CLEARLY *RISING...*
...IT CAN ONLY MEAN HAPPINESS BEING *CREATED ANEW!*
HE'S... HE'S *RIGHT!*
THAT'S WHY KEIICHI'S DISASTERS ALWAYS TURN INTO GOOD FORTUNE!
AND THE SOURCE OF THAT NEW HAPPINESS? OF *COURSE...*
...THAT DAMN BELLDANDY!
I'VE GOT TO *SUPPRESS* HER *POWER!*
OOG...
ACK...
I... I'VE GOT TO... *WARN* HER...

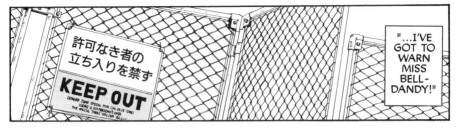

許可なき者の
立ち入りを禁ず

KEEP OUT

DANGER ZONE SPECIAL FOR CAR-GUNS ONLY
HERE & NO PARKING OVER
THE SPECIAL TRIBE GILINO ALL

" ...I'VE GOT TO WARN MISS BELL-DANDY!"

BY TEST... YOU MEANT *THIS*?!

WHUD YA THINK, HUH? WHY ELSE WOULD WE CALL YUH?

SO, UHM...

WHY DO YOUR QUARTER-MILE ENGINE TESTING IN A *TRUCK*? KINDA WEIRD, IF YOU ASK ME...

YEAH! DAT'S DUH *REASON*, KIDDO!

BEING *NORMAL* FAST AIN'T INTERESTIN', GEDDIT?

OUR MOTOR CLUB DON'T DO *NOTHIN'* DAT AIN'T *INTERESTIN'*!

"EXPECT DUH UN-EXPECTED!" DAT'S OUR NEW MOTTO!

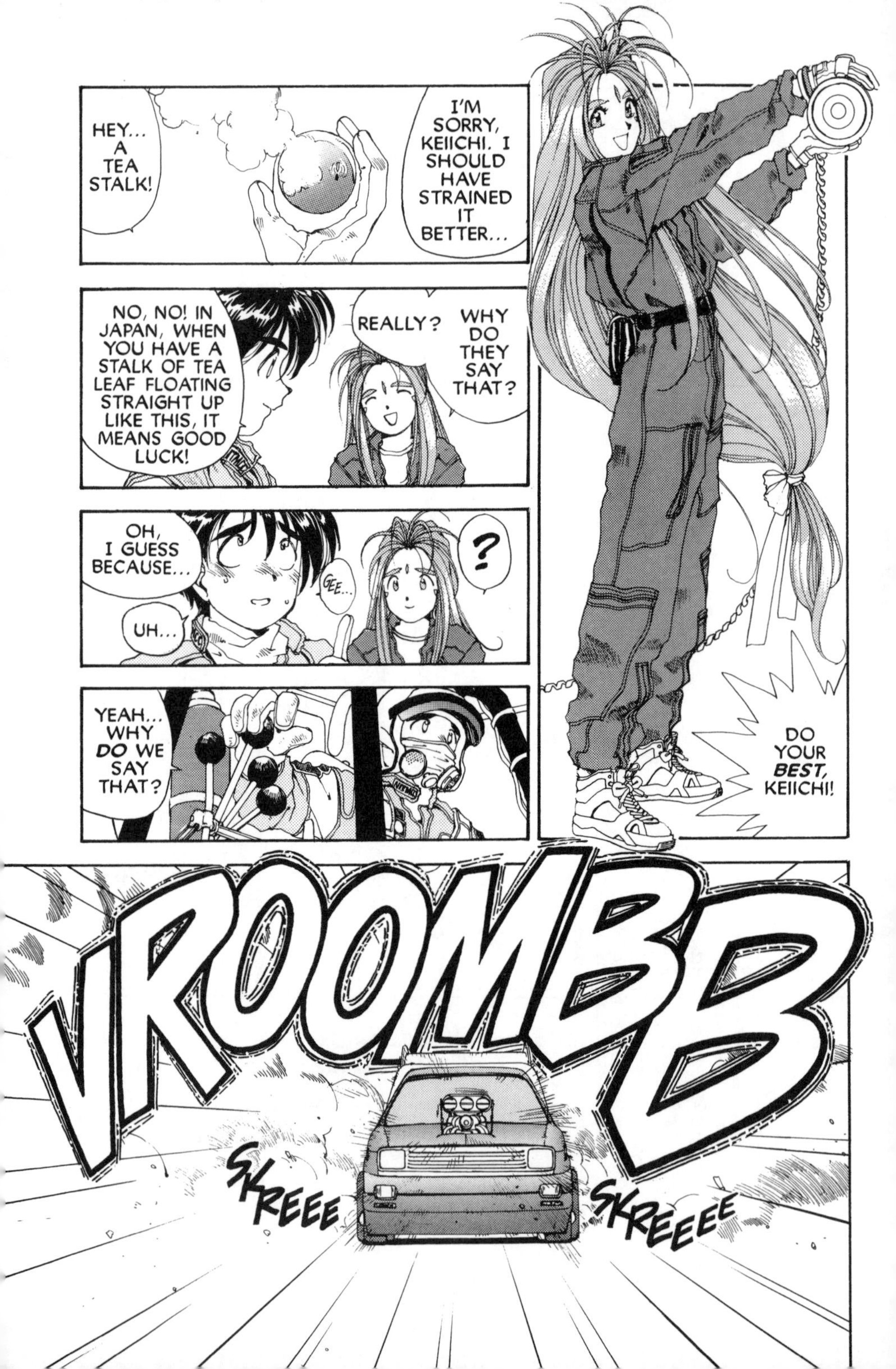
HEY... A TEA STALK!
I'M SORRY, KEIICHI. I SHOULD HAVE STRAINED IT BETTER...
NO, NO! IN JAPAN, WHEN YOU HAVE A STALK OF TEA LEAF FLOATING STRAIGHT UP LIKE THIS, IT MEANS GOOD LUCK!
REALLY?
WHY DO THEY SAY THAT?
OH, I GUESS BECAUSE...
UH...
GEE...
?
YEAH... WHY *DO* WE SAY THAT?
DO YOUR *BEST,* KEIICHI!
VROOMBB
SKREEEE
SKREEEEE

VROOOMMBB
SKREEEEE

OKAY, SENBEI... *DO* IT.

I'M DAMPING BELLDANDY'S POWER, SO...

ATTACK!!

GRP!

FRAP!

BLORT!

DAMN IT! WHAT THE...?!

GRP! GRP!

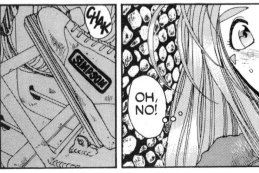

CHAK

SIMPSON

OH, NO!

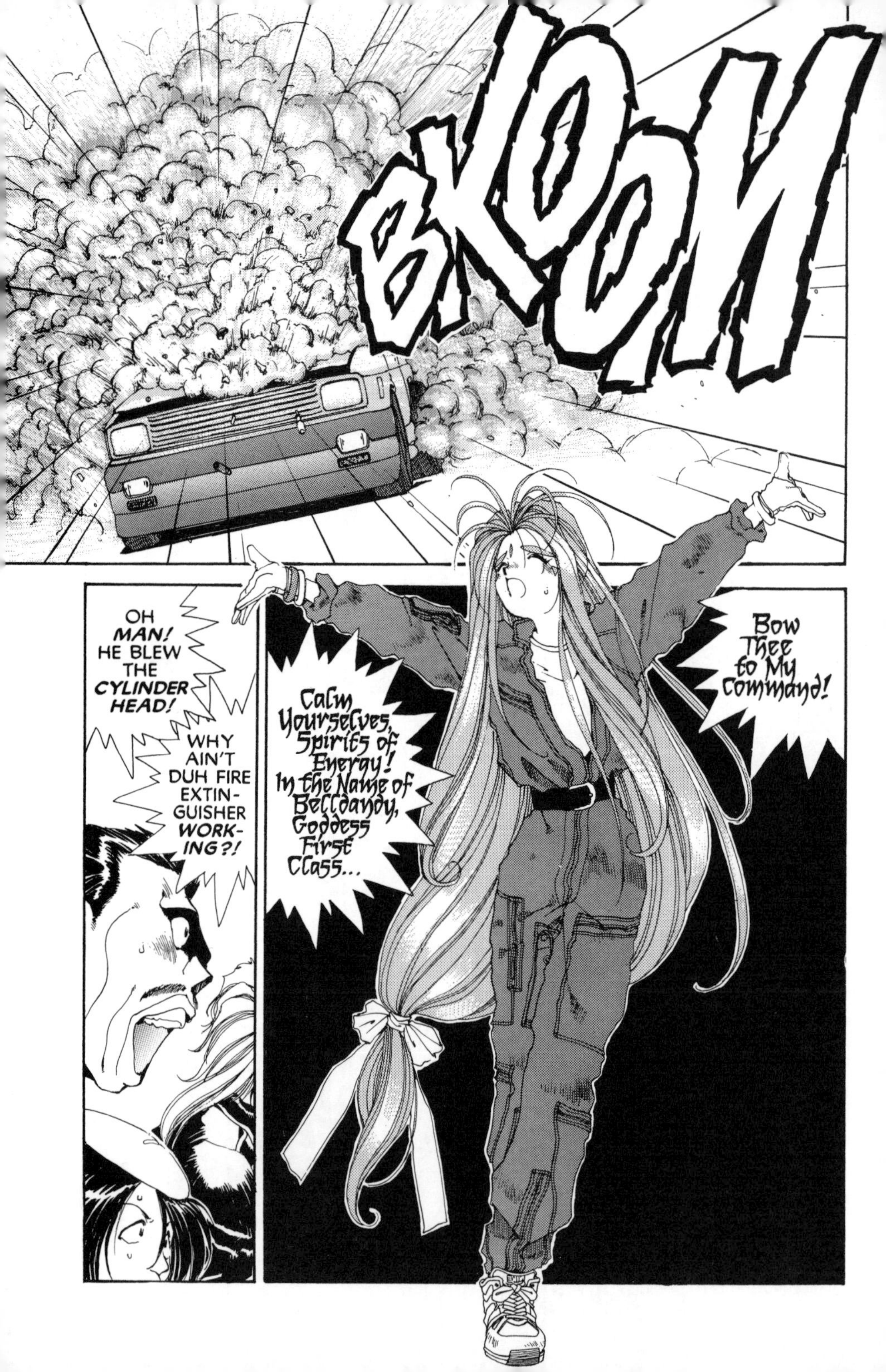
BKOOM
OH MAN! HE BLEW THE CYLINDER HEAD!
WHY AIN'T DUH FIRE EXTIN-GUISHER WORK-ING?!
Calm Yourselves, Spirits of Energy! In the Name of Belldandy, Goddess First Class...
Bow Thee to My Command!

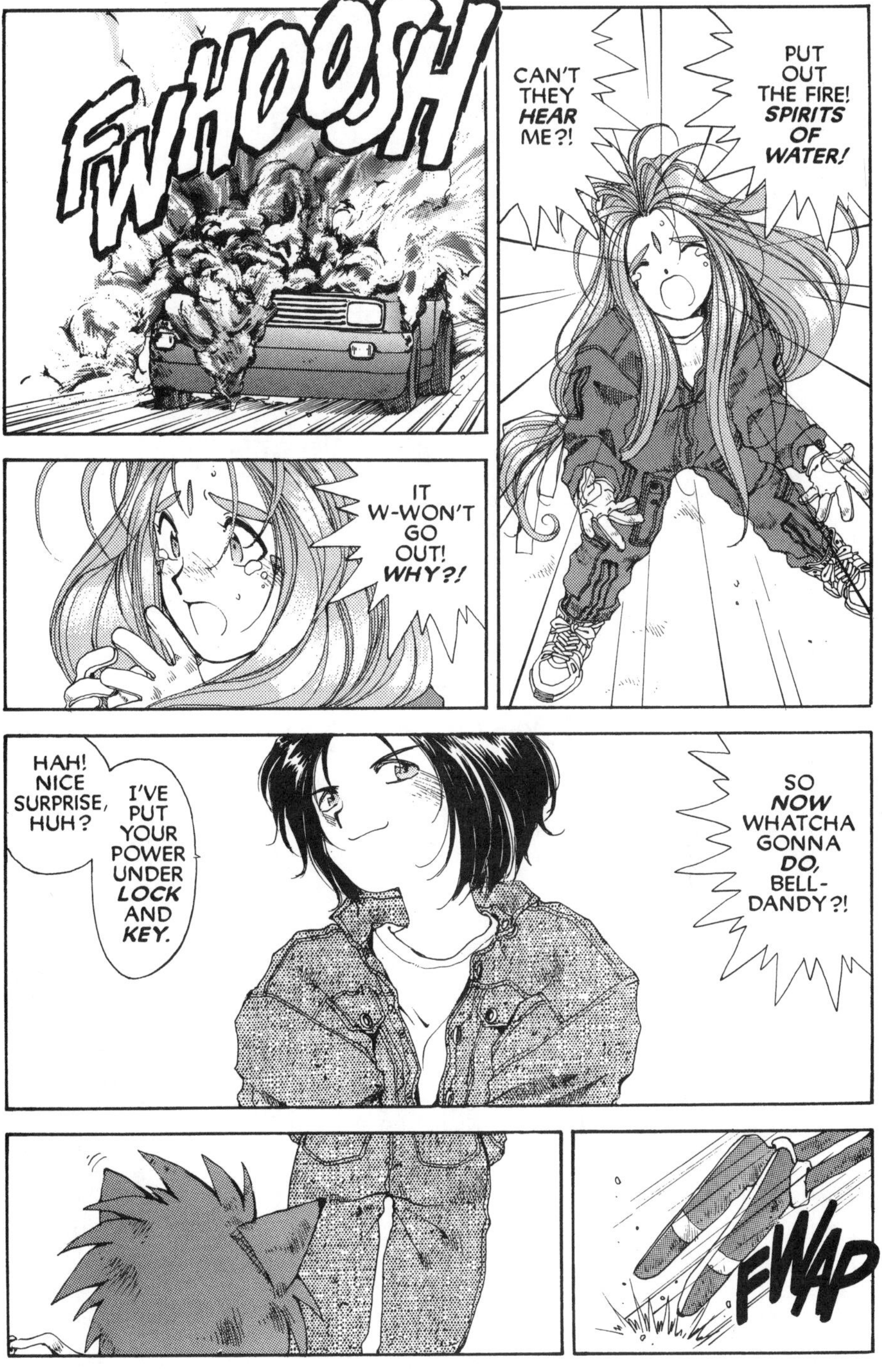
FWHOOSH
IT W-WON'T GO OUT! WHY?!
CAN'T THEY HEAR ME?!
PUT OUT THE FIRE! SPIRITS OF WATER!
HAH! NICE SURPRISE, HUH?
I'VE PUT YOUR POWER UNDER LOCK AND KEY.
SO NOW WHATCHA GONNA DO, BELL-DANDY?!
FWAP

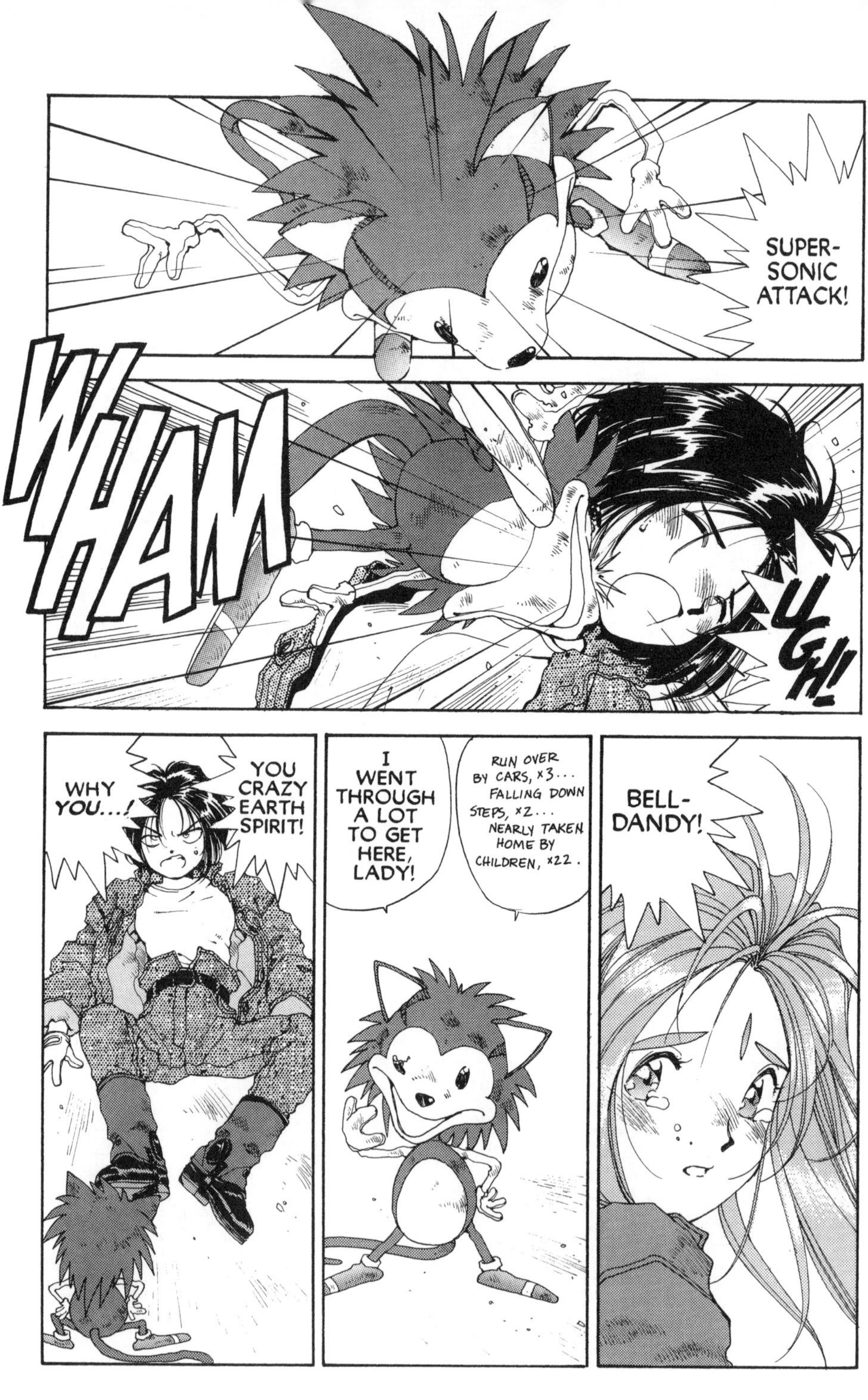
SUPER-SONIC ATTACK!
WHAM
UGH!
WHY YOU...!
YOU CRAZY EARTH SPIRIT!
I WENT THROUGH A LOT TO GET HERE, LADY!
RUN OVER BY CARS, ×3... FALLING DOWN STEPS, ×2... NEARLY TAKEN HOME BY CHILDREN, ×22.
BELL-DANDY!

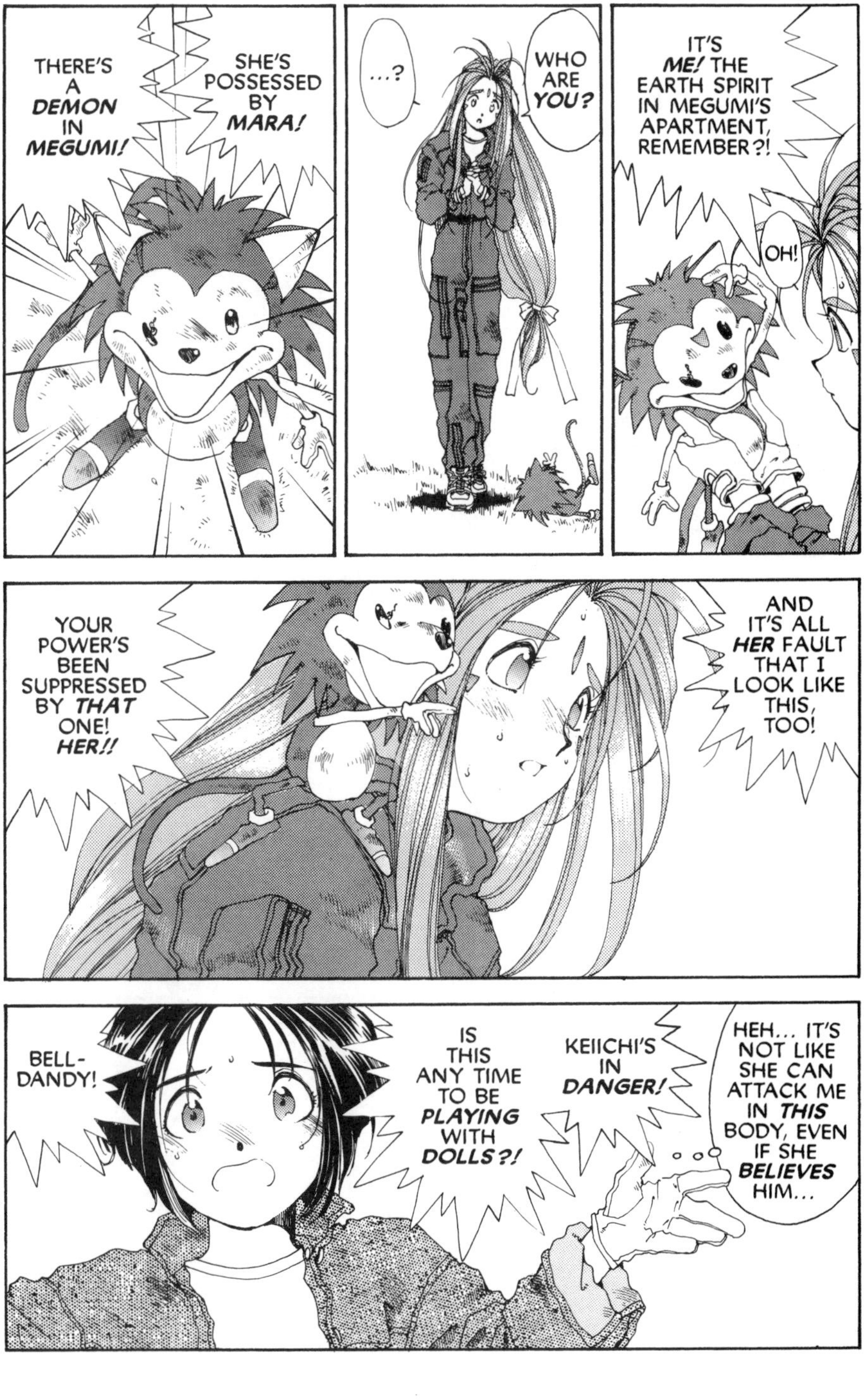
THERE'S A *DEMON* IN *MEGUMI!*
SHE'S POSSESSED BY *MARA!*
...?
WHO ARE *YOU?*
IT'S *ME!* THE EARTH SPIRIT IN MEGUMI'S APARTMENT, REMEMBER?!
OH!
YOUR POWER'S BEEN SUPPRESSED BY *THAT* ONE! *HER!!*
AND IT'S ALL *HER* FAULT THAT I LOOK LIKE THIS, TOO!
BELL-DANDY!
IS THIS ANY TIME TO BE *PLAYING* WITH *DOLLS?!*
KEIICHI'S IN *DANGER!*
HEH... IT'S NOT LIKE SHE CAN ATTACK ME IN *THIS* BODY, EVEN IF SHE *BELIEVES* HIM...

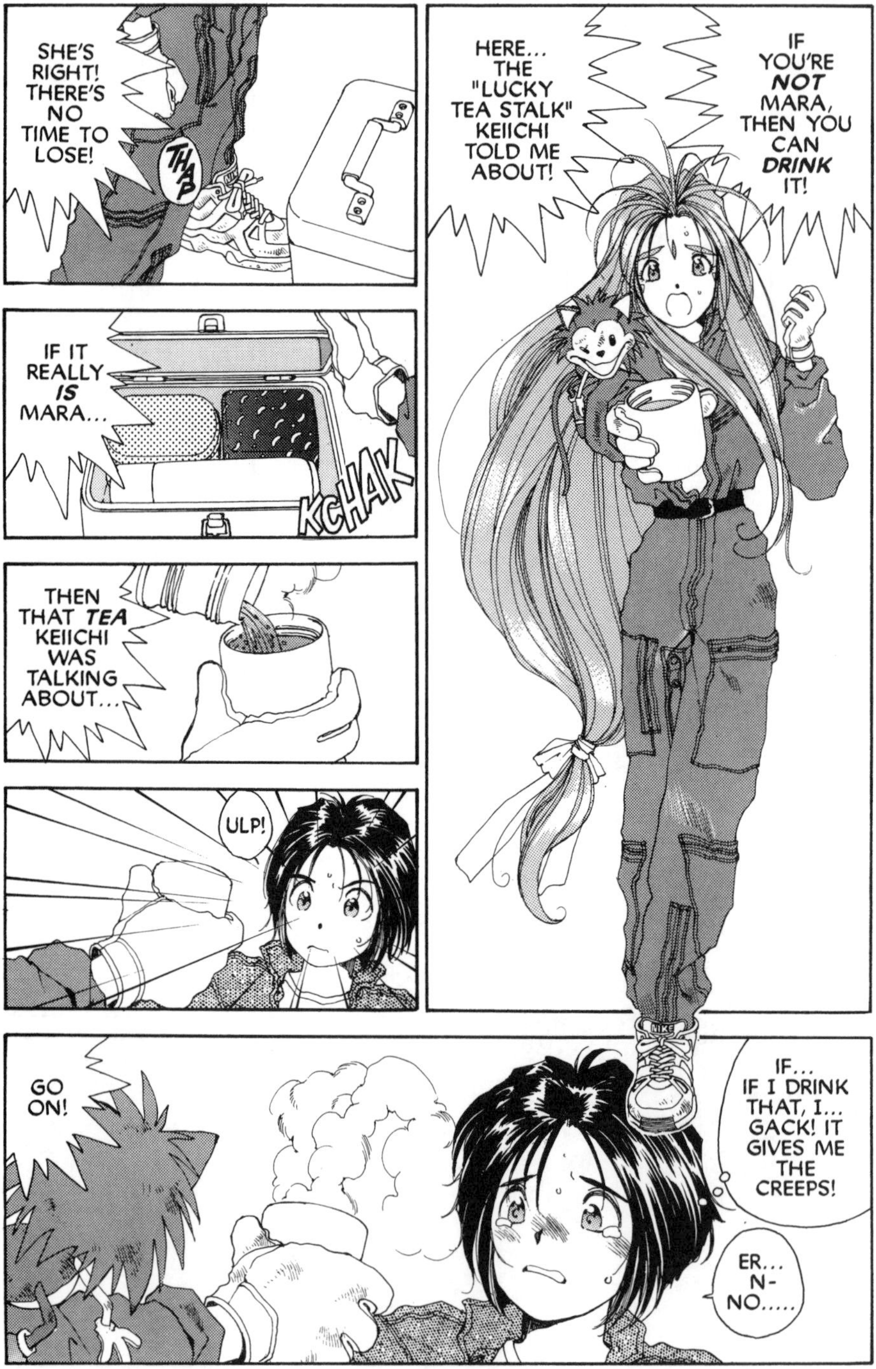
SHE'S RIGHT! THERE'S NO TIME TO LOSE!
THAP
IF IT REALLY IS MARA...
KCHAK
THEN THAT TEA KEIICHI WAS TALKING ABOUT...
ULP!
HERE... THE "LUCKY TEA STALK" KEIICHI TOLD ME ABOUT!
IF YOU'RE NOT MARA, THEN YOU CAN DRINK IT!
GO ON!
IF... IF I DRINK THAT, I... GACK! IT GIVES ME THE CREEPS!
ER... N- NO.....

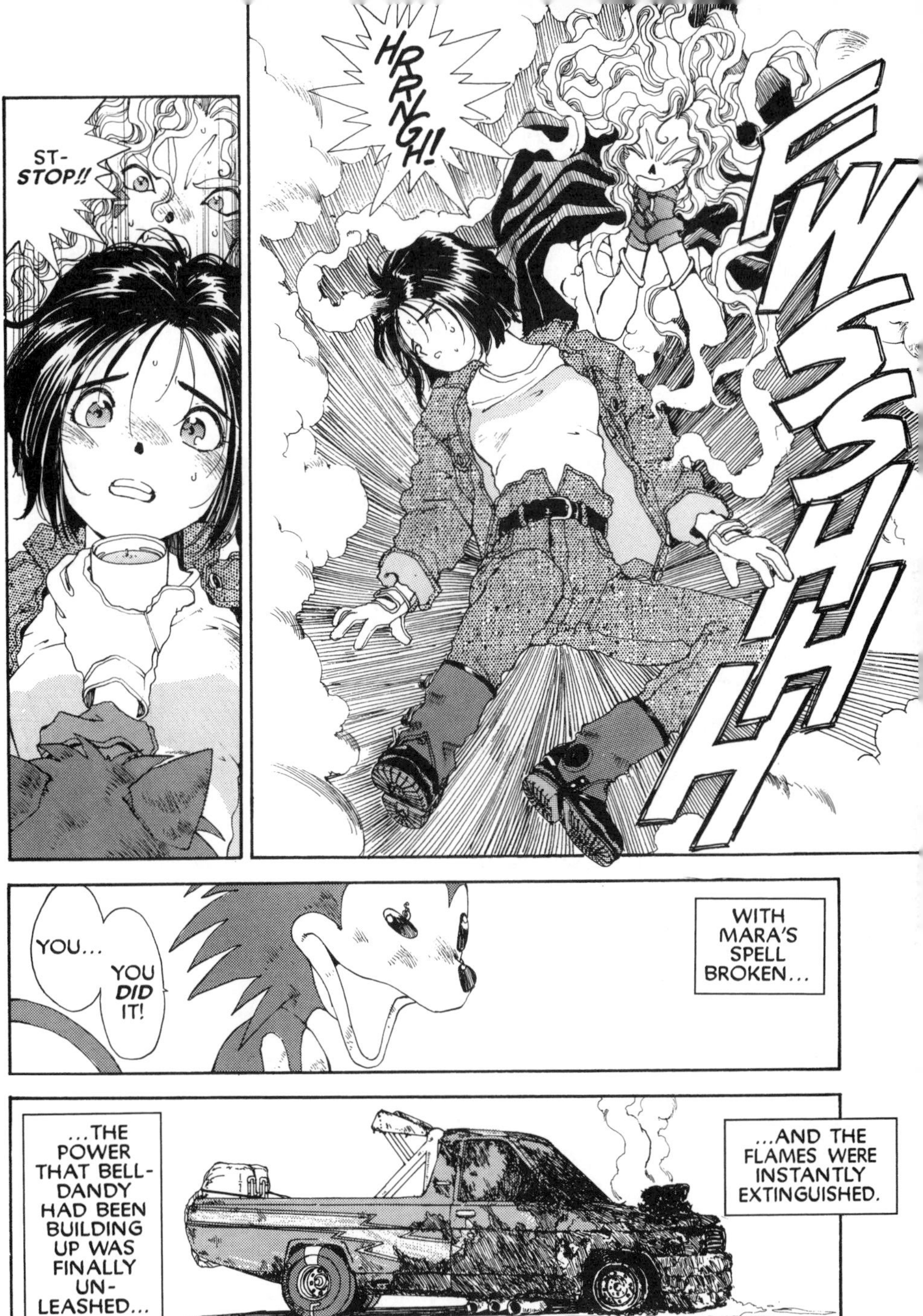
ST-
STOP!!
HRRNGH!!
FWSSHHHH
YOU...
YOU DID IT!
WITH MARA'S SPELL BROKEN...
...THE POWER THAT BELL-DANDY HAD BEEN BUILDING UP WAS FINALLY UN-LEASHED...
...AND THE FLAMES WERE INSTANTLY EXTINGUISHED.

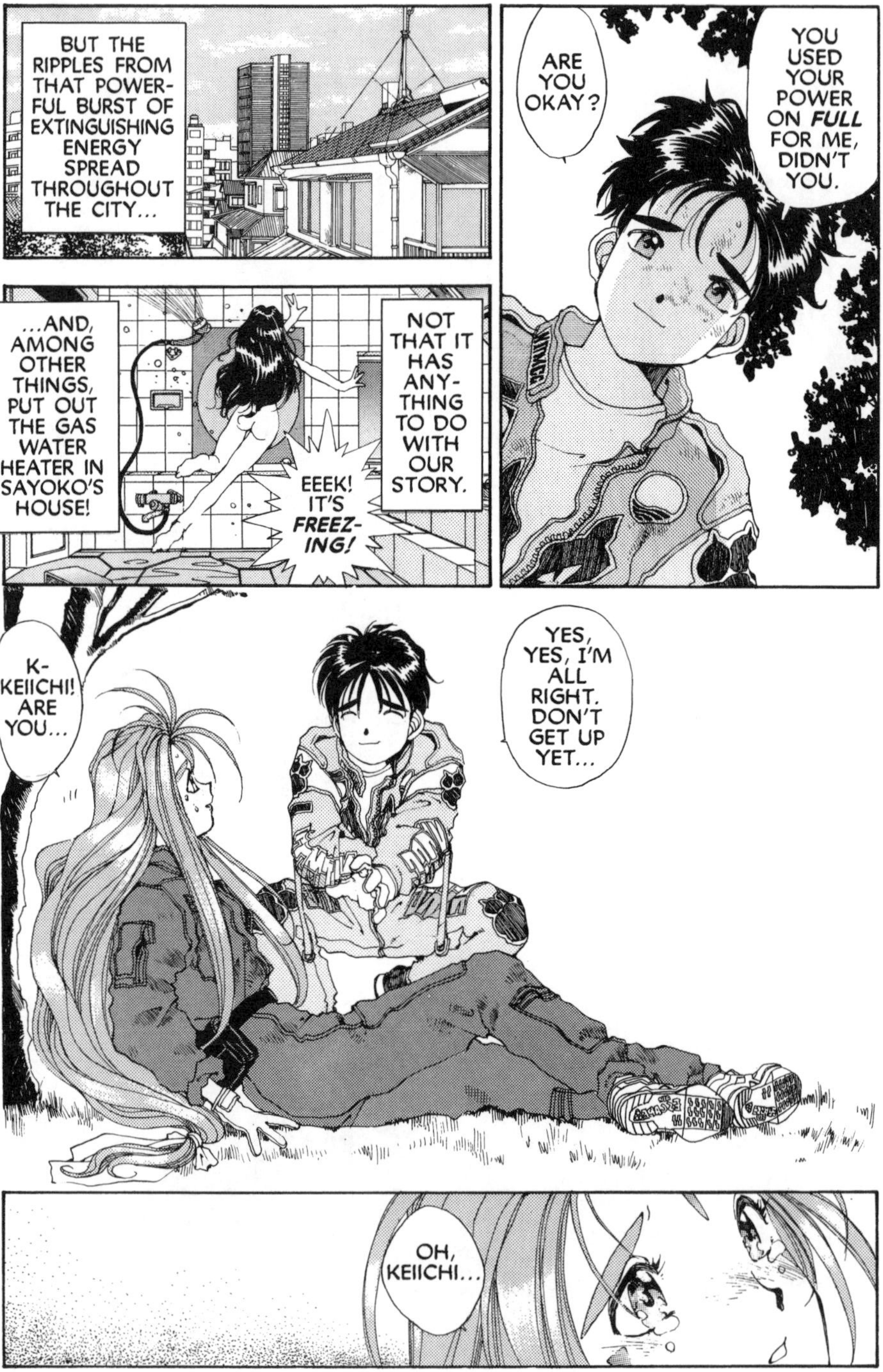
BUT THE RIPPLES FROM THAT POWERFUL BURST OF EXTINGUISHING ENERGY SPREAD THROUGHOUT THE CITY...
...AND, AMONG OTHER THINGS, PUT OUT THE GAS WATER HEATER IN SAYOKO'S HOUSE!
EEEK! IT'S *FREEZING!*
NOT THAT IT HAS ANYTHING TO DO WITH OUR STORY.
ARE YOU OKAY?
YOU USED YOUR POWER ON *FULL* FOR ME, DIDN'T YOU.
K-KEIICHI! ARE YOU...
YES, YES, I'M ALL RIGHT. DON'T GET UP YET...
OH, KEIICHI...

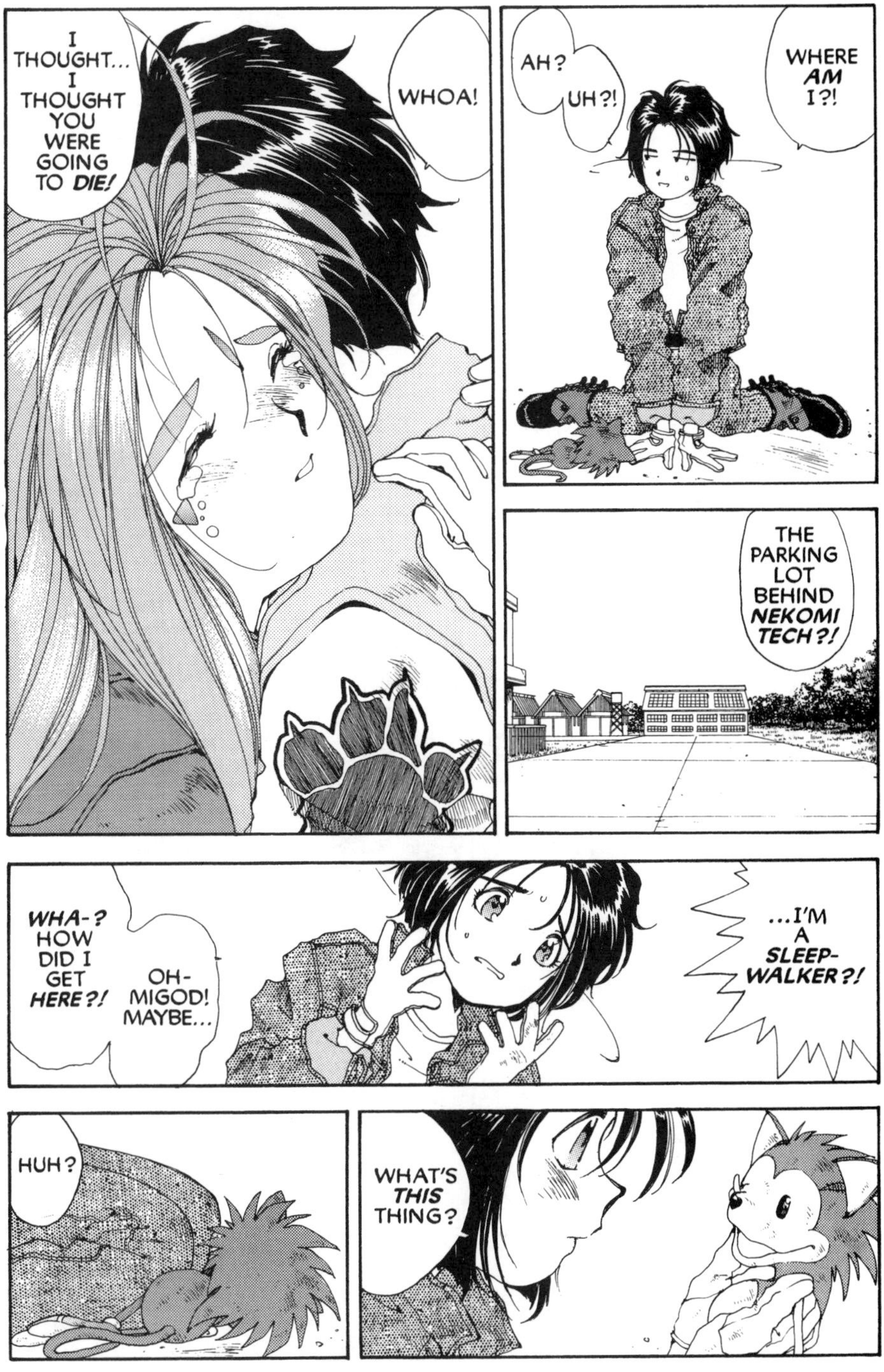
I THOUGHT... I THOUGHT YOU WERE GOING TO DIE!
WHOA!
AH?
UH?!
WHERE AM I?!
THE PARKING LOT BEHIND NEKOMI TECH?!
WHA-? HOW DID I GET HERE?!
OH-MIGOD! MAYBE...
...I'M A SLEEP-WALKER?!
HUH?
WHAT'S THIS THING?

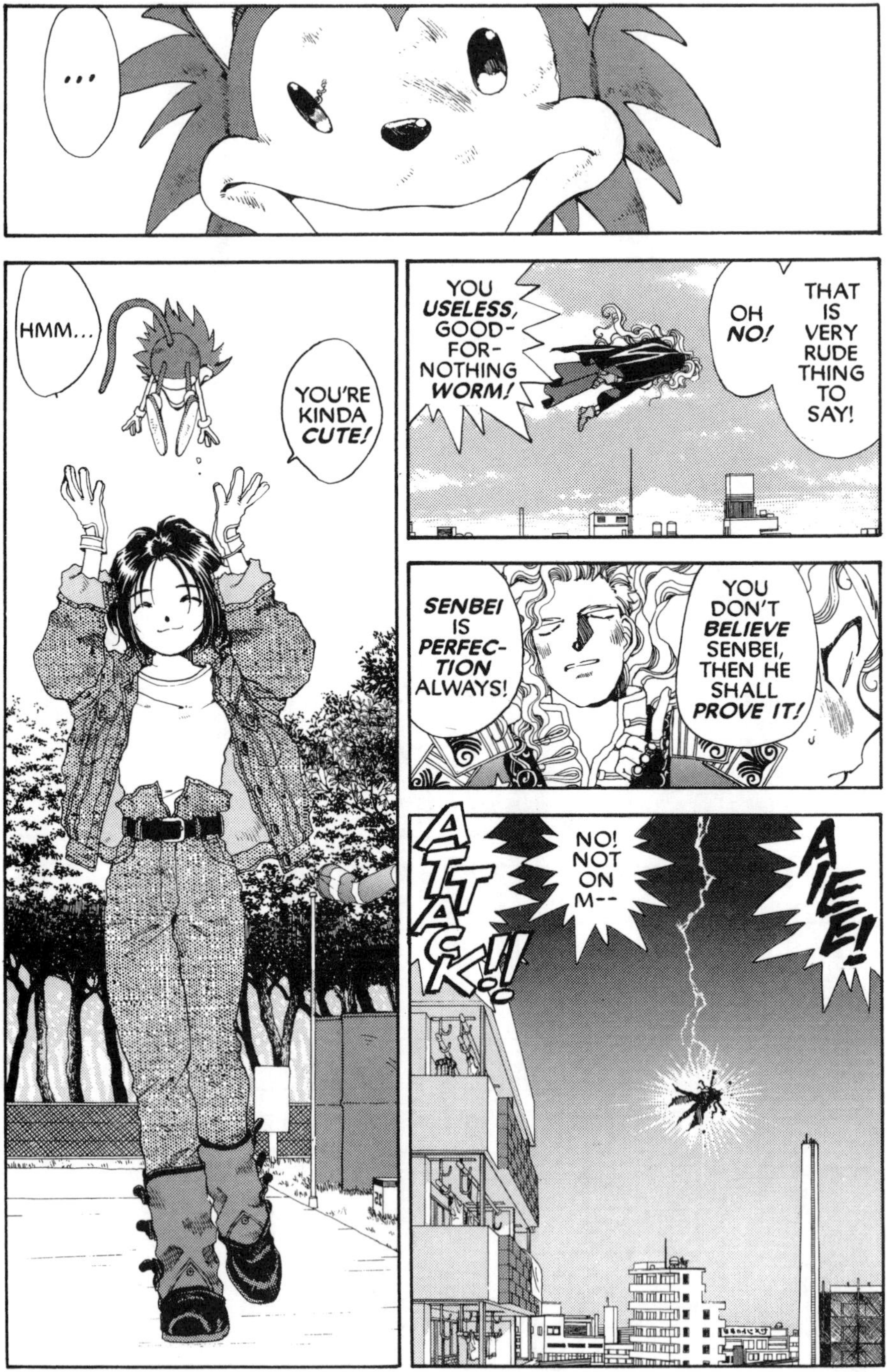
...
HMM...
YOU'RE KINDA CUTE!
YOU USELESS, GOOD-FOR-NOTHING WORM!
OH NO!
THAT IS VERY RUDE THING TO SAY!
SENBEI IS PERFECTION ALWAYS!
YOU DON'T BELIEVE SENBEI, THEN HE SHALL PROVE IT!
ATTACK!!
NO! NOT ON M--
AIEEE!

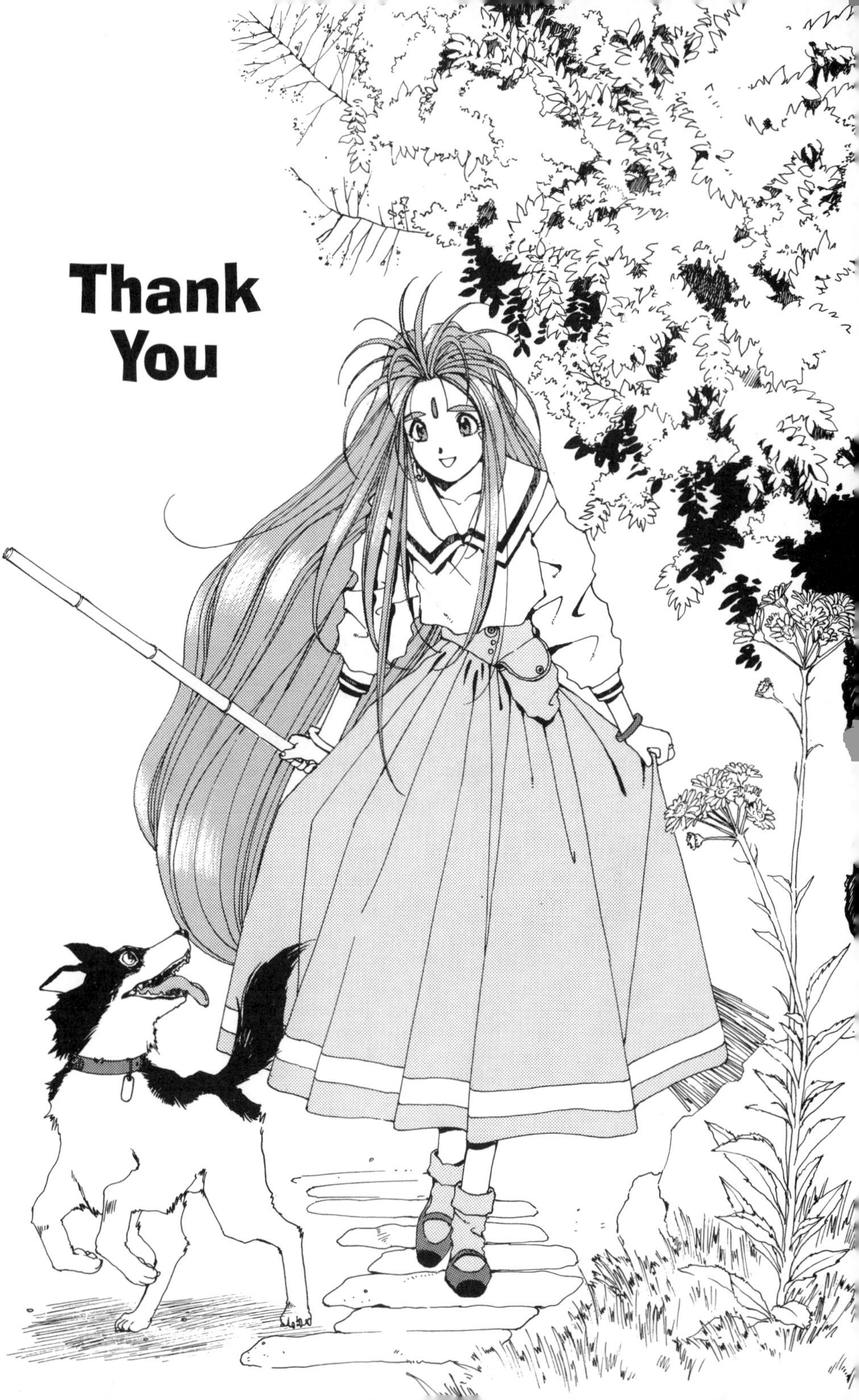
Thank You

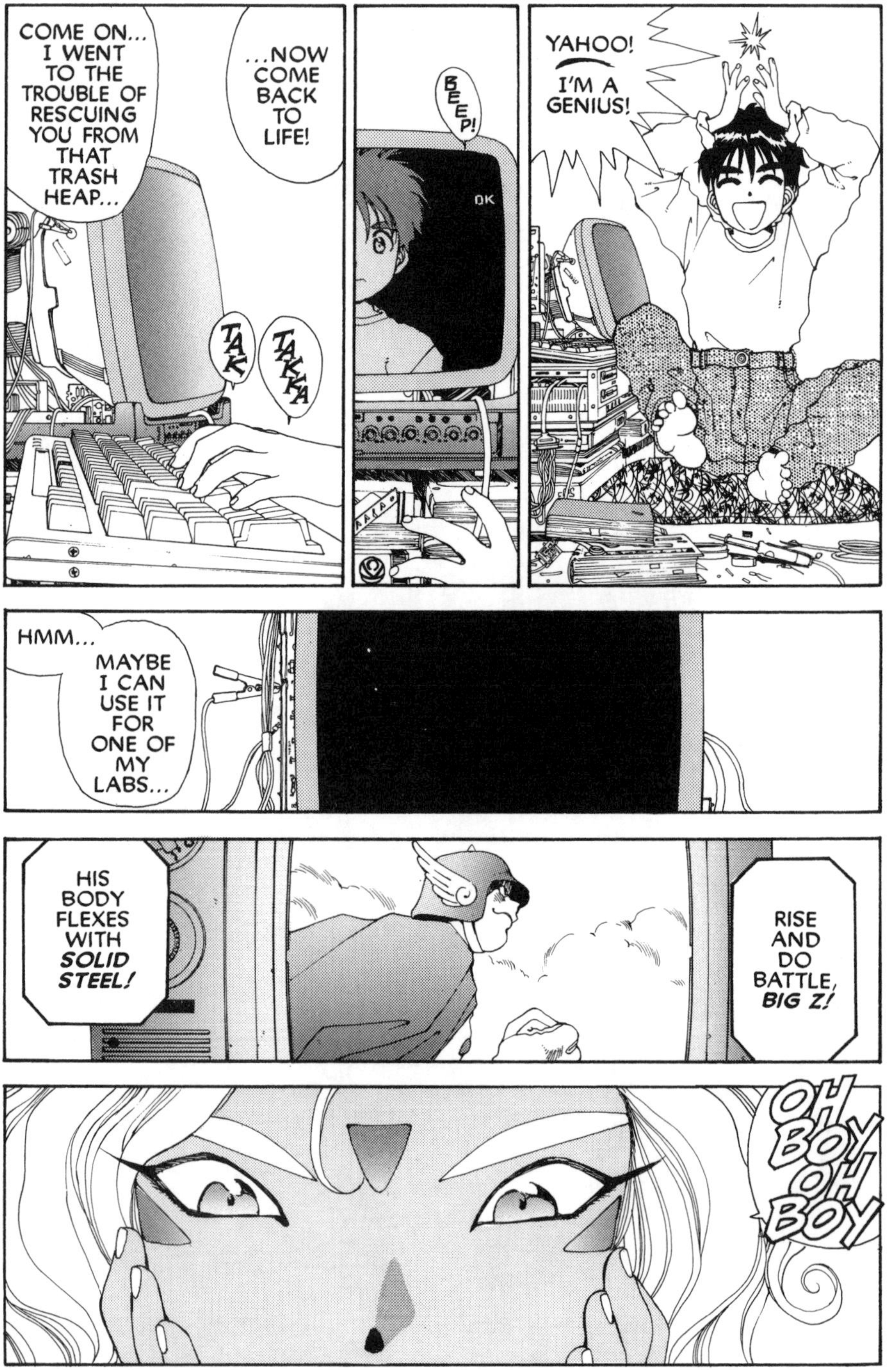
COME ON... I WENT TO THE TROUBLE OF RESCUING YOU FROM THAT TRASH HEAP...
...NOW COME BACK TO LIFE!
TAK
TAKKA
BEEP!
OK
YAHOO! I'M A GENIUS!
HMM... MAYBE I CAN USE IT FOR ONE OF MY LABS...
HIS BODY FLEXES WITH SOLID STEEL!
RISE AND DO BATTLE, BIG Z!
OH BOY OH BOY

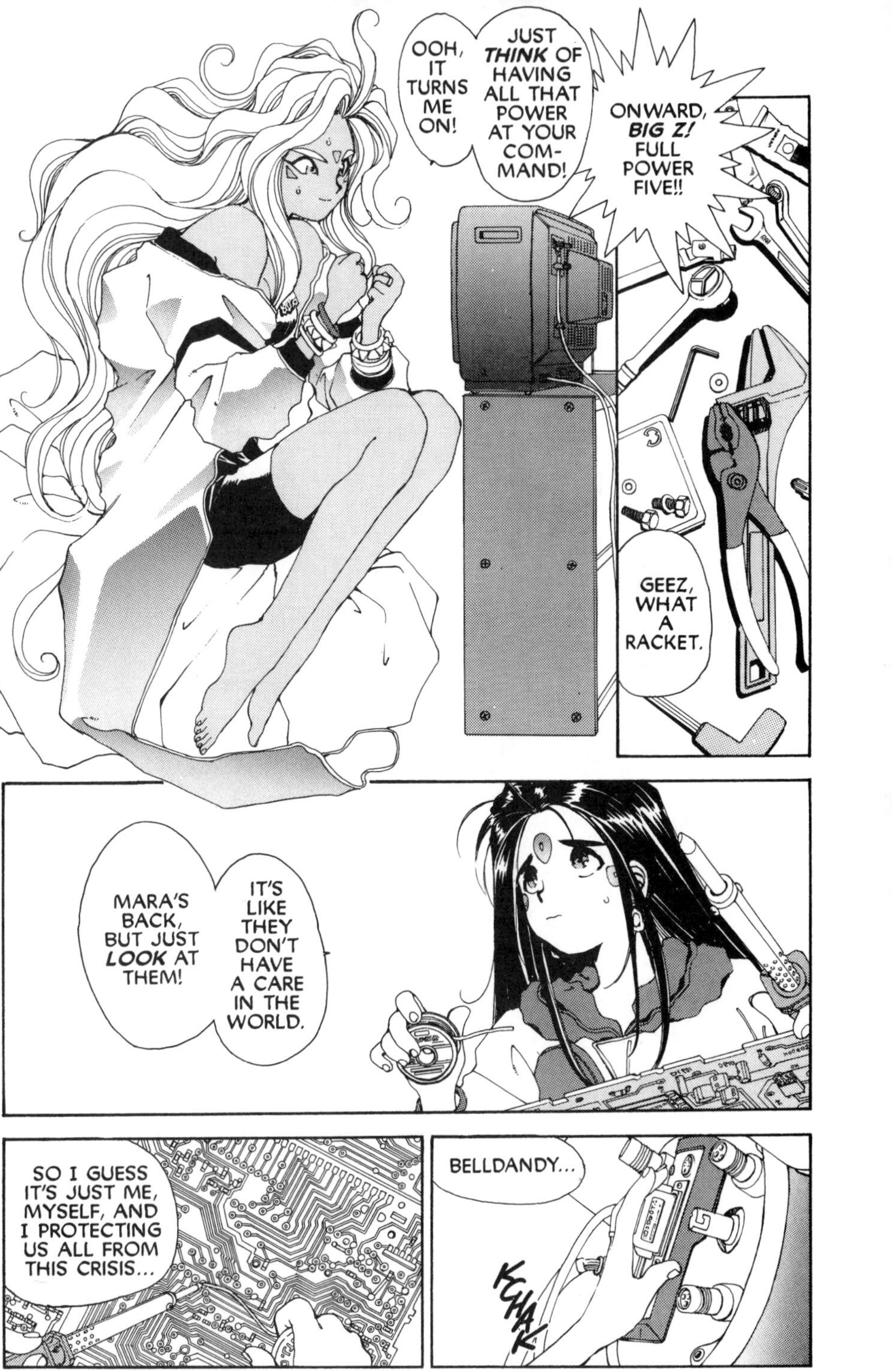

OOH, IT TURNS ME ON!
JUST *THINK* OF HAVING ALL THAT POWER AT YOUR COM-MAND!
ONWARD, *BIG Z!* FULL POWER FIVE!!
GEEZ, WHAT A RACKET.
MARA'S BACK, BUT JUST *LOOK* AT THEM!
IT'S LIKE THEY DON'T HAVE A CARE IN THE WORLD.
SO I GUESS IT'S JUST ME, MYSELF, AND I PROTECTING US ALL FROM THIS CRISIS...
BELLDANDY...
KCHAK

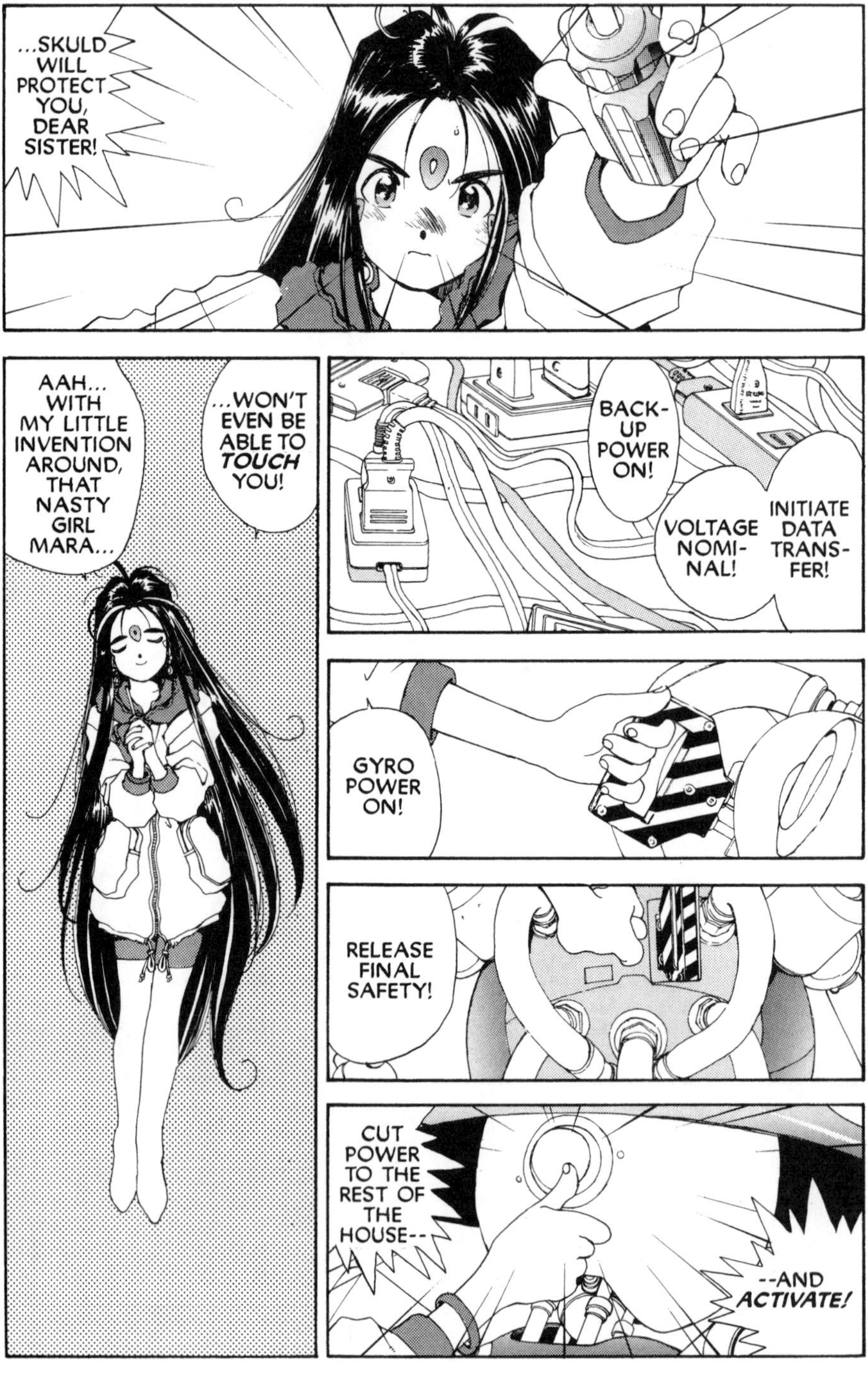
...SKULD WILL PROTECT YOU, DEAR SISTER!
AAH... WITH MY LITTLE INVENTION AROUND, THAT NASTY GIRL MARA...
...WON'T EVEN BE ABLE TO *TOUCH* YOU!
BACK-UP POWER ON!
VOLTAGE NOMI-NAL!
INITIATE DATA TRANS-FER!
GYRO POWER ON!
RELEASE FINAL SAFETY!
CUT POWER TO THE REST OF THE HOUSE--
--AND *ACTIVATE!*

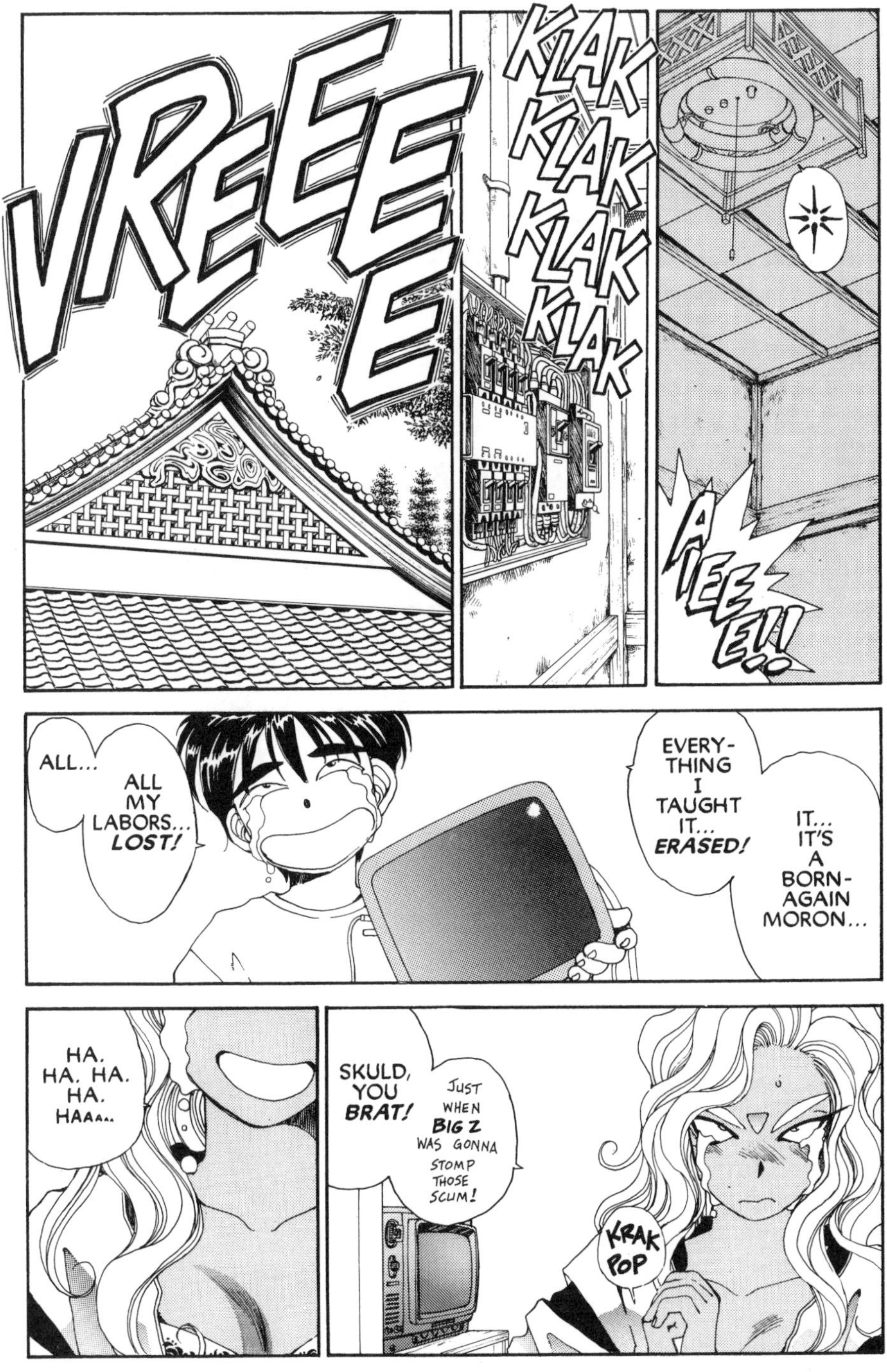
VREEEE
KLAK KLAK KLAK KLAK KLAK
AIEEEE!!
ALL... ALL MY LABORS... LOST!
EVERYTHING I TAUGHT IT... ERASED!
IT... IT'S A BORN-AGAIN MORON...
HA. HA. HA. HA. HAAA..
SKULD, YOU BRAT!
JUST WHEN BIG Z WAS GONNA STOMP THOSE SCUM!
KRAK POP

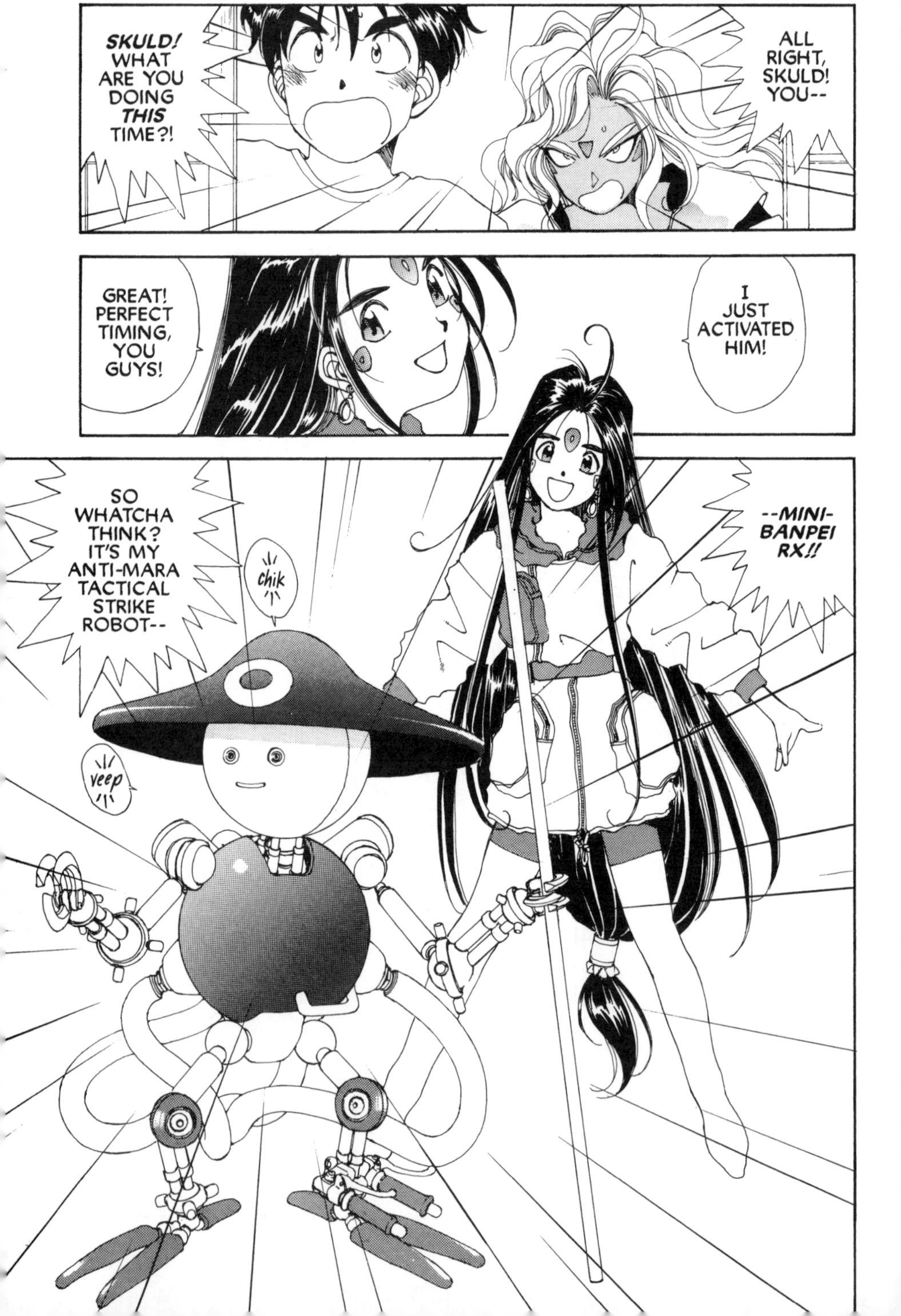
SKULD! WHAT ARE YOU DOING THIS TIME?!
ALL RIGHT, SKULD! YOU--
GREAT! PERFECT TIMING, YOU GUYS!
I JUST ACTIVATED HIM!
SO WHATCHA THINK? IT'S MY ANTI-MARA TACTICAL STRIKE ROBOT--
chik
--MINI-BANPEI RX!!
veep

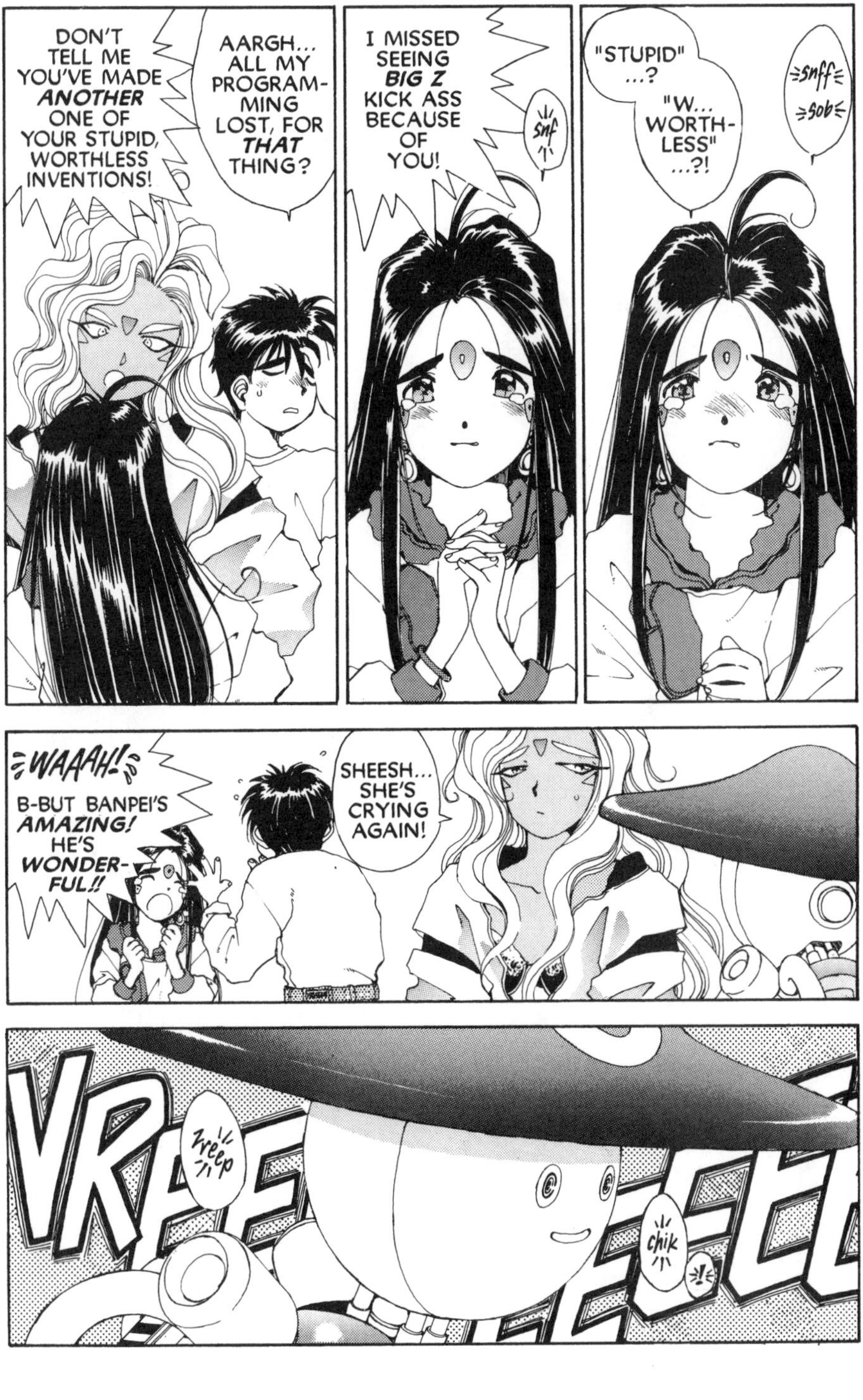
DON'T TELL ME YOU'VE MADE ANOTHER ONE OF YOUR STUPID, WORTHLESS INVENTIONS!
AARGH... ALL MY PROGRAMMING LOST, FOR THAT THING?
I MISSED SEEING BIG Z KICK ASS BECAUSE OF YOU!
snf
"STUPID"...?
"W... WORTHLESS"...?!
snff
sob
WAAAH!
B-BUT BANPEI'S AMAZING! HE'S WONDERFUL!!
SHEESH... SHE'S CRYING AGAIN!
VREEEEEEE
zreep
chik

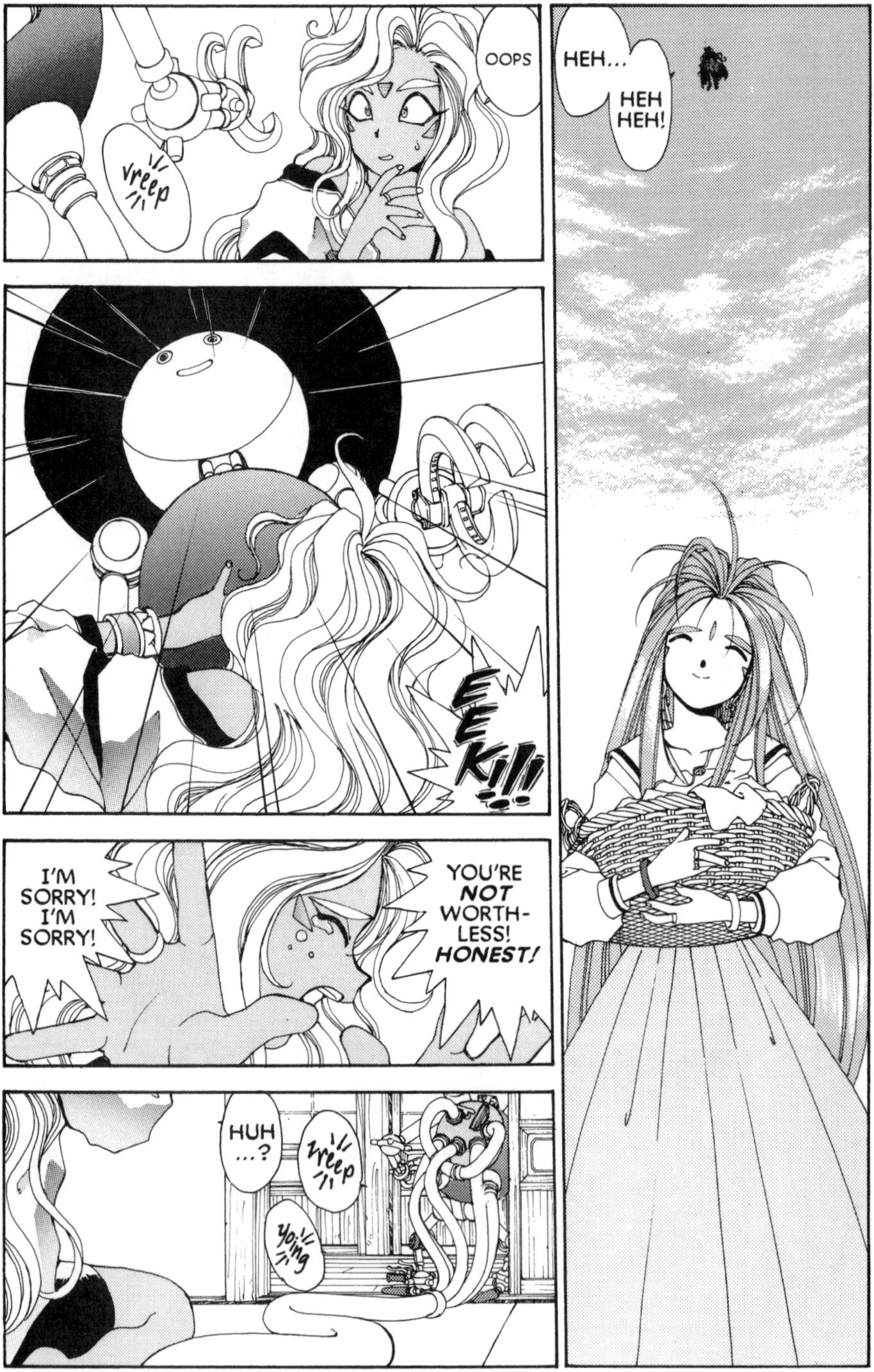
vreep
OOPS
EEK!!!
I'M SORRY! I'M SORRY!
YOU'RE NOT WORTH-LESS! HONEST!
HUH ...?
vreep
yoing
HEH...
HEH HEH!

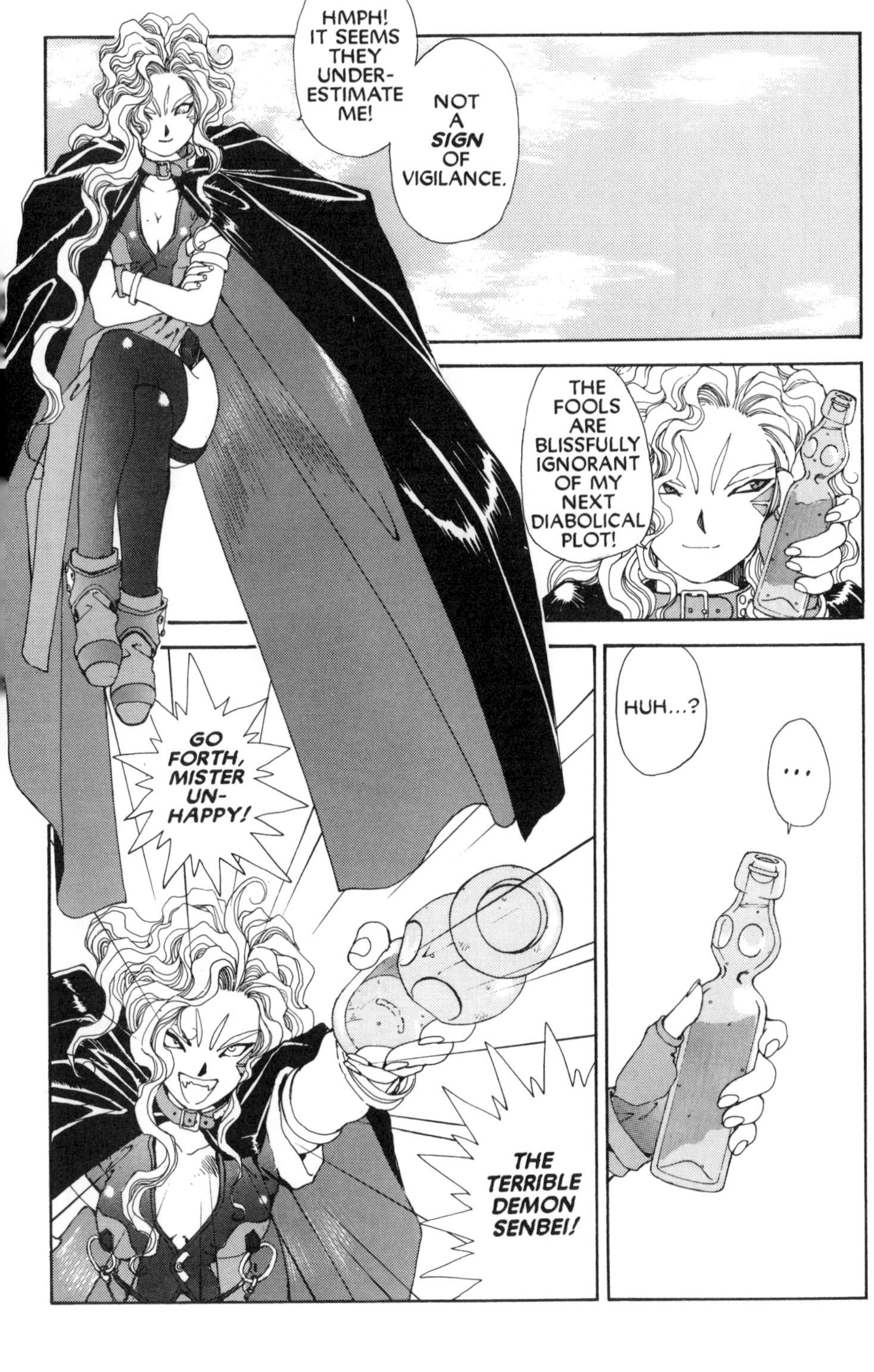
HMPH! IT SEEMS THEY UNDER-ESTIMATE ME!
NOT A *SIGN* OF VIGILANCE.
THE FOOLS ARE BLISSFULLY IGNORANT OF MY NEXT DIABOLICAL PLOT!
GO FORTH, MISTER UN-HAPPY!
THE TERRIBLE DEMON SENBEI!
HUH...?
...

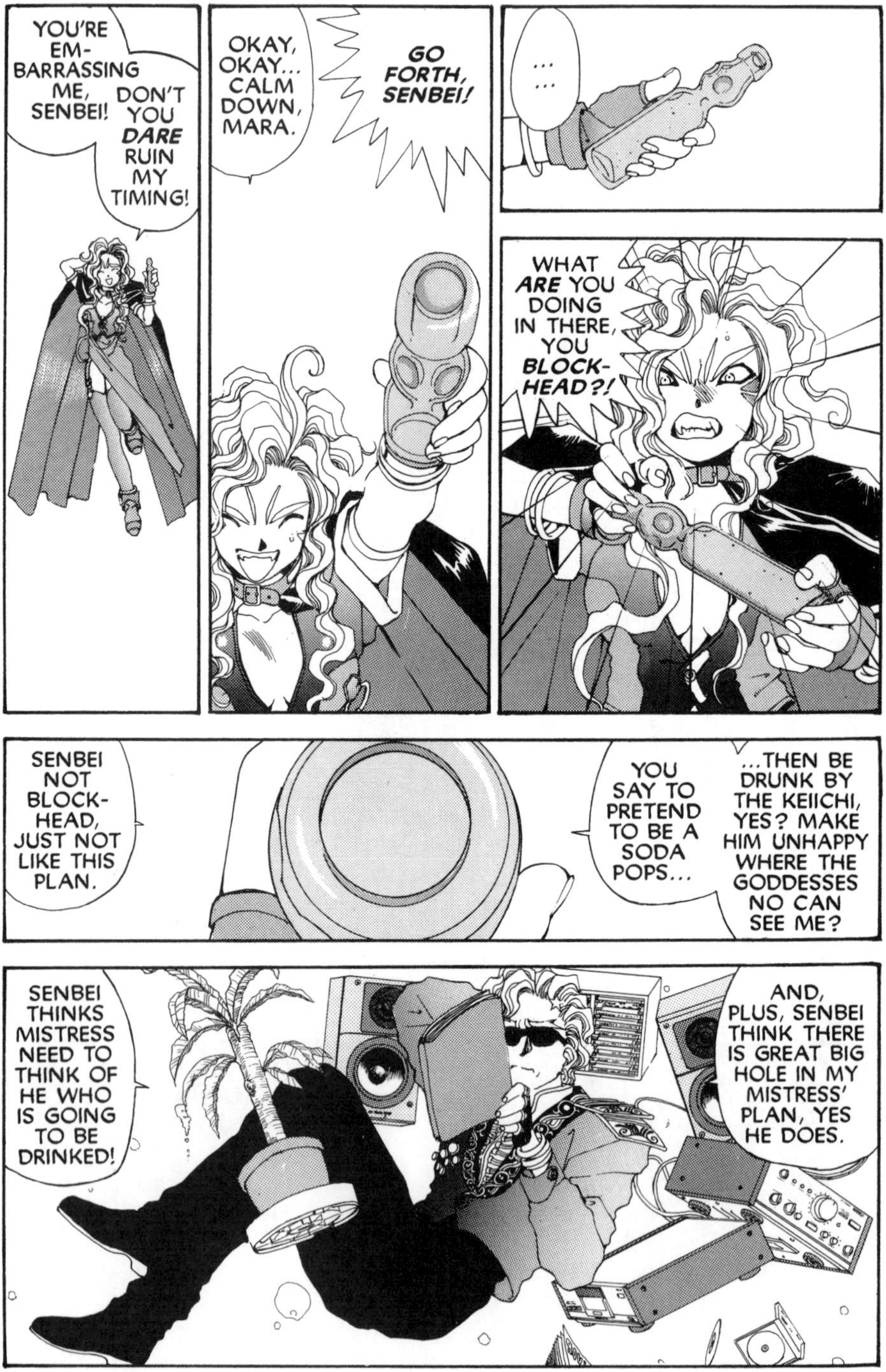
YOU'RE EM-BARRASSING ME, SENBEI!
DON'T YOU DARE RUIN MY TIMING!
OKAY, OKAY... CALM DOWN, MARA.
GO FORTH, SENBEI!
... ...
WHAT ARE YOU DOING IN THERE, YOU BLOCK-HEAD?!
SENBEI NOT BLOCK-HEAD, JUST NOT LIKE THIS PLAN.
YOU SAY TO PRETEND TO BE A SODA POPS...
...THEN BE DRUNK BY THE KEIICHI, YES? MAKE HIM UNHAPPY WHERE THE GODDESSES NO CAN SEE ME?
SENBEI THINKS MISTRESS NEED TO THINK OF HE WHO IS GOING TO BE DRINKED!
AND, PLUS, SENBEI THINK THERE IS GREAT BIG HOLE IN MY MISTRESS' PLAN, YES HE DOES.

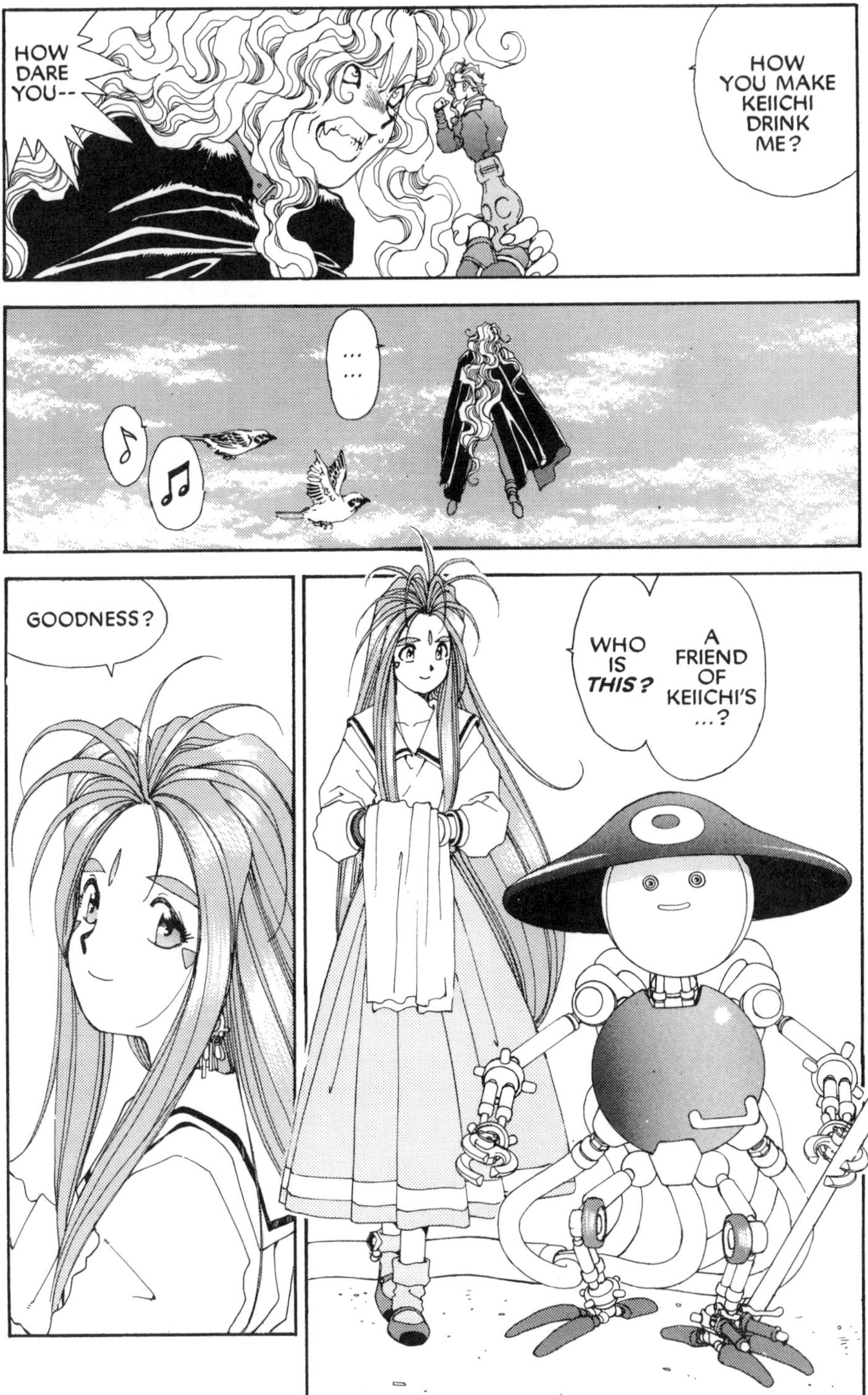

HOW DARE YOU--
HOW YOU MAKE KEIICHI DRINK ME?
... ...
GOODNESS?
WHO IS *THIS?*
A FRIEND OF KEIICHI'S ...?

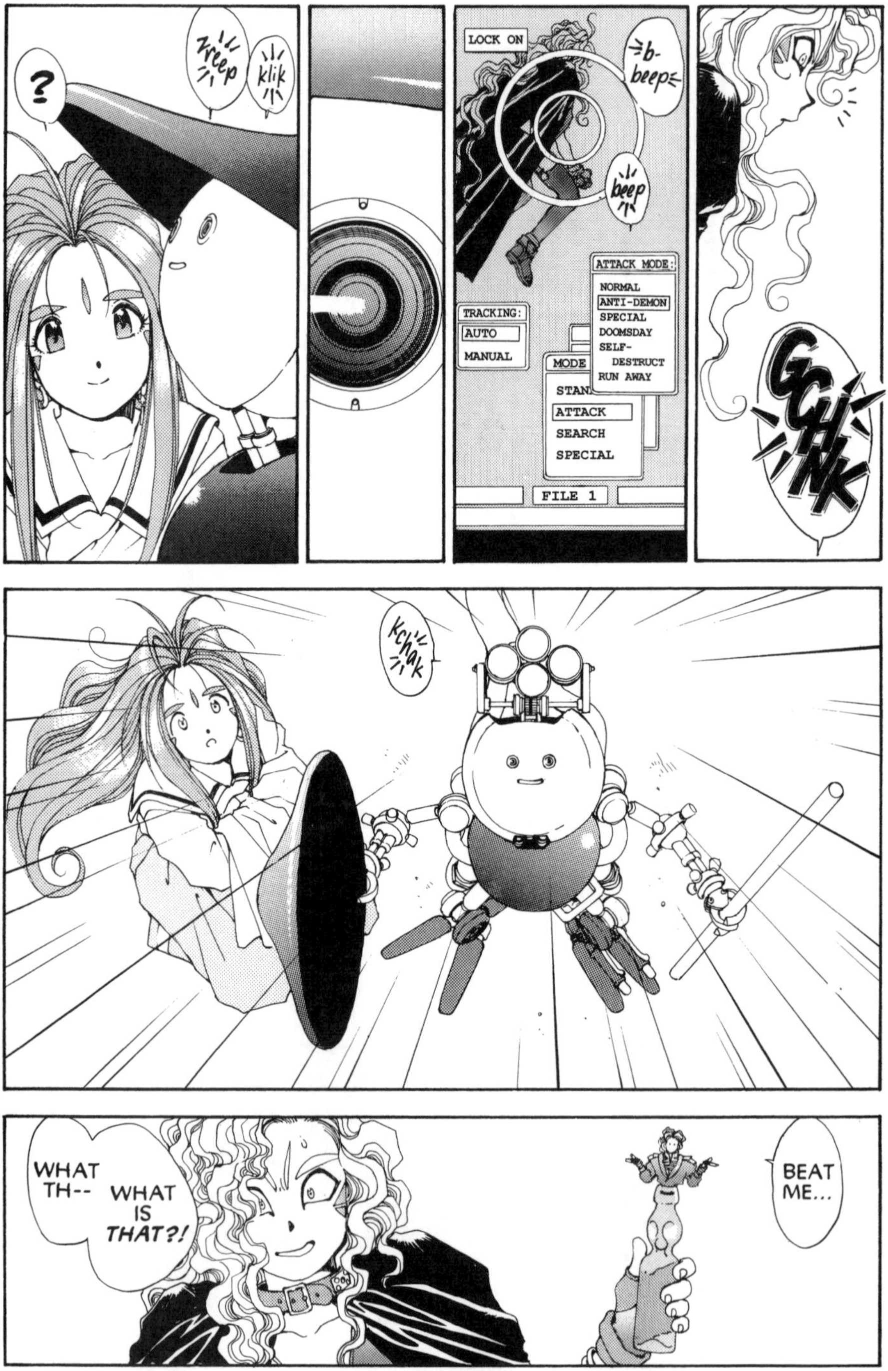
?
zreep
klik
LOCK ON
b-beep
beep
ATTACK MODE:
NORMAL
ANTI-DEMON
SPECIAL
DOOMSDAY
SELF-DESTRUCT
RUN AWAY
TRACKING:
AUTO
MANUAL
MODE
STAN
ATTACK
SEARCH
SPECIAL
FILE 1
GCHINK
kchak
WHAT TH-- WHAT IS *THAT?!*
BEAT ME...

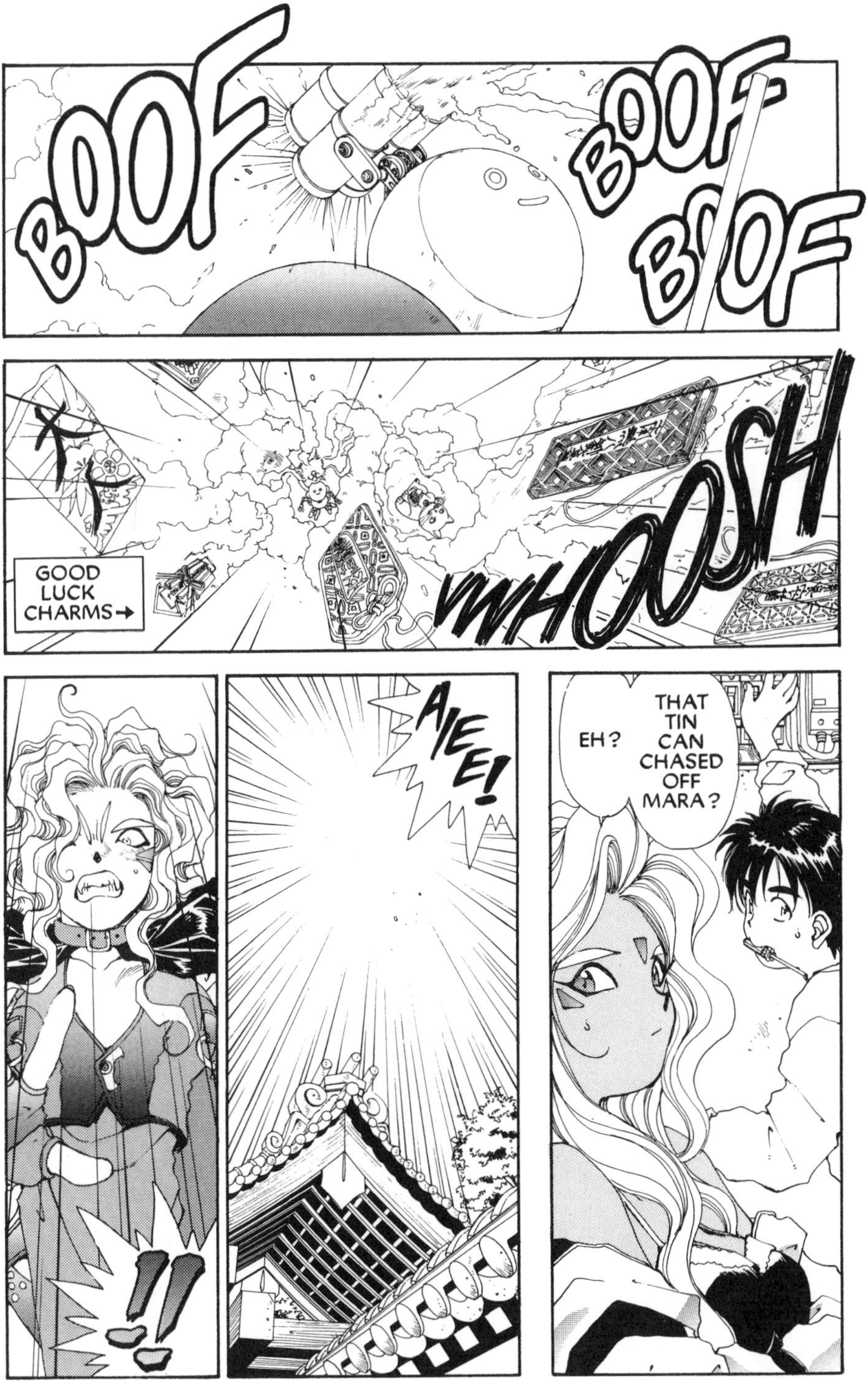
BOOF
BOOF
BOOF
GOOD LUCK CHARMS →
VWHOOSH
!!
AIEEE!
EH?
THAT TIN CAN CHASED OFF MARA?

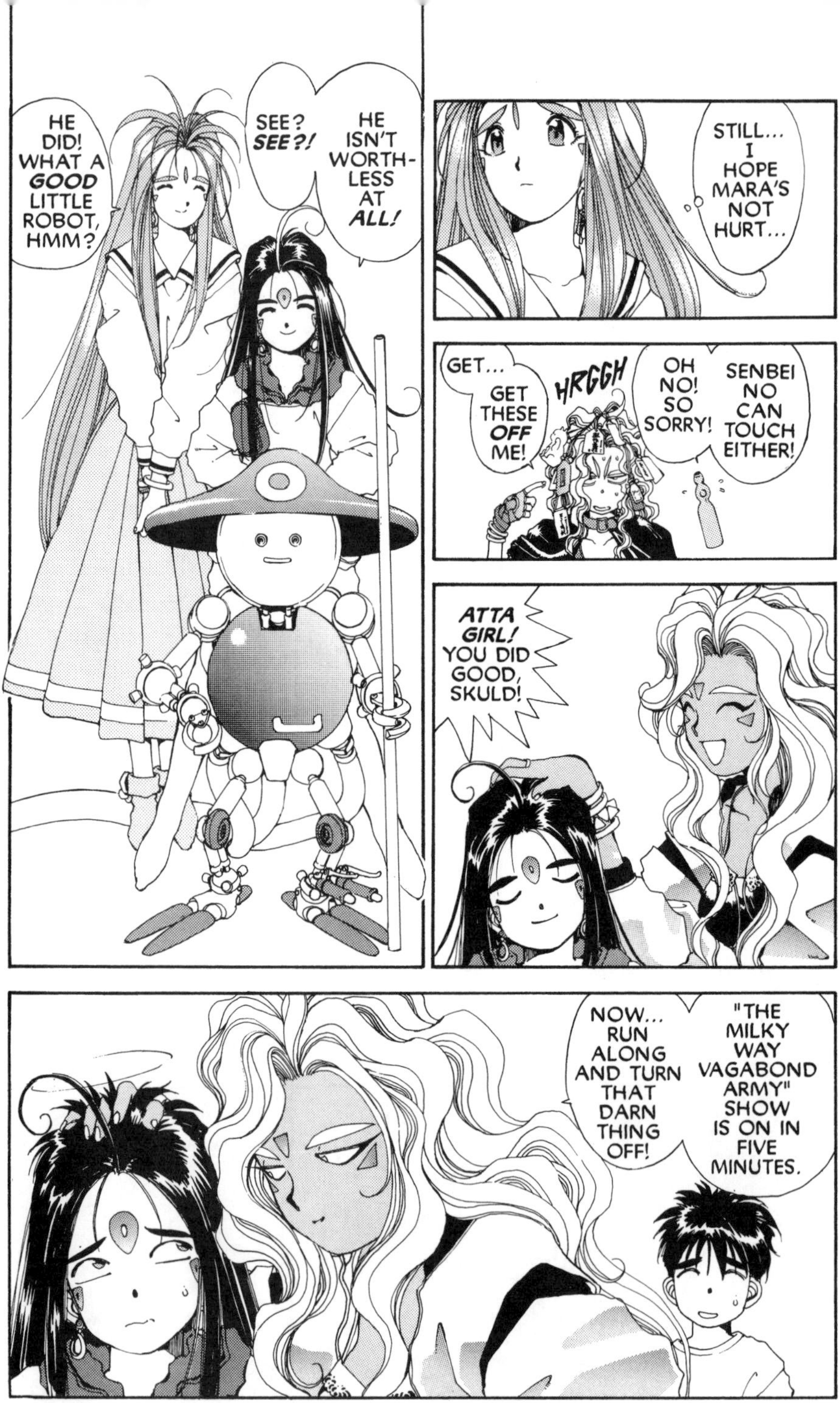
HE DID! WHAT A **GOOD** LITTLE ROBOT, HMM?
SEE? ***SEE?!***
HE ISN'T WORTH-LESS AT ***ALL!***
STILL... I HOPE MARA'S NOT HURT...
GET...
GET THESE ***OFF*** ME!
HRGGH
OH NO! SO SORRY!
SENBEI NO CAN TOUCH EITHER!
ATTA GIRL! YOU DID GOOD, SKULD!
NOW... RUN ALONG AND TURN THAT DARN THING OFF!
"THE MILKY WAY VAGABOND ARMY" SHOW IS ON IN FIVE MINUTES.

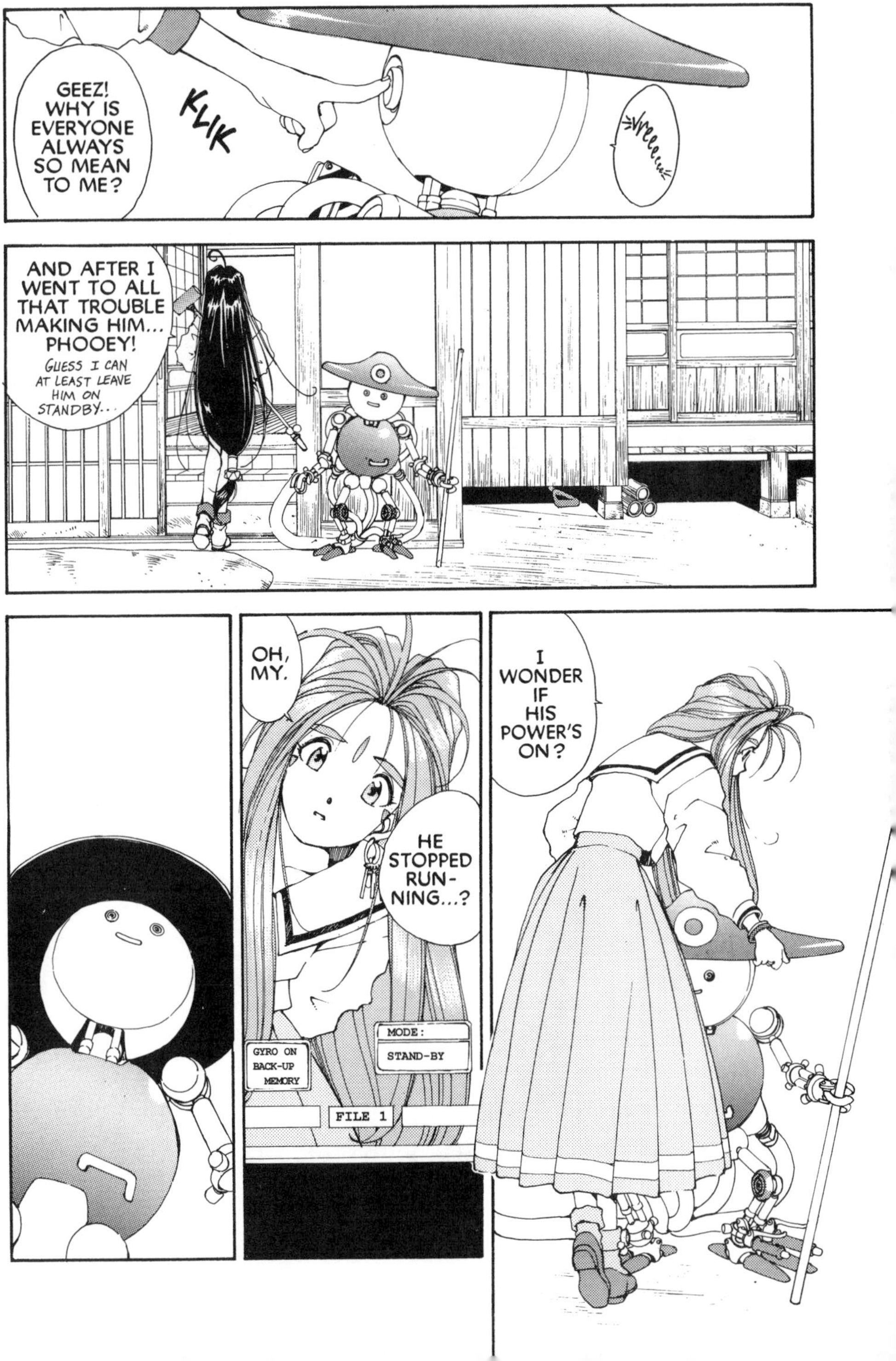

GEEZ! WHY IS EVERYONE ALWAYS SO MEAN TO ME?
KLIK
Vreeeee
AND AFTER I WENT TO ALL THAT TROUBLE MAKING HIM... PHOOEY!
GUESS I CAN AT LEAST LEAVE HIM ON STANDBY...
OH, MY.
HE STOPPED RUN-NING...?
MODE:
STAND-BY
GYRO ON
BACK-UP MEMORY
FILE 1
I WONDER IF HIS POWER'S ON?

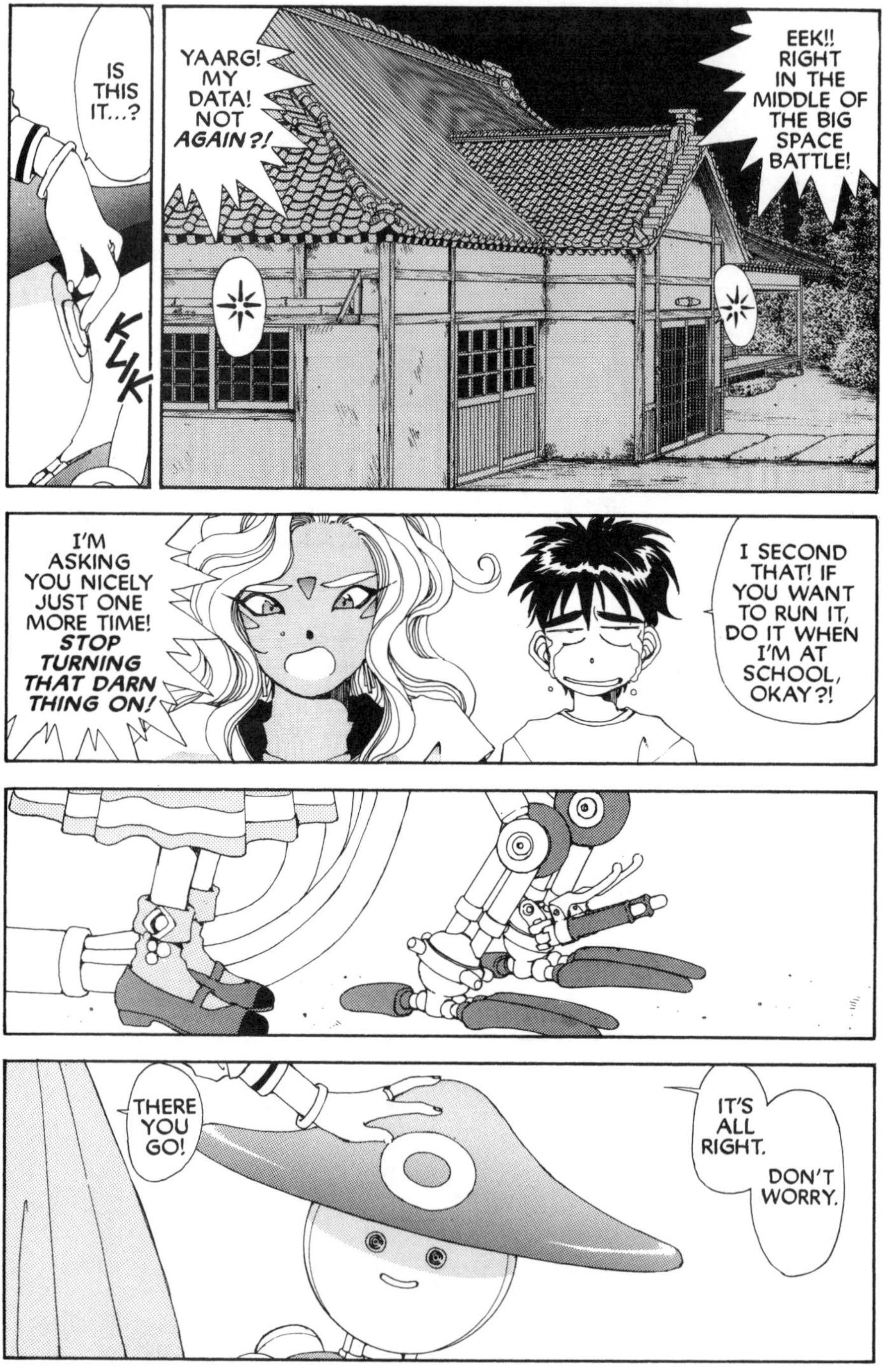

IS THIS IT...?
KLIK
YAARG! MY DATA! NOT AGAIN?!
EEK!! RIGHT IN THE MIDDLE OF THE BIG SPACE BATTLE!
I'M ASKING YOU NICELY JUST ONE MORE TIME! STOP TURNING THAT DARN THING ON!
I SECOND THAT! IF YOU WANT TO RUN IT, DO IT WHEN I'M AT SCHOOL, OKAY?!
THERE YOU GO!
IT'S ALL RIGHT.
DON'T WORRY.

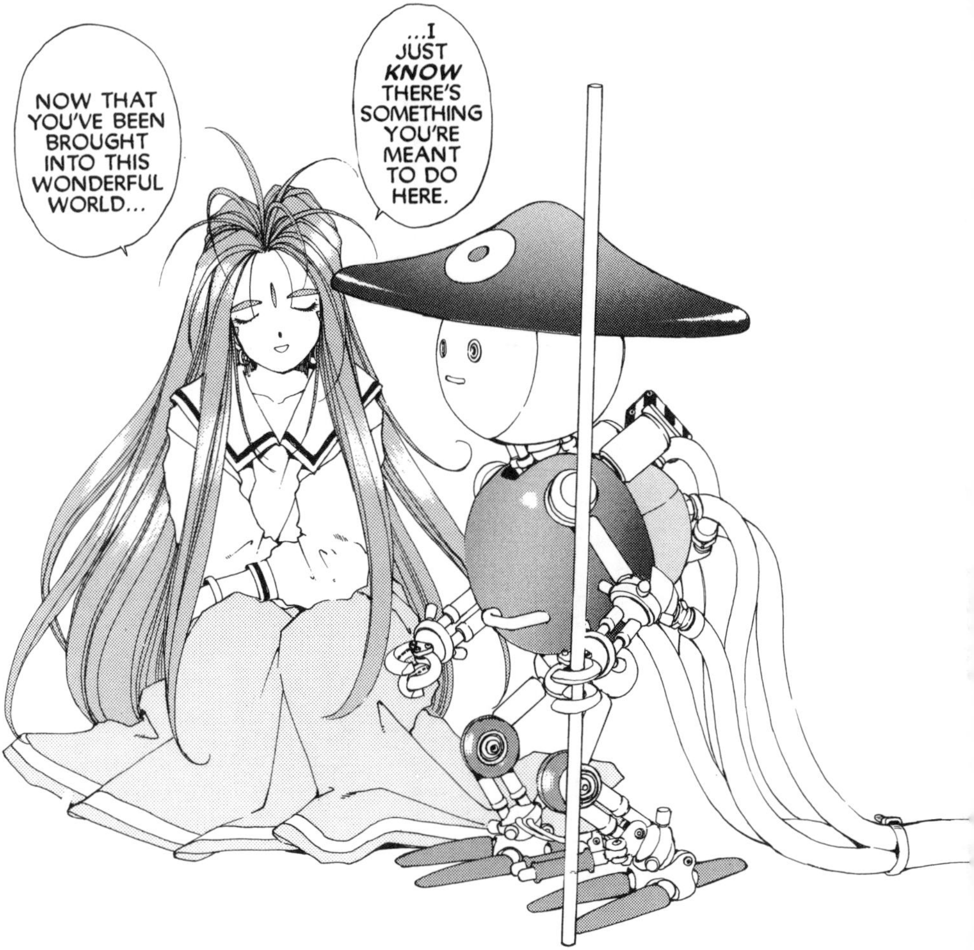
NOW THAT YOU'VE BEEN BROUGHT INTO THIS WONDERFUL WORLD...
...I JUST ***KNOW*** THERE'S SOMETHING YOU'RE MEANT TO DO HERE.

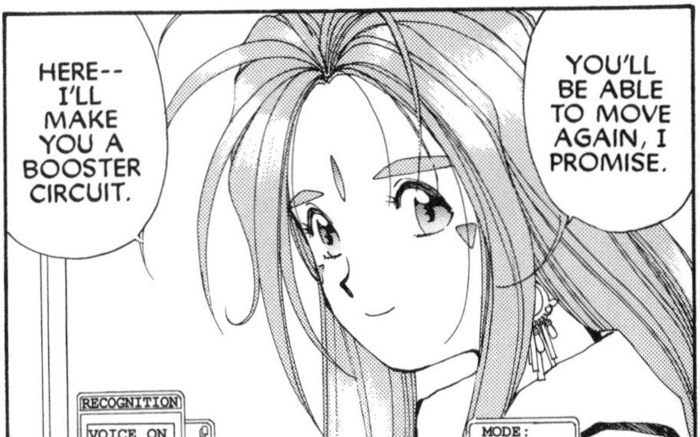
HERE-- I'LL MAKE YOU A BOOSTER CIRCUIT.
YOU'LL BE ABLE TO MOVE AGAIN, I PROMISE.
RECOGNITION
VOICE ON
MODE:
STAND-BY

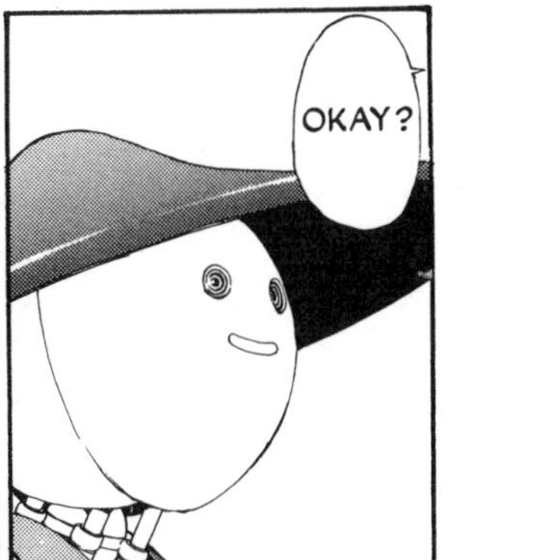
OKAY?

Come Together Little Parts Awaken Now to Ace Your Callings

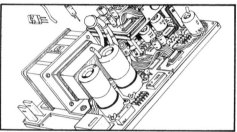

Join Your Hands Become as One

Become the Power Unleashing Greater Power Still!

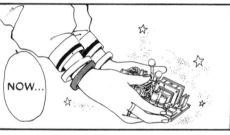

NOW...

ALL WE DO IS PLUG THIS IN...

hahh

hahh

?

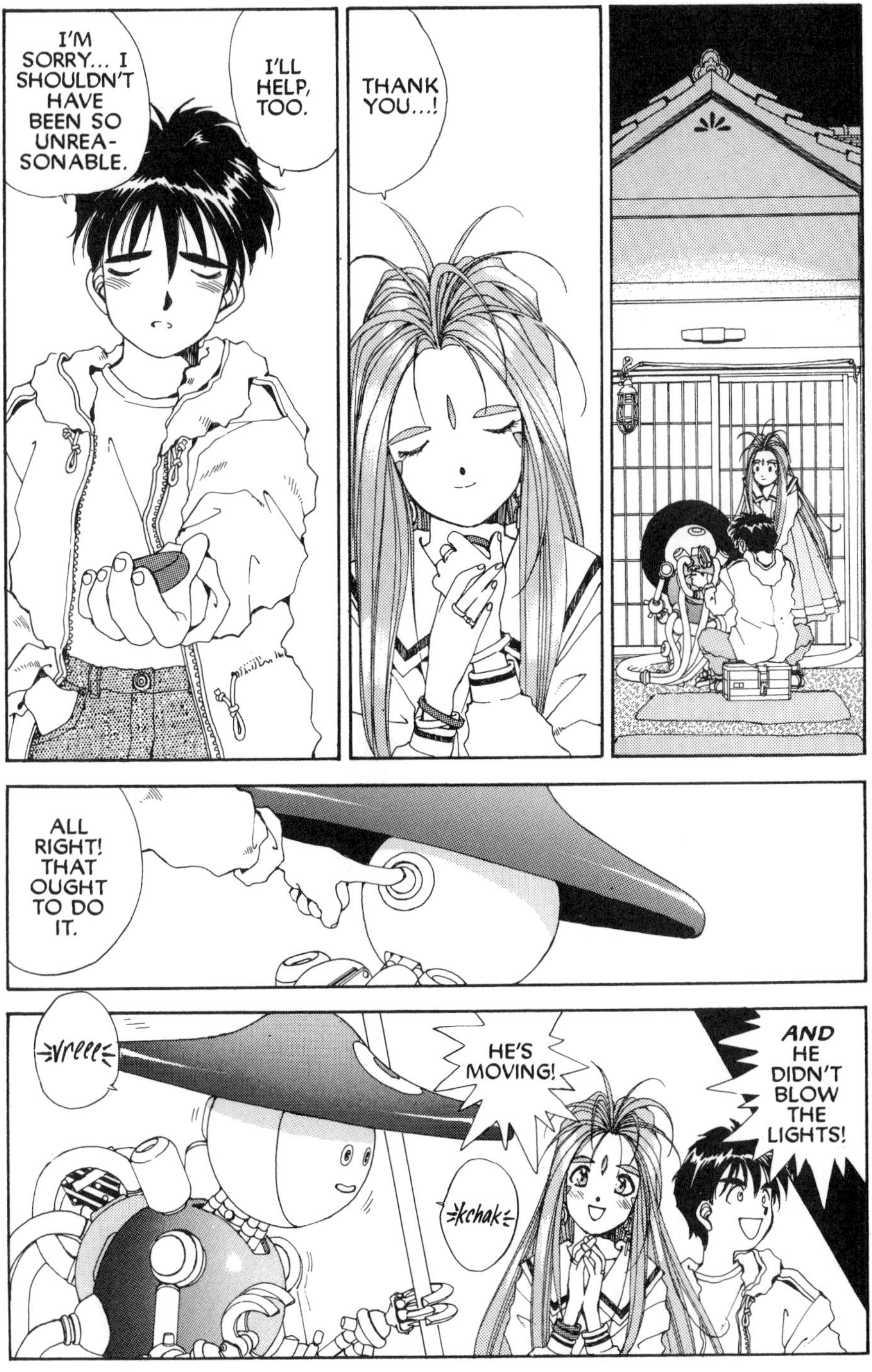
I'M SORRY... I SHOULDN'T HAVE BEEN SO UNREA-SONABLE.
I'LL HELP, TOO.
THANK YOU...!
ALL RIGHT! THAT OUGHT TO DO IT.
vreee
HE'S MOVING!
AND HE DIDN'T BLOW THE LIGHTS!
kchak

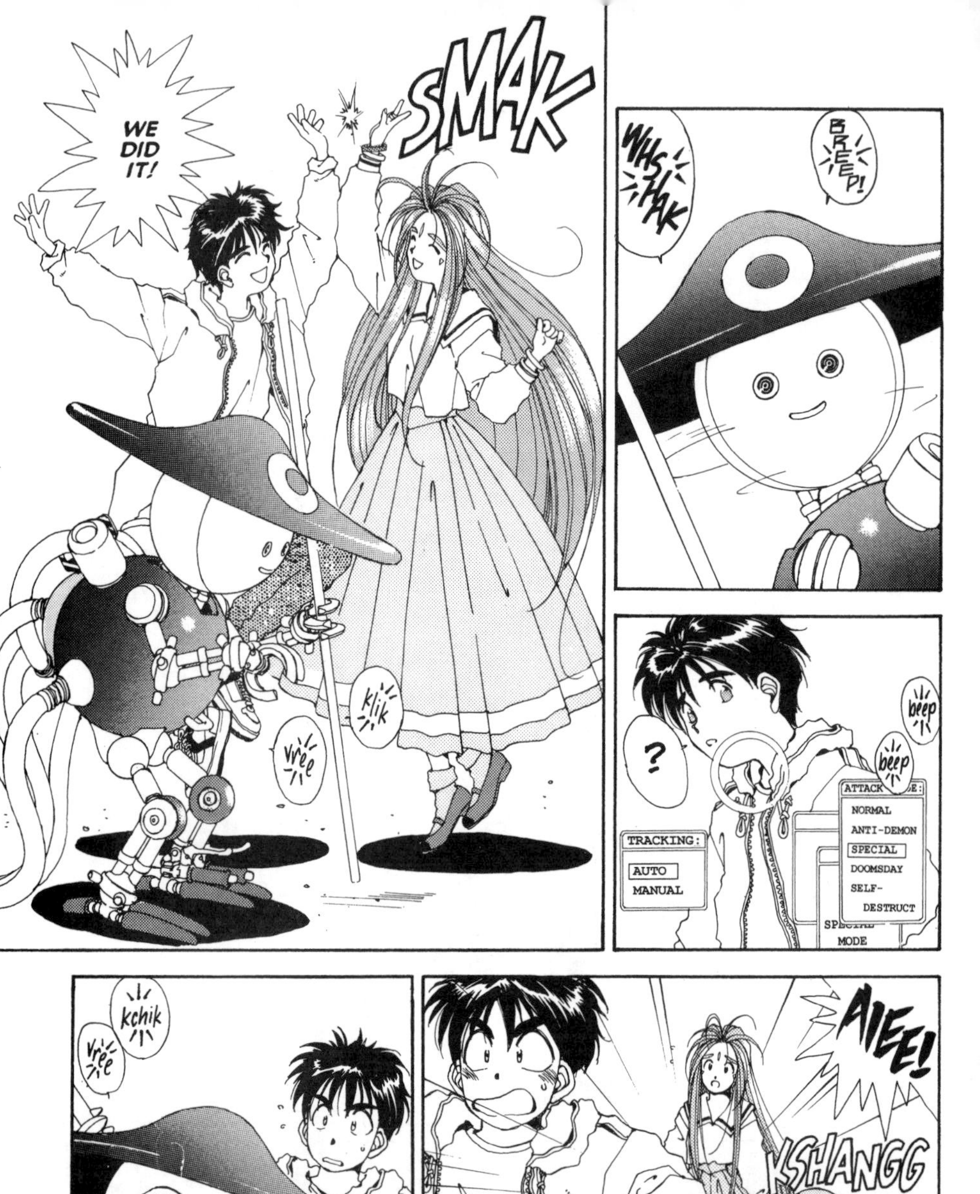
WE DID IT!
SMAK
klik
vree
WHSHAK
BREEP!
?
beep
beep
TRACKING:
AUTO
MANUAL
ATTACK
NORMAL
ANTI-DEMON
SPECIAL
DOOMSDAY
SELF-DESTRUCT
SPECIAL MODE
kchik
vree
AIEE!
KSHANGG

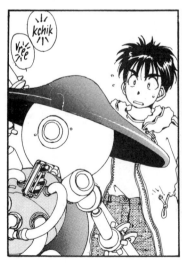

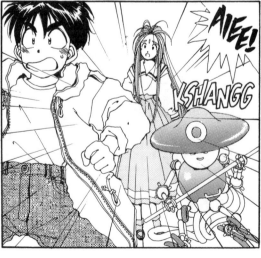

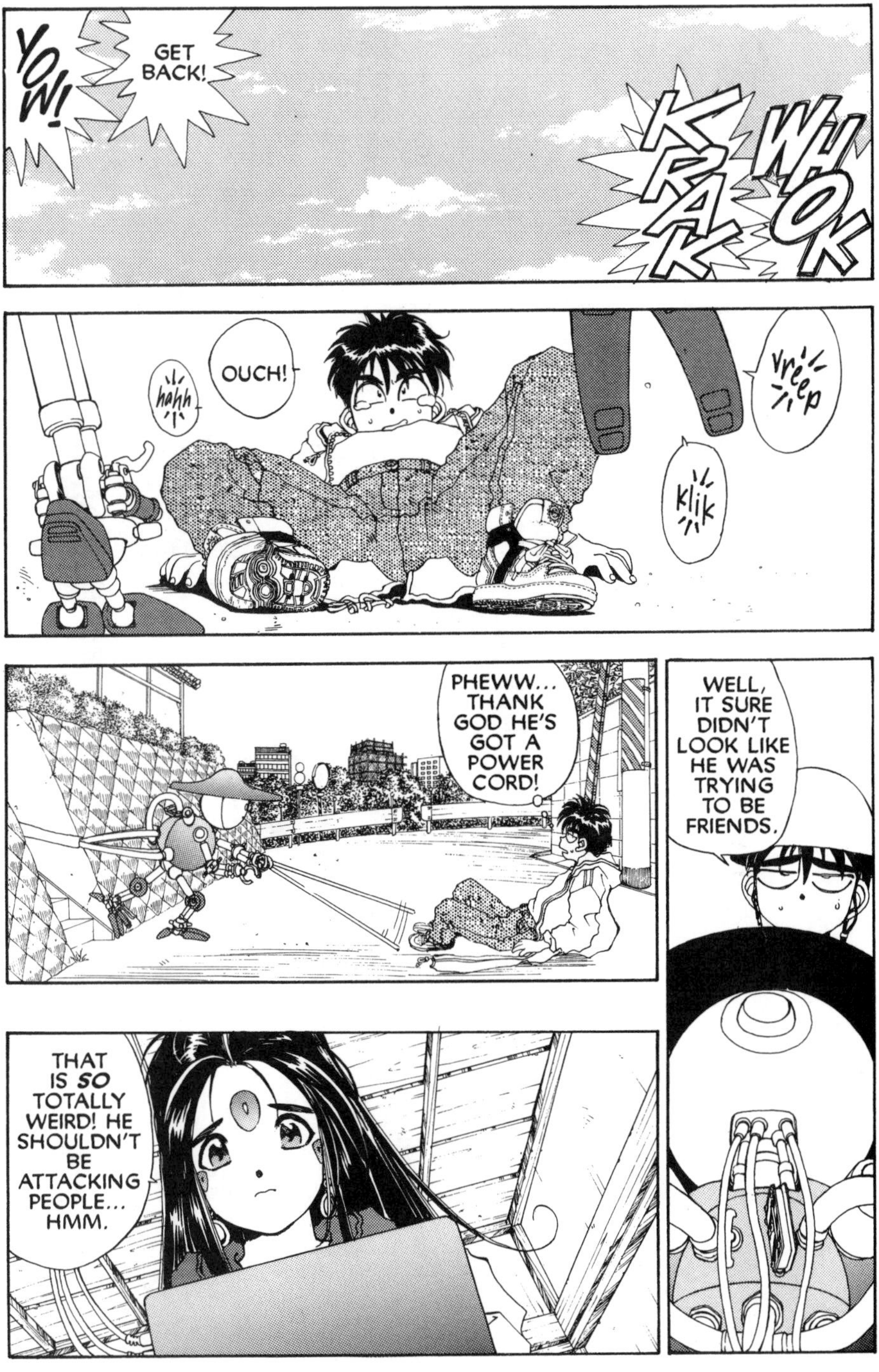
YOW!
GET BACK!
KRAK
WHOK
hahh
OUCH!
vreep
klik
PHEWW... THANK GOD HE'S GOT A POWER CORD!
WELL, IT SURE DIDN'T LOOK LIKE HE WAS TRYING TO BE FRIENDS.
THAT IS *SO* TOTALLY WEIRD! HE SHOULDN'T BE ATTACKING PEOPLE... HMM.

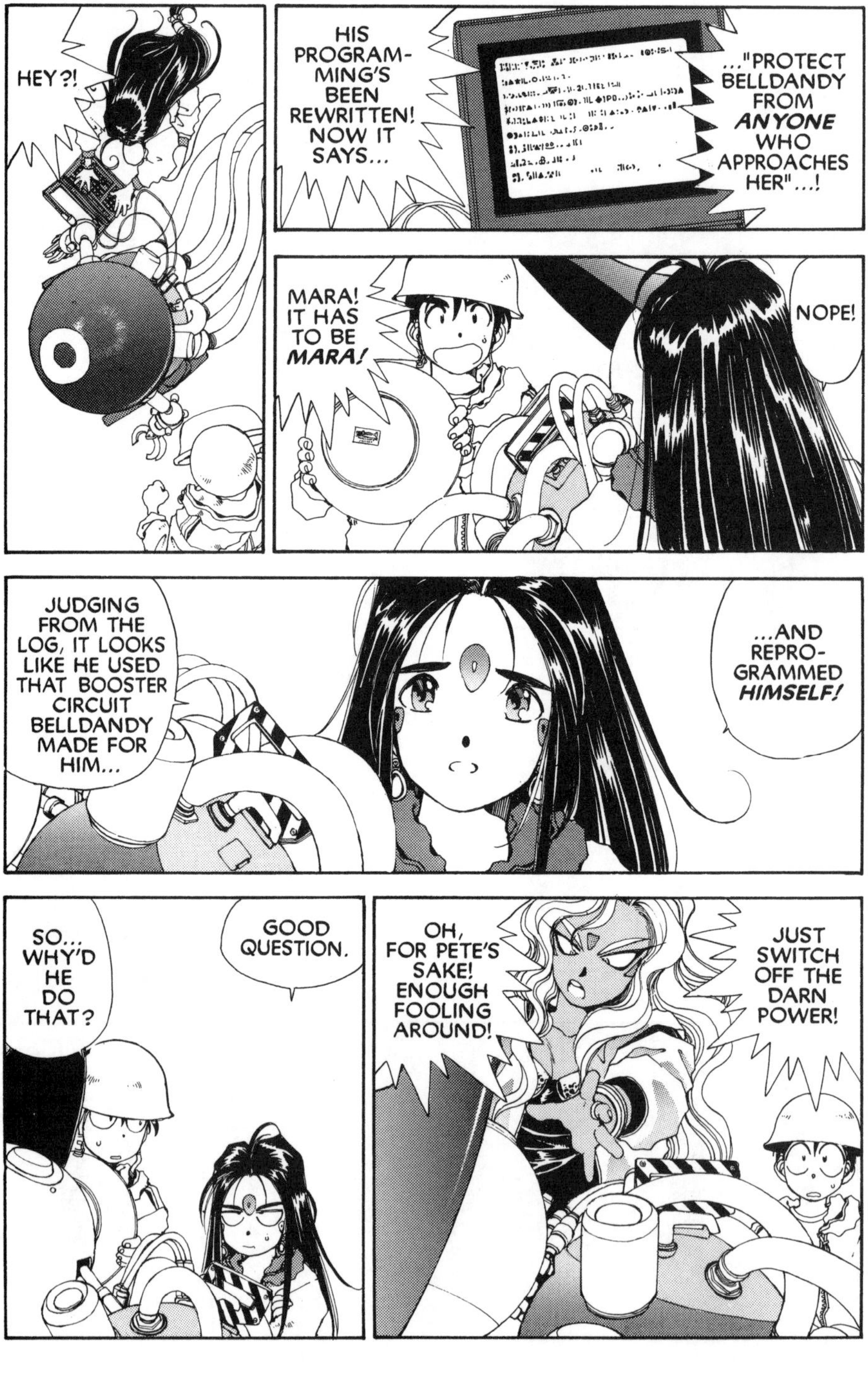
HEY?!
HIS PROGRAM-MING'S BEEN REWRITTEN! NOW IT SAYS...
..."PROTECT BELLDANDY FROM *ANYONE* WHO APPROACHES HER"...!
MARA! IT HAS TO BE *MARA!*
NOPE!
JUDGING FROM THE LOG, IT LOOKS LIKE HE USED THAT BOOSTER CIRCUIT BELLDANDY MADE FOR HIM...
...AND REPRO-GRAMMED *HIMSELF!*
SO... WHY'D HE DO THAT?
GOOD QUESTION.
OH, FOR PETE'S SAKE! ENOUGH FOOLING AROUND!
JUST SWITCH OFF THE DARN POWER!

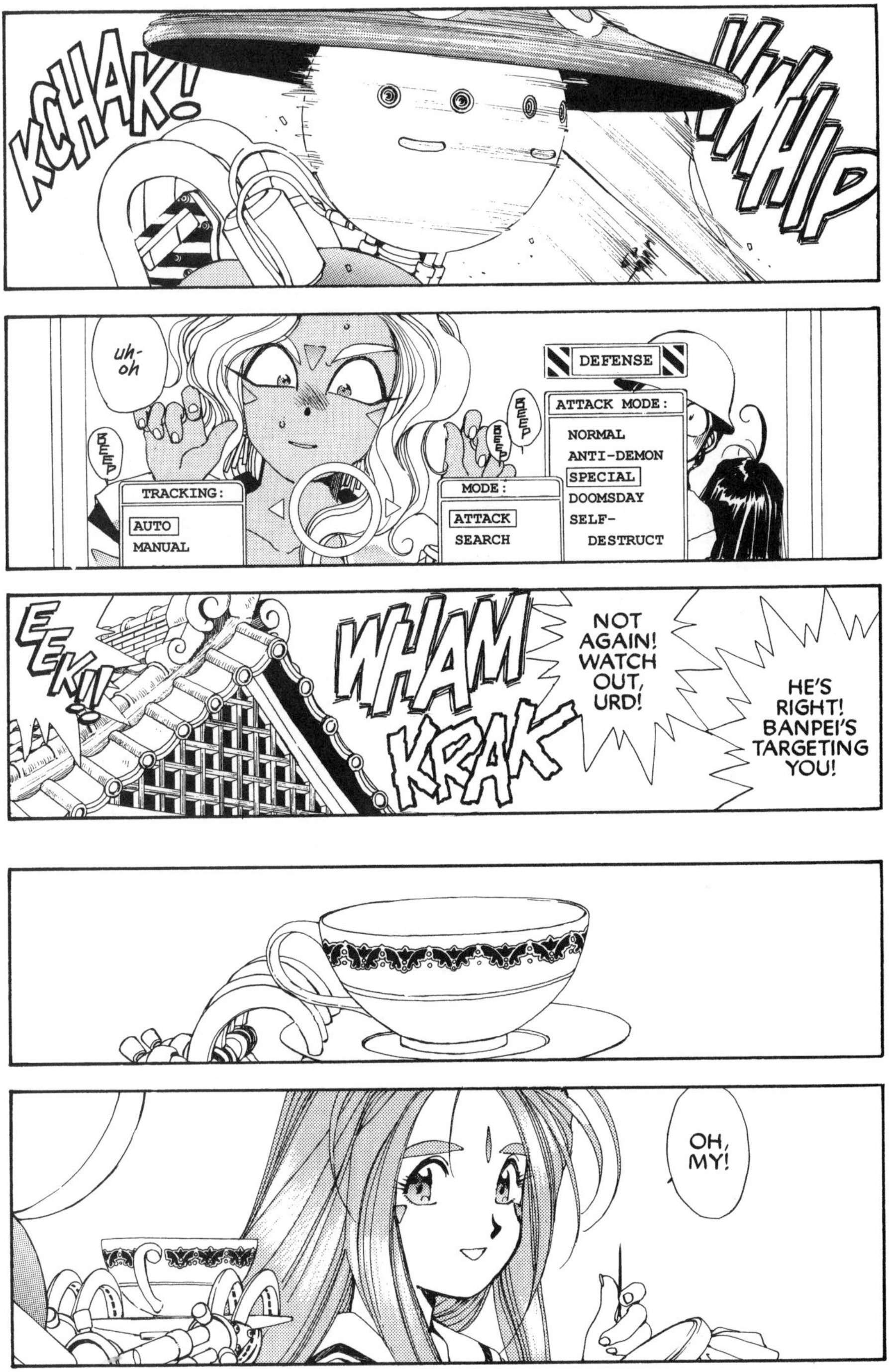
KCHAK!
WHIP
uh-oh
BEEP
BEEP
BEEP
TRACKING:
AUTO
MANUAL
MODE:
ATTACK
SEARCH
DEFENSE
ATTACK MODE:
NORMAL
ANTI-DEMON
SPECIAL
DOOMSDAY
SELF-DESTRUCT
EEK!!
WHAM
KRAK
NOT AGAIN! WATCH OUT, URD!
HE'S RIGHT! BANPEI'S TARGETING YOU!
OH, MY!

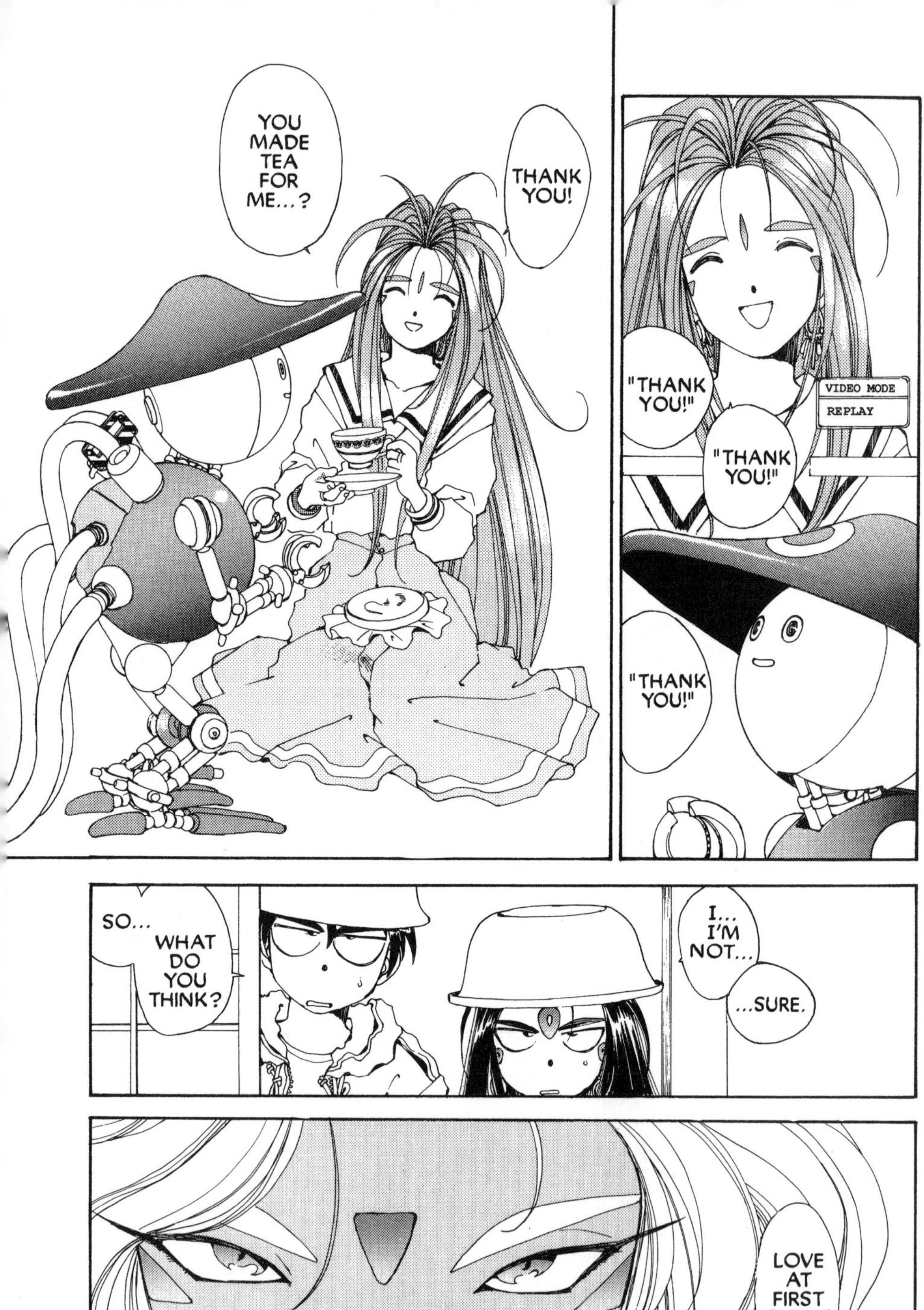
YOU MADE TEA FOR ME...?
THANK YOU!
"THANK YOU!"
VIDEO MODE
REPLAY
"THANK YOU!"
"THANK YOU!"
SO... WHAT DO YOU THINK?
I... I'M NOT...
...SURE.
LOVE AT FIRST SIGHT!

THAT'S WHAT I WAS AFRAID YOU'D SAY.

SORRY, BUT NO DOUBT. LOOK AT HIS EYES!

SKULD... BELLDANDY'S SORT OF SPECIAL, YOU KNOW? THERE'S SOMETHING ABOUT HER THAT DRAWS ANYONE-- OR *ANYTHING*-- IN.

AN EMOTION CIRCUIT...? IT'S NOT IN MY DESIGN...

OH, HI!

WHY DON'T YOU ALL COME AND JOIN US HERE?

HUH? OH NO! WE'RE SAFE-- I MEAN, OKAY OUT HERE!

SHE CAN ALSO BE ESPECIALLY CLUE-LESS...

THE NEXT DAY

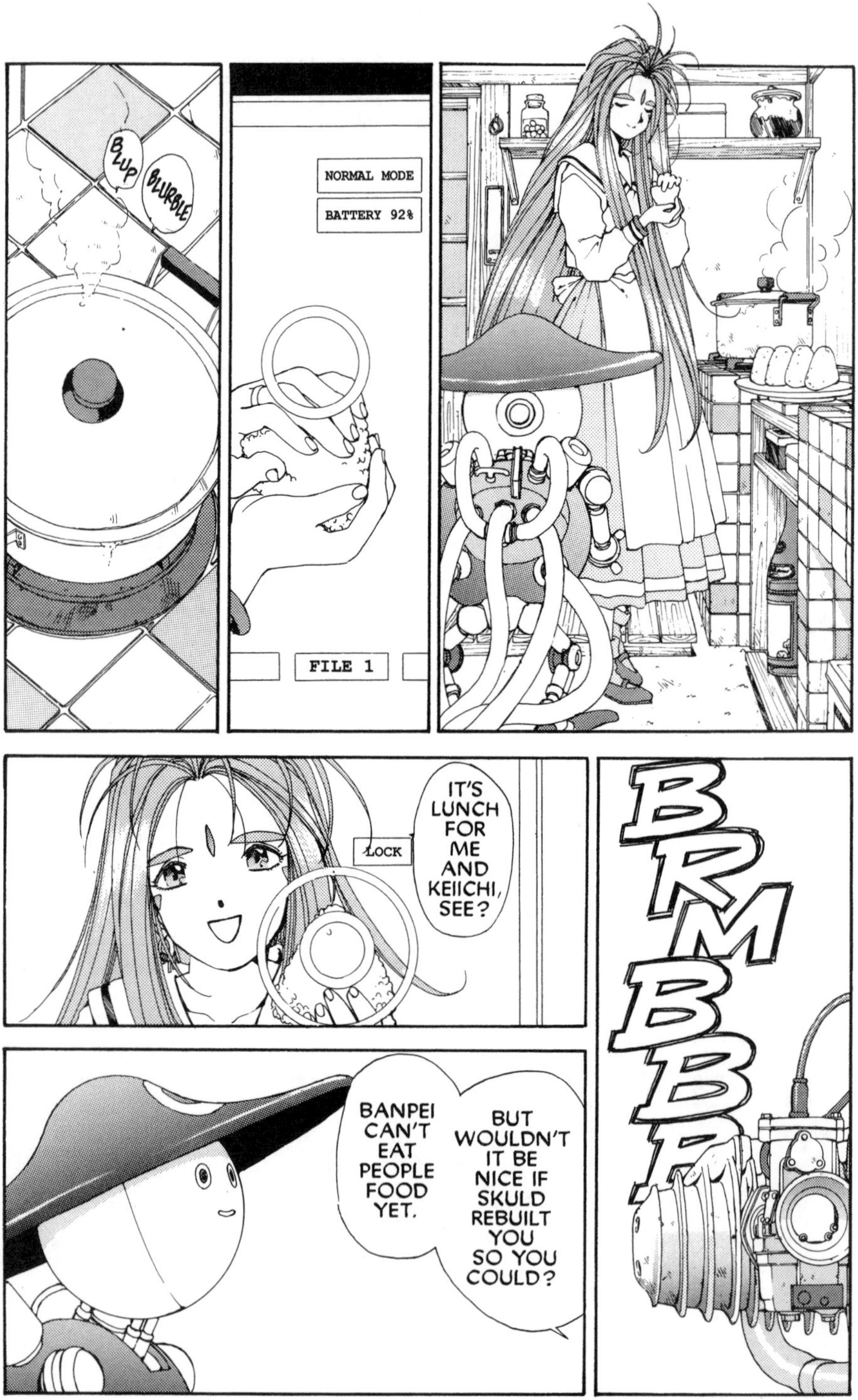
BLUP
BLURBLE
NORMAL MODE
BATTERY 92%
FILE 1
LOCK
IT'S LUNCH FOR ME AND KEIICHI, SEE?
BRMBBB
BANPEI CAN'T EAT PEOPLE FOOD YET.
BUT WOULDN'T IT BE NICE IF SKULD REBUILT YOU SO YOU COULD?

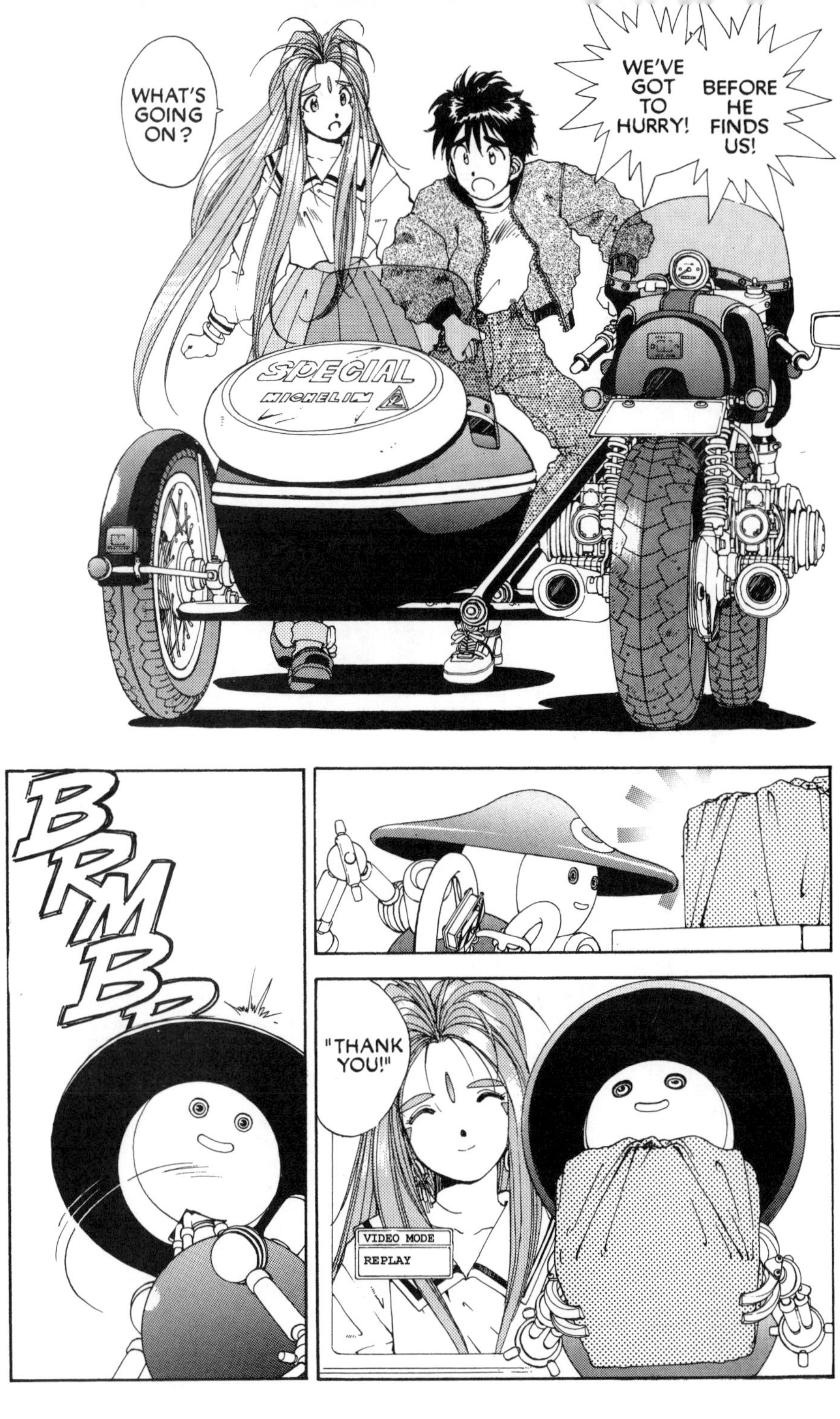
WHAT'S GOING ON?
WE'VE GOT TO HURRY!
BEFORE HE FINDS US!
SPECIAL
MICHELIN
BRMB
"THANK YOU!"
VIDEO MODE
REPLAY

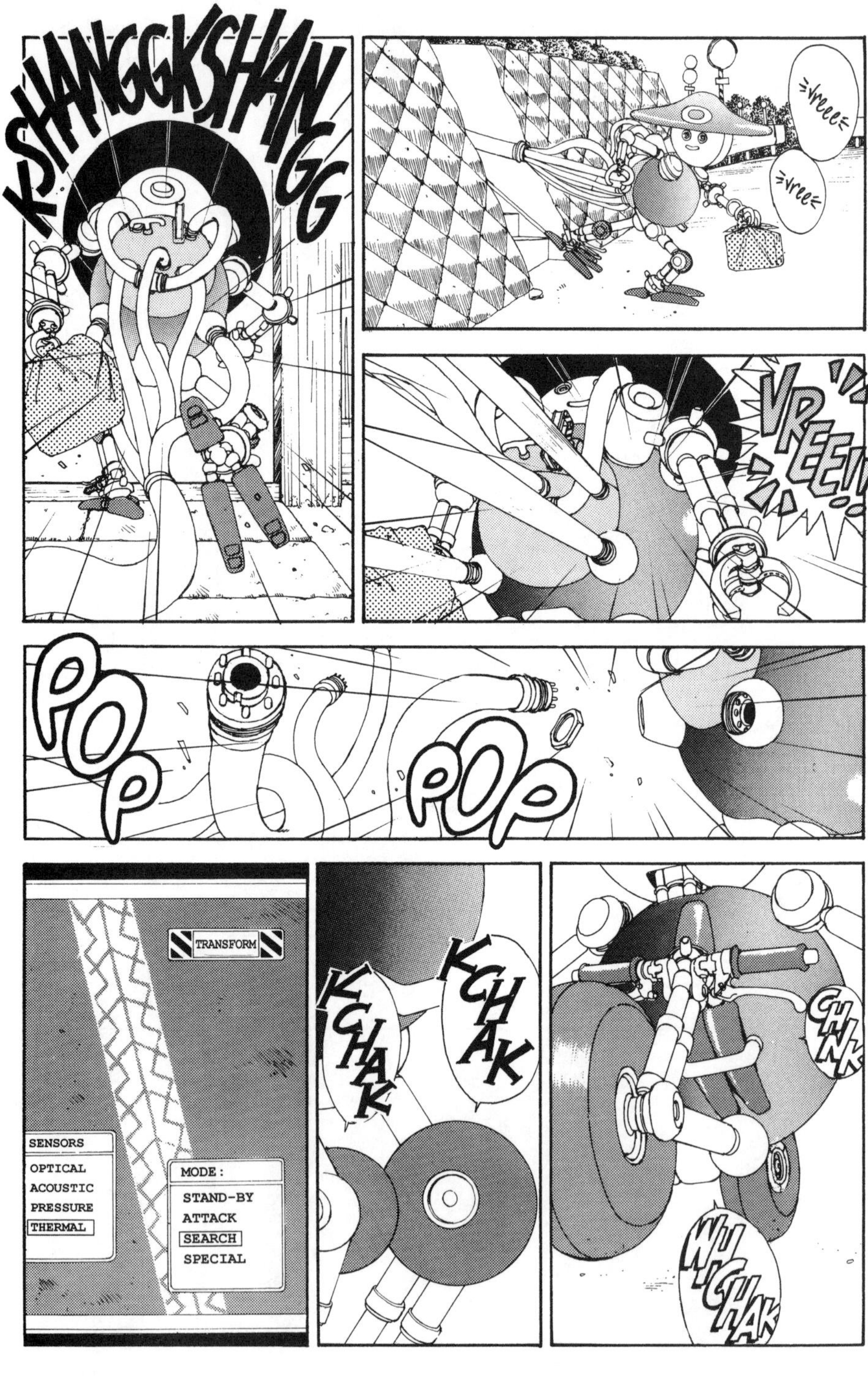
SHANGGKSHANGG
vreee
vree
VREEE!!
POP
POP
TRANSFORM
SENSORS
OPTICAL
ACOUSTIC
PRESSURE
THERMAL
MODE:
STAND-BY
ATTACK
SEARCH
SPECIAL
KCHAK
KCHAK
CHNK
WHCHAK

VREE

WHSSH

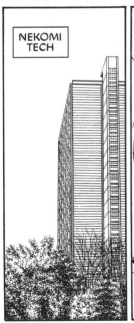

NEKOMI
TECH

?? BANPEI IS IN *LOVE* WITH ME?

THAT'S RIGHT.

THAT'S WHY I HAVEN'T BEEN ABLE TO GET CLOSE TO YOU.

AT LEAST HE STILL NEEDS A POWER CORD...

...SO THERE'S NO WAY HE CAN FOLLOW US.

AH, WELL...

...IT'S NOT LIKE HE MEANS BADLY, IT'S JUST--

≠vreep≠

YAIEE!

breep

breep

BANPEI, DEAR? ARE YOU ALL RIGHT?

WARNING!
BATTERY CHARGE: 0.1%

breep

breep

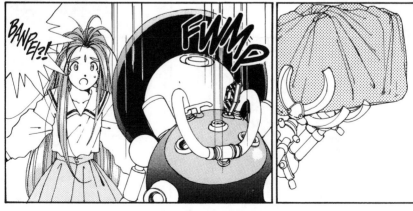

BANPEI?!

FWMP

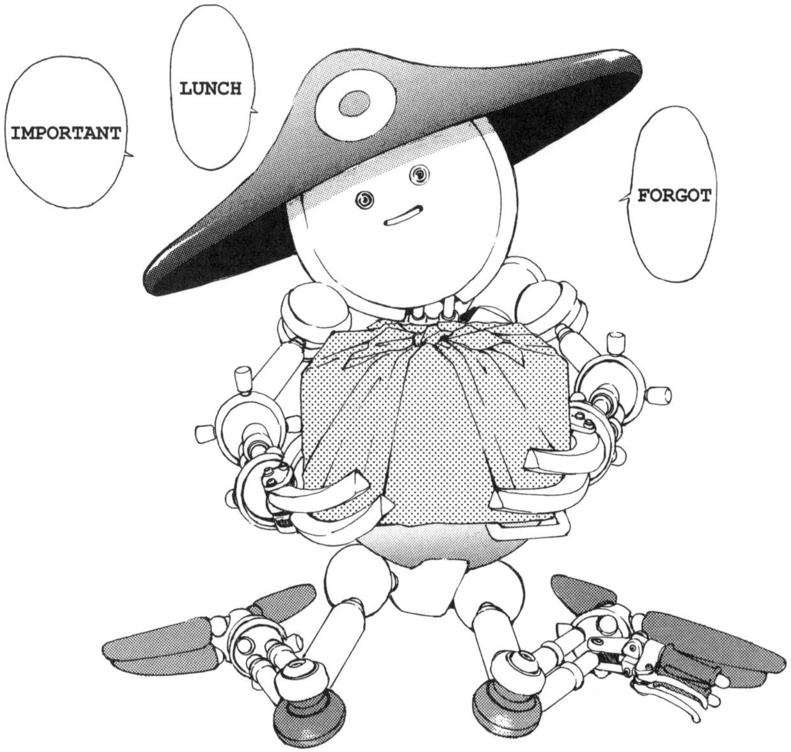
IMPORTANT
LUNCH
FORGOT

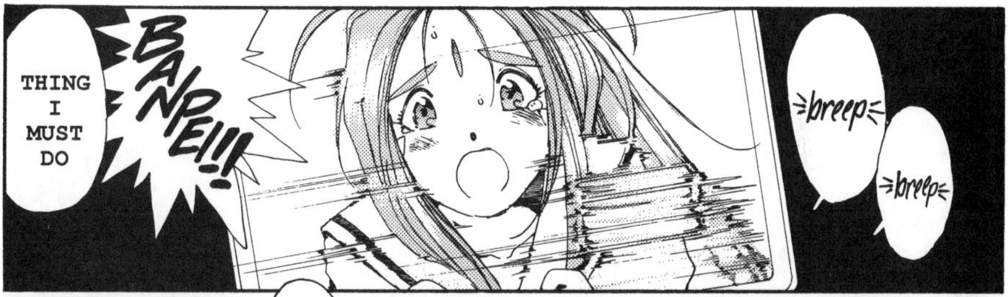
THING I MUST DO
BANPEI!!
breep
breep

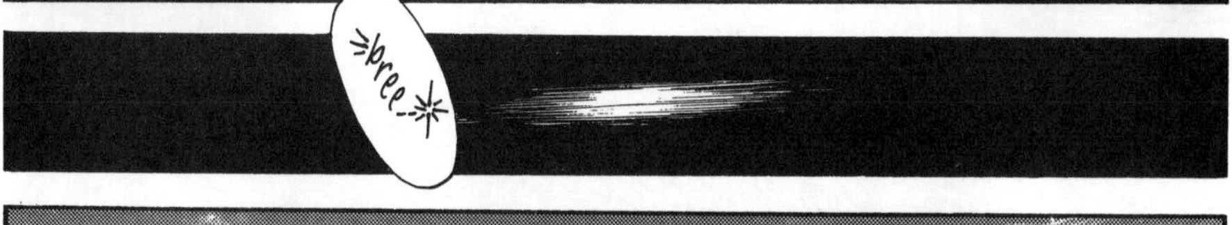
bree-

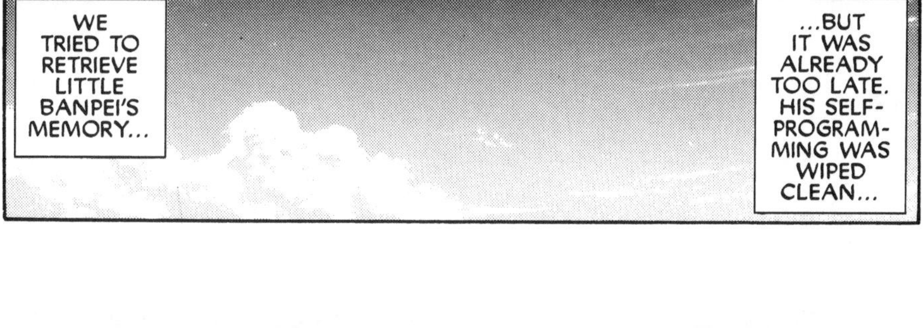
WE TRIED TO RETRIEVE LITTLE BANPEI'S MEMORY...
...BUT IT WAS ALREADY TOO LATE. HIS SELF-PROGRAMMING WAS WIPED CLEAN...

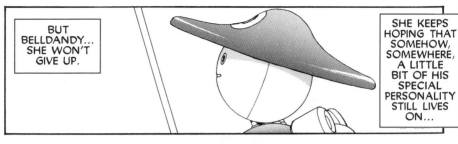

BUT BELLDANDY... SHE WON'T GIVE UP.

SHE KEEPS HOPING THAT SOMEHOW, SOMEWHERE, A LITTLE BIT OF HIS SPECIAL PERSONALITY STILL LIVES ON...

SEE YOU LATER, BANPEI!

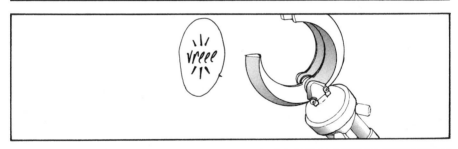

vreee

COME BACK SOON

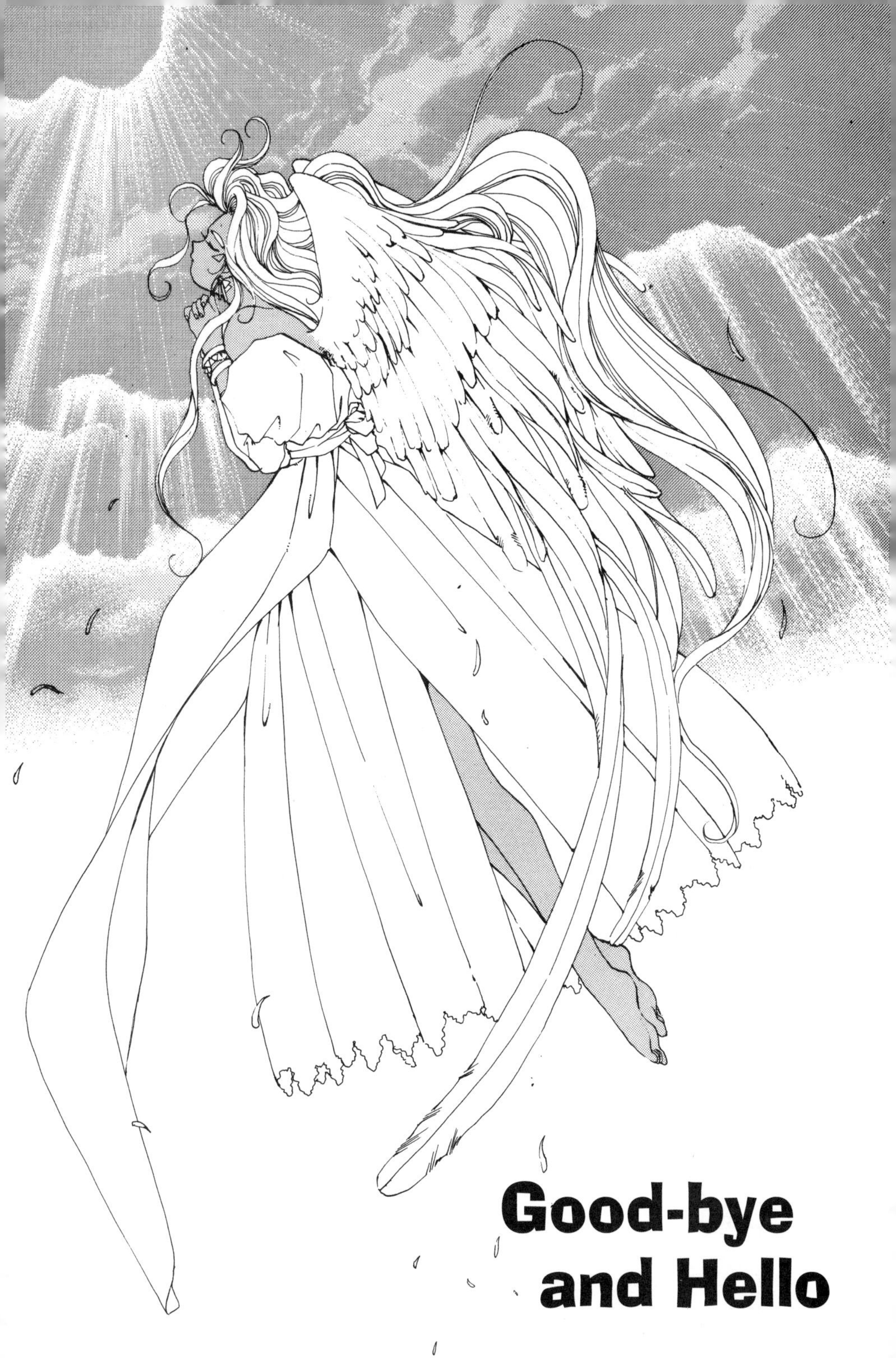

Good-bye and Hello

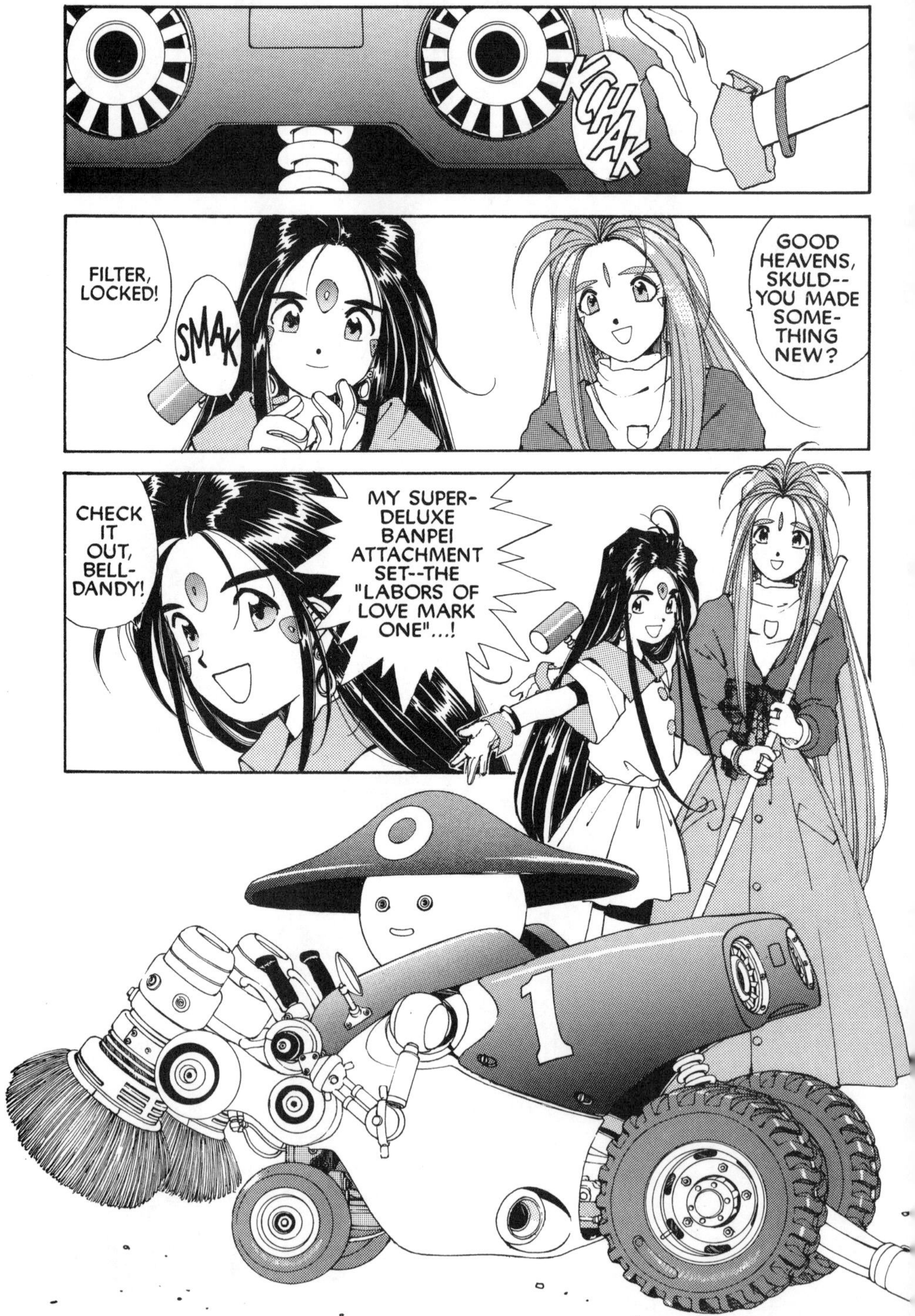
KCHAK
FILTER, LOCKED!
SMAK
GOOD HEAVENS, SKULD-- YOU MADE SOME-THING NEW?
CHECK IT OUT, BELL-DANDY!
MY SUPER-DELUXE BANPEI ATTACHMENT SET--THE "LABORS OF LOVE MARK ONE"...!
1

AND NOW I HIT THE SWITCH!

BANPEI RX... GO!

VREEEEE

MY LATEST LOVE POTION...

...IS JUST A LITTLE BIT DIFFERENT, EH?

MMM... SMELLS PERFECT...!

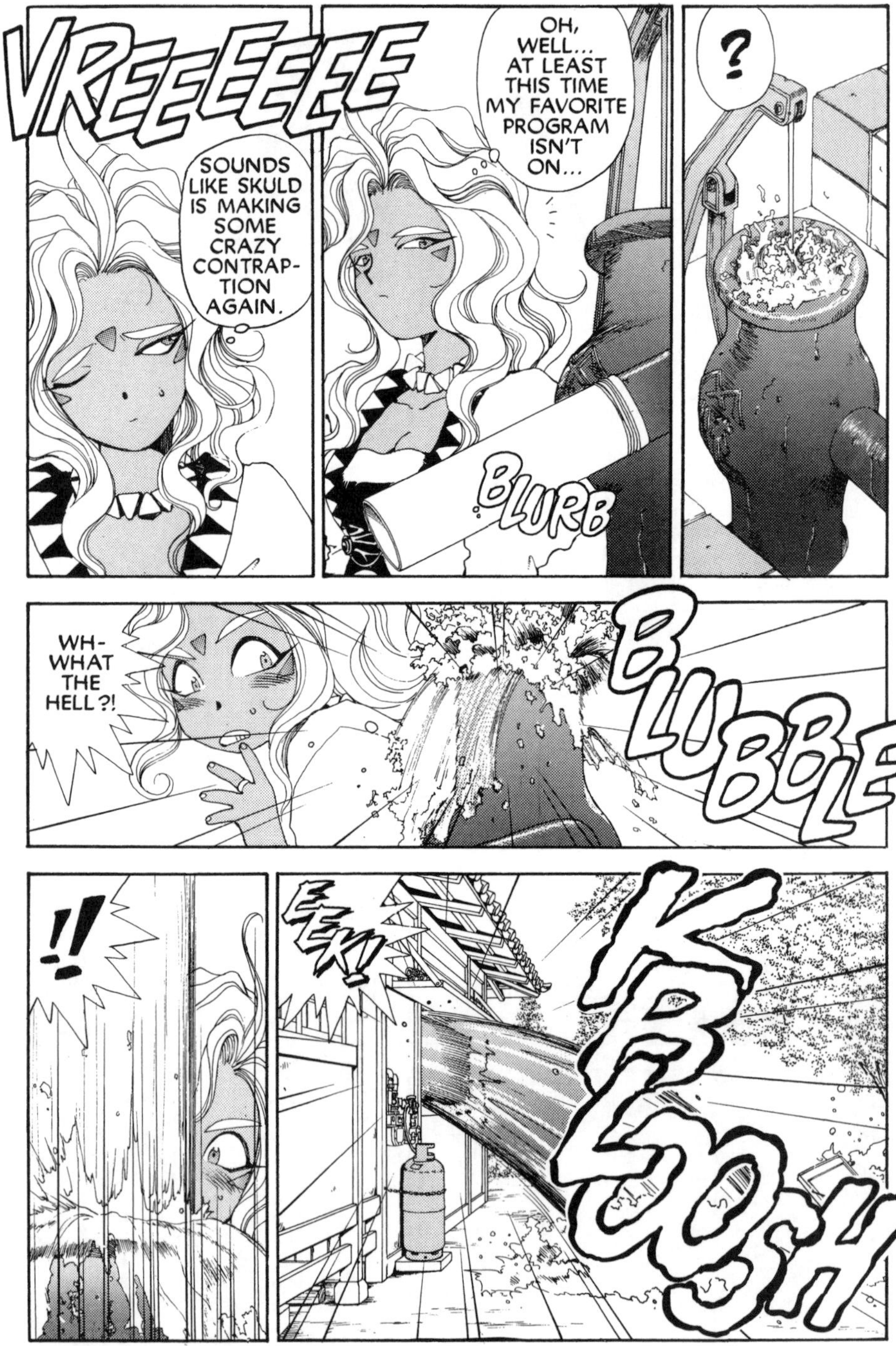
VREEEEEEE
SOUNDS LIKE SKULD IS MAKING SOME CRAZY CONTRAPTION AGAIN.
OH, WELL... AT LEAST THIS TIME MY FAVORITE PROGRAM ISN'T ON...
BLURB
?
WH- WHAT THE HELL?!
BLUBBLE
!!
EEK!
KRSOOSH

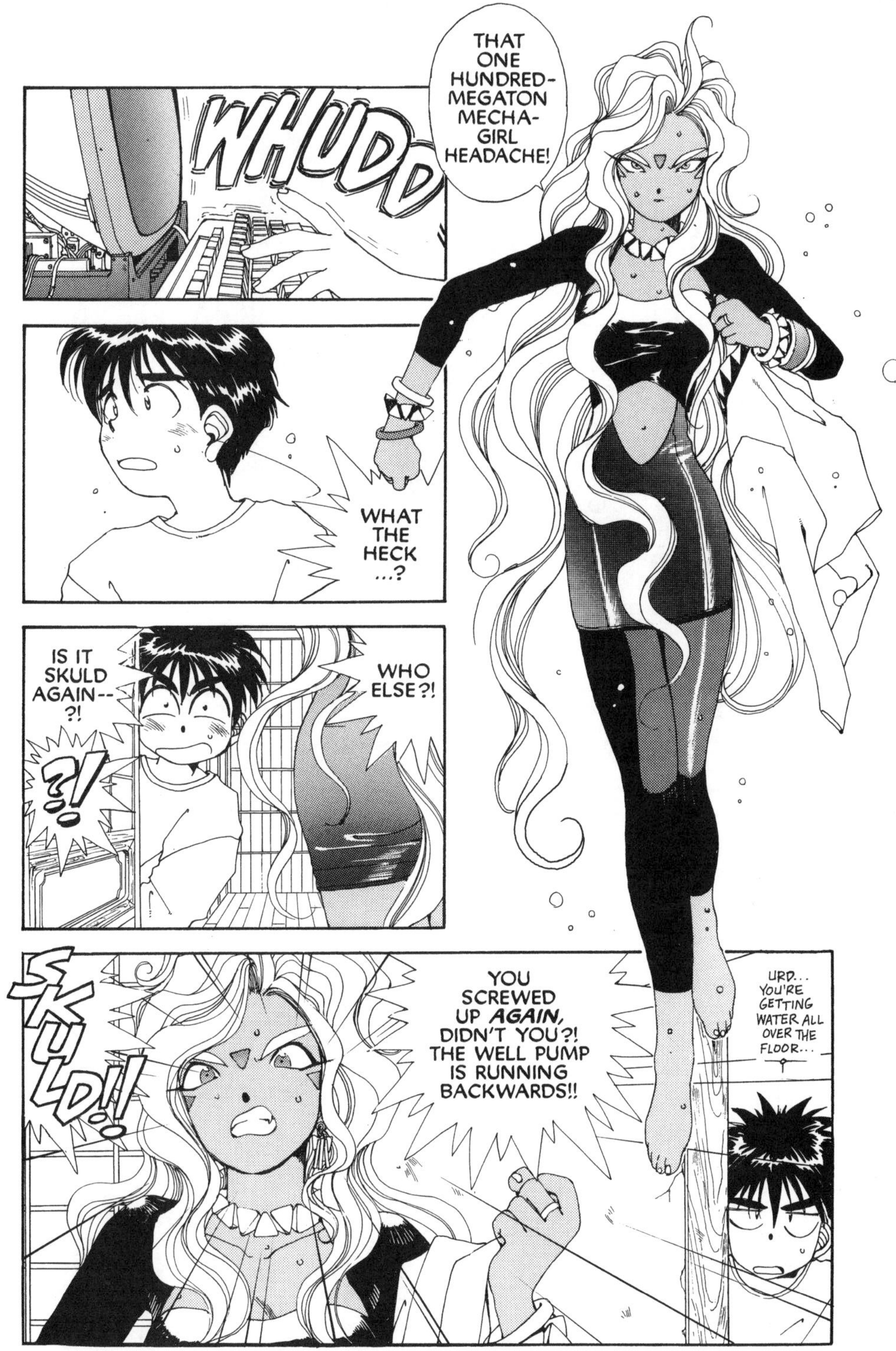
WHUDD
WHAT THE HECK ...?
IS IT SKULD AGAIN-- ?!
?!
WHO ELSE?!
THAT ONE HUNDRED-MEGATON MECHA-GIRL HEADACHE!
SKULD!!
YOU SCREWED UP *AGAIN*, DIDN'T YOU?! THE WELL PUMP IS RUNNING BACKWARDS!!
URD... YOU'RE GETTING WATER ALL OVER THE FLOOR...

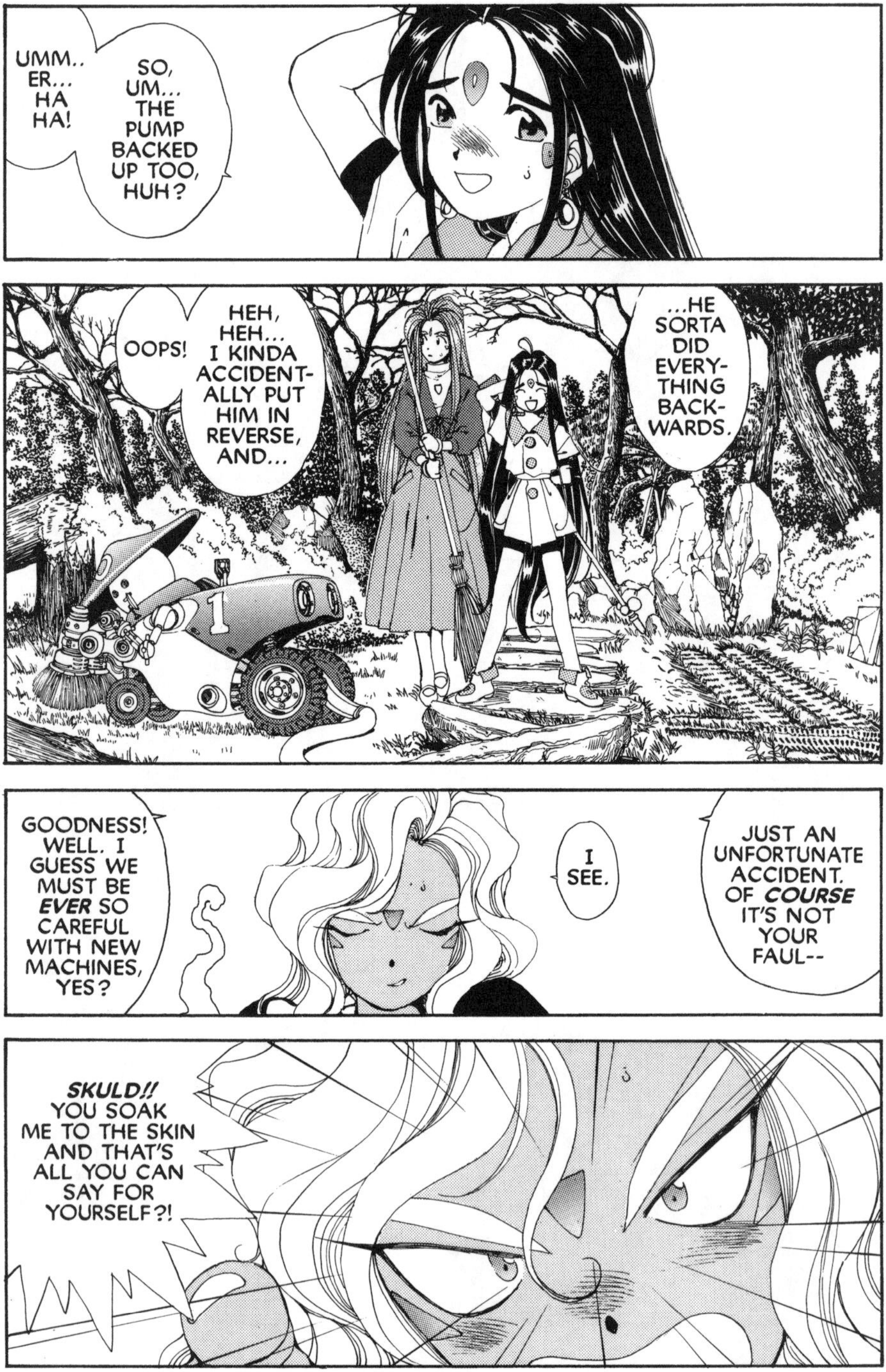
UMM.. ER... HA HA!
SO, UM... THE PUMP BACKED UP TOO, HUH?
OOPS!
HEH, HEH... I KINDA ACCIDENTALLY PUT HIM IN REVERSE, AND...
...HE SORTA DID EVERYTHING BACKWARDS.
GOODNESS! WELL. I GUESS WE MUST BE *EVER* SO CAREFUL WITH NEW MACHINES, YES?
I SEE.
JUST AN UNFORTUNATE ACCIDENT. OF *COURSE* IT'S NOT YOUR FAUL--
SKULD!! YOU SOAK ME TO THE SKIN AND THAT'S ALL YOU CAN SAY FOR YOURSELF?!

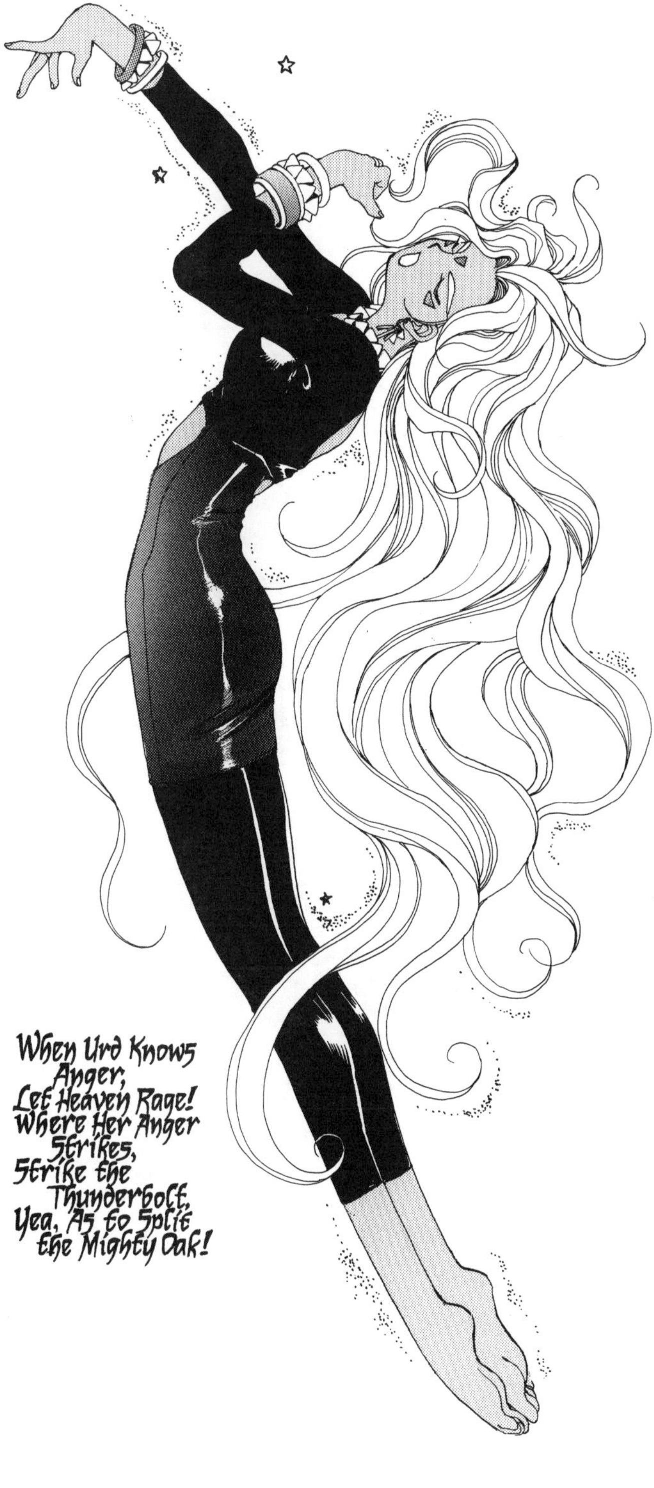
When Urd Knows Anger, Let Heaven Rage! Where Her Anger Strikes, Strike the Thunderbolt, Yea, As to Split the Mighty Oak!
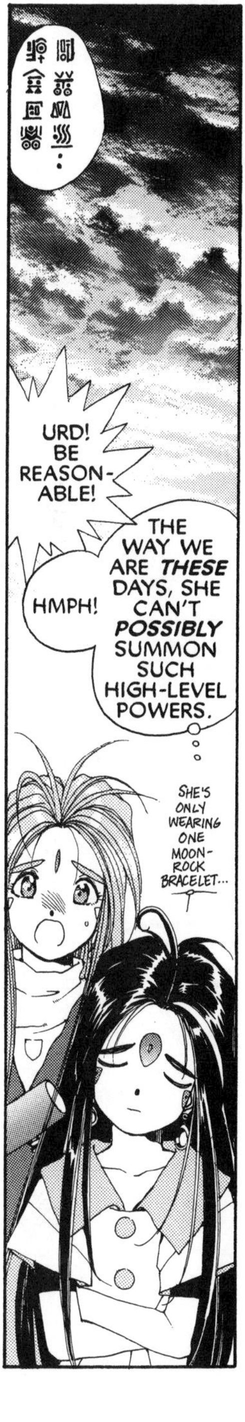
URD! BE REASON-ABLE!
HMPH!
THE WAY WE ARE *THESE* DAYS, SHE CAN'T *POSSIBLY* SUMMON SUCH HIGH-LEVEL POWERS.
SHE'S ONLY WEARING ONE MOON-ROCK BRACELET...

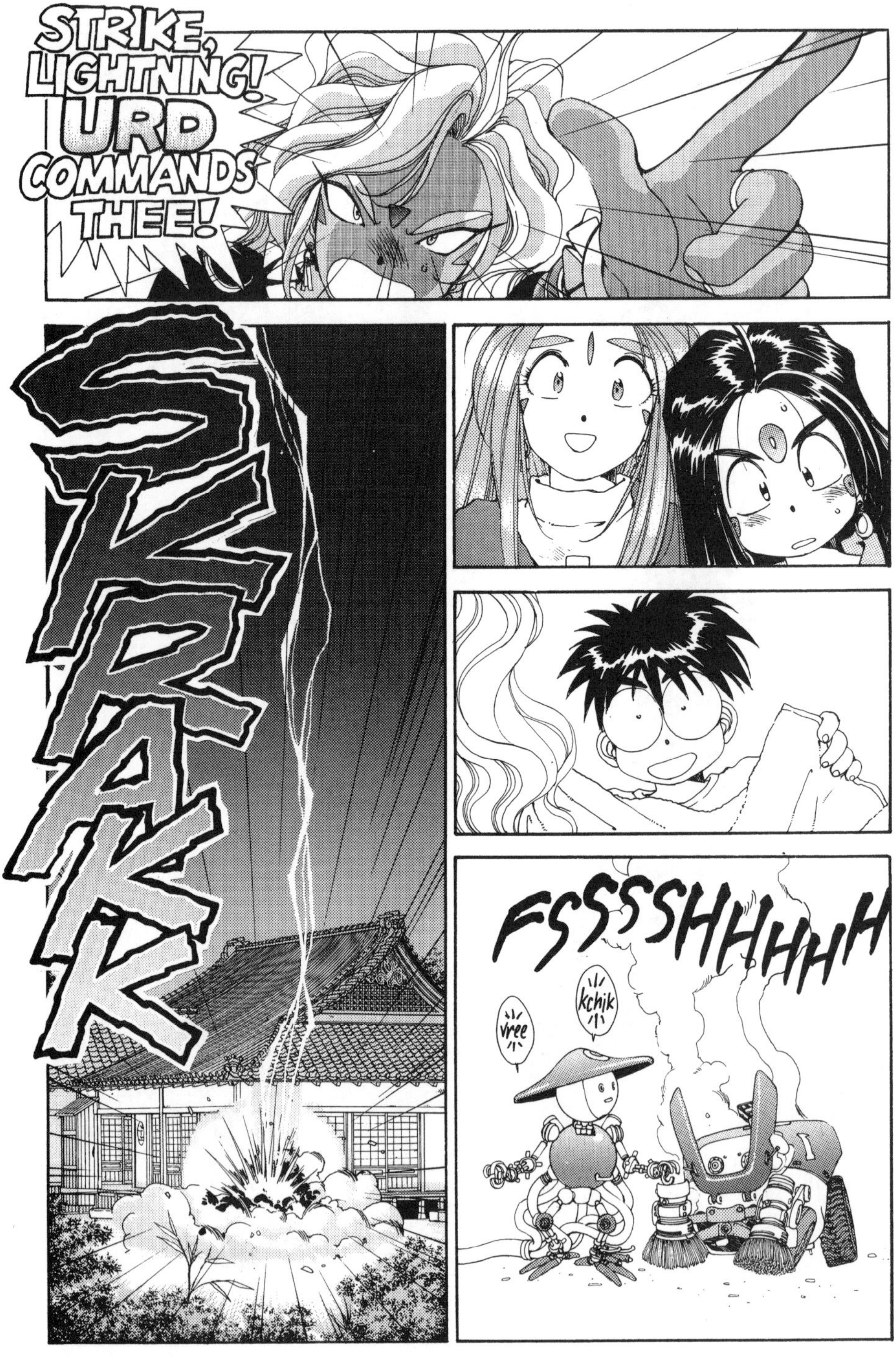
STRIKE, LIGHTNING! URD COMMANDS THEE!
SKRAKK
FSSSSHHHHHH
vree
kchik

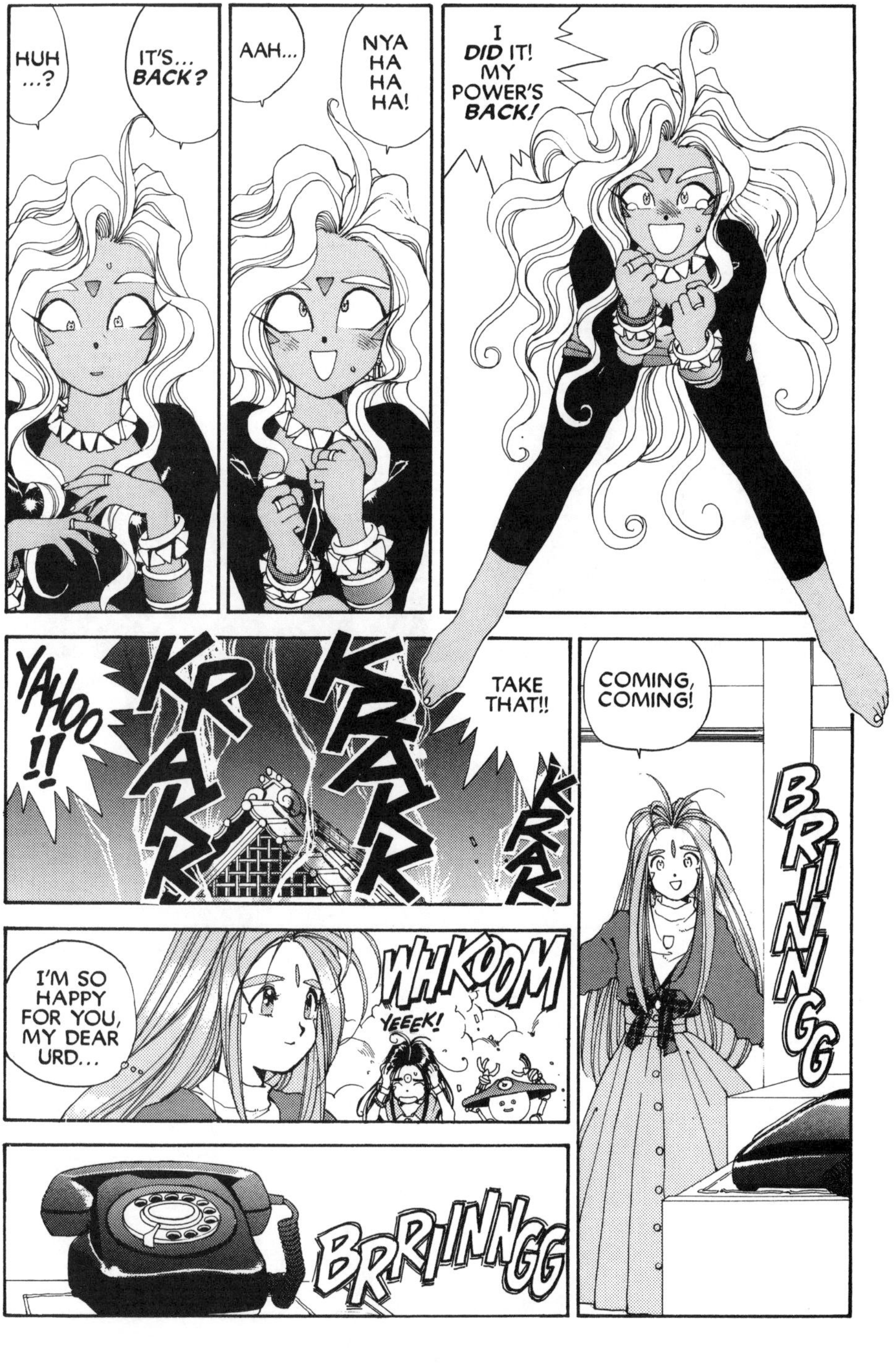
HUH ...?
IT'S... BACK?
AAH...
NYA HA HA HA!
I DID IT! MY POWER'S BACK!
YAHOO!!
KRAK
KRAK
TAKE THAT!!
KRAK
COMING, COMING!
BRRINNGG
I'M SO HAPPY FOR YOU, MY DEAR URD...
WHKOOM
YEEEK!
BRRIINNGG

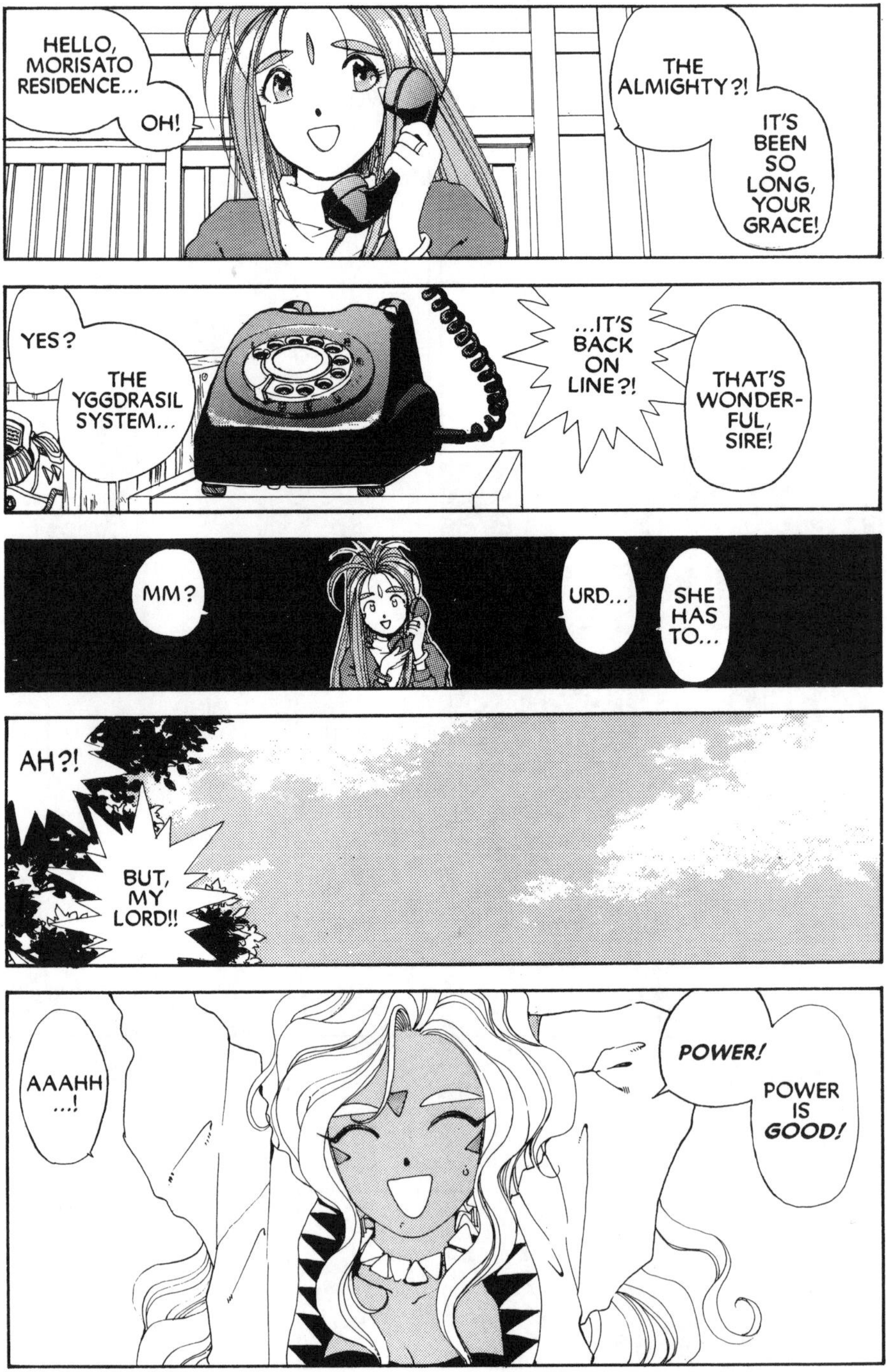
HELLO, MORISATO RESIDENCE...
OH!
THE ALMIGHTY?!
IT'S BEEN SO LONG, YOUR GRACE!
YES?
THE YGGDRASIL SYSTEM...
...IT'S BACK ON LINE?!
THAT'S WONDER-FUL, SIRE!
MM?
URD...
SHE HAS TO...
AH?!
BUT, MY LORD!!
AAAHH ...!
POWER!
POWER IS GOOD!

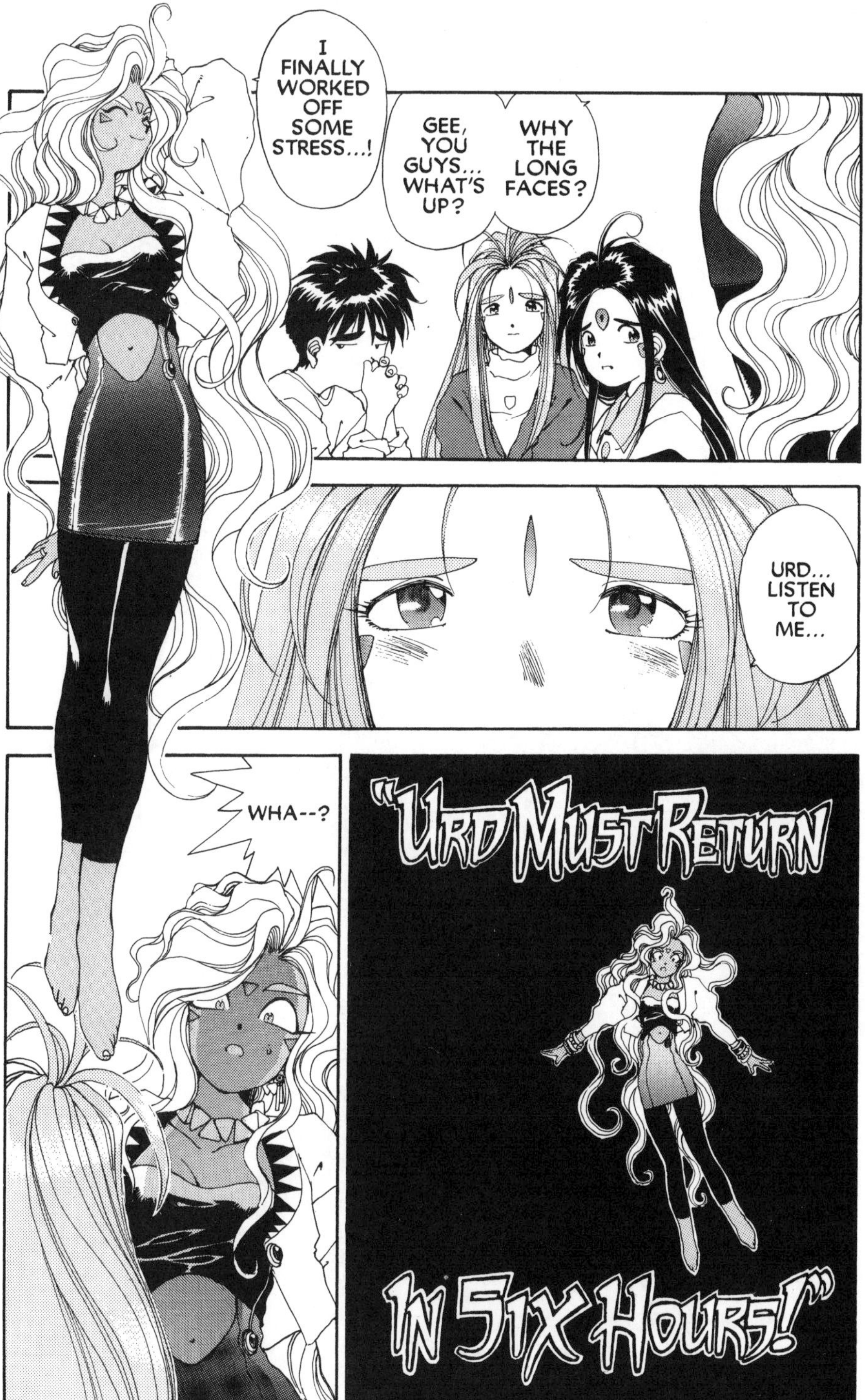
I FINALLY WORKED OFF SOME STRESS...!
GEE, YOU GUYS... WHAT'S UP?
WHY THE LONG FACES?
URD... LISTEN TO ME...
WHA--?
"URD MUST RETURN IN SIX HOURS!"

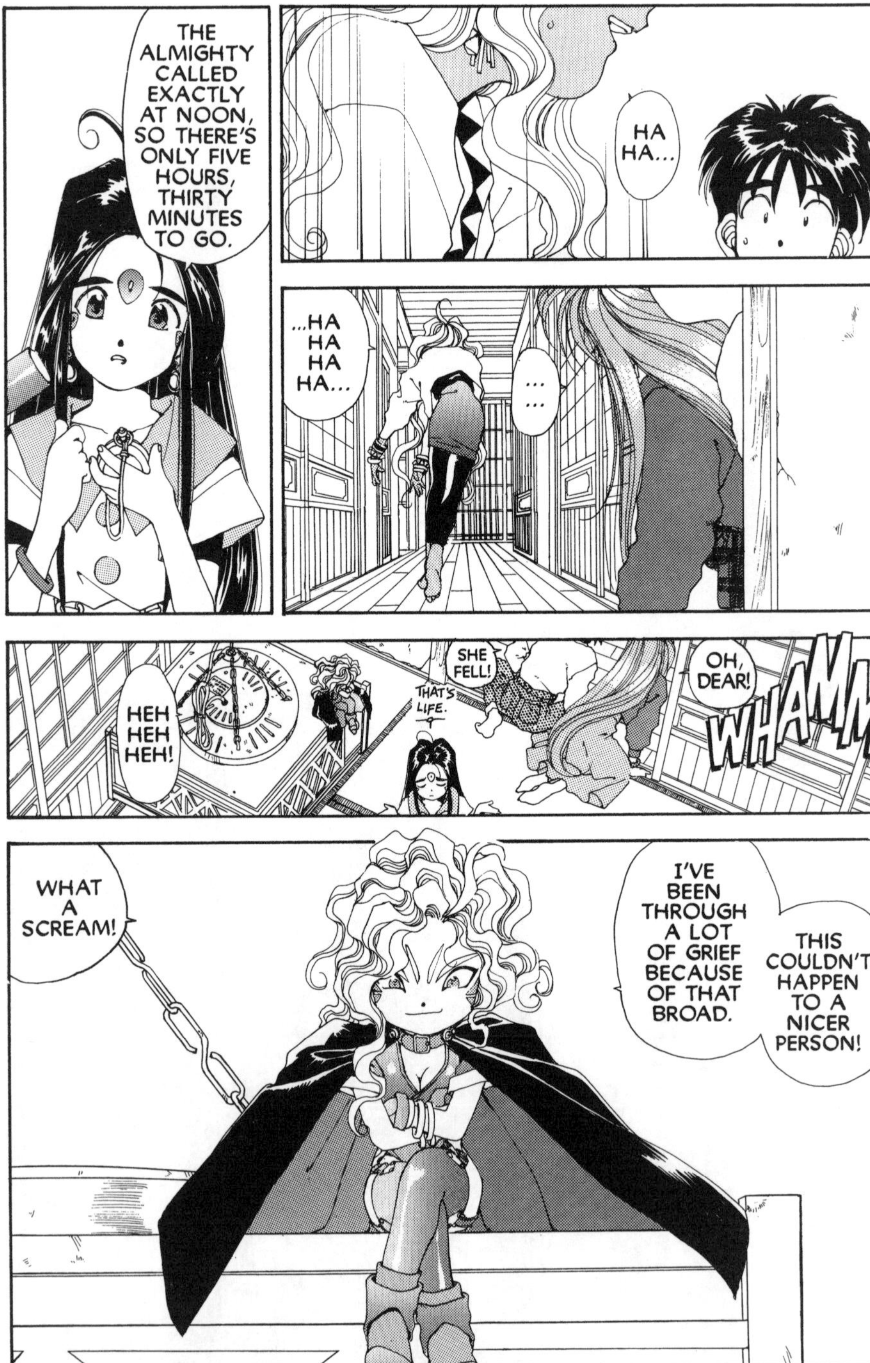
THE ALMIGHTY CALLED EXACTLY AT NOON, SO THERE'S ONLY FIVE HOURS, THIRTY MINUTES TO GO.
HA HA...
...HA HA HA HA...
......
HEH HEH HEH!
THAT'S LIFE.
SHE FELL!
OH, DEAR!
WHAMM
WHAT A SCREAM!
I'VE BEEN THROUGH A LOT OF GRIEF BECAUSE OF THAT BROAD.
THIS COULDN'T HAPPEN TO A NICER PERSON!

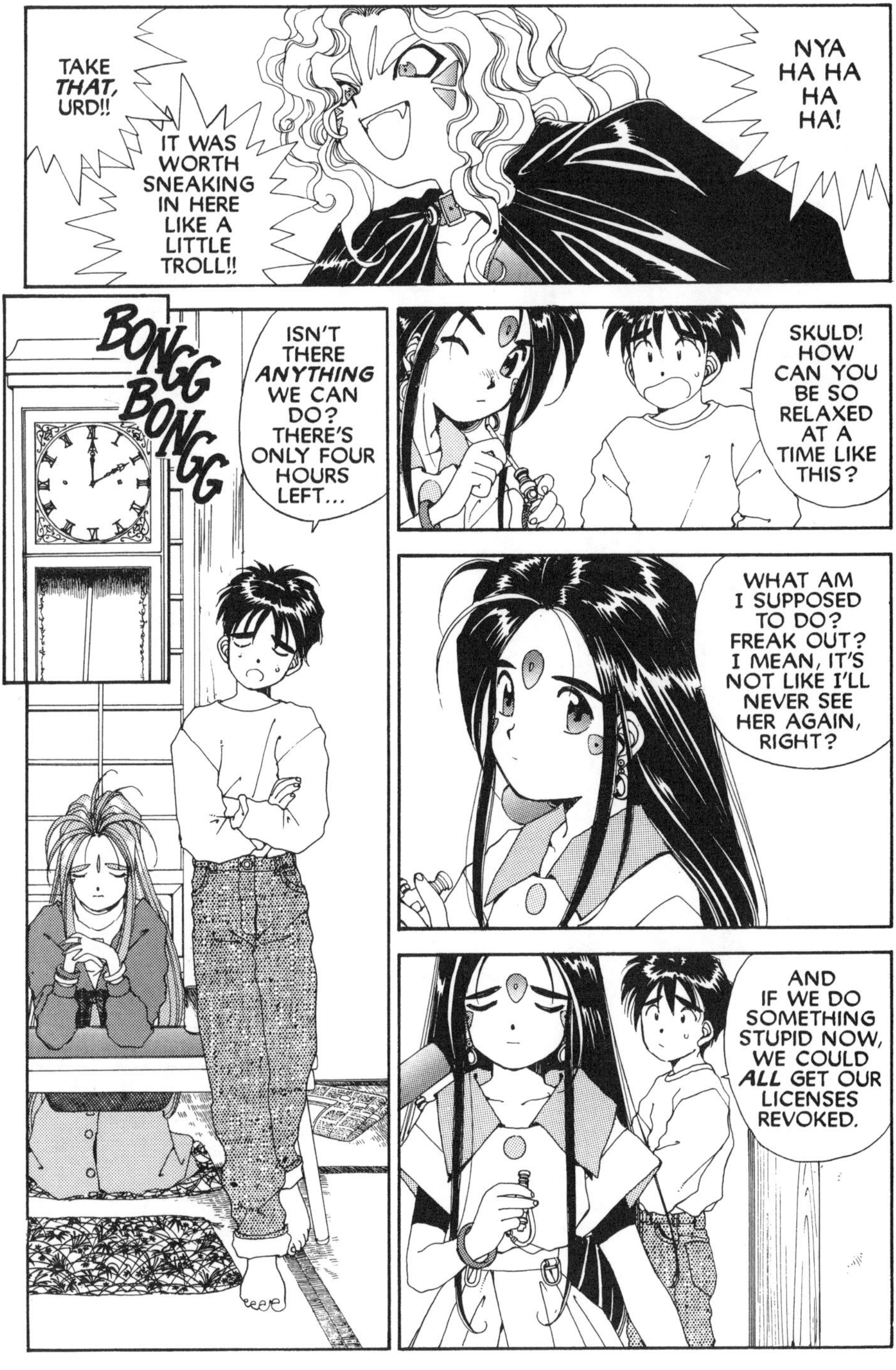
TAKE THAT, URD!!
IT WAS WORTH SNEAKING IN HERE LIKE A LITTLE TROLL!!
NYA HA HA HA HA!
BONGG BONGG
ISN'T THERE ANYTHING WE CAN DO? THERE'S ONLY FOUR HOURS LEFT...
SKULD! HOW CAN YOU BE SO RELAXED AT A TIME LIKE THIS?
WHAT AM I SUPPOSED TO DO? FREAK OUT? I MEAN, IT'S NOT LIKE I'LL NEVER SEE HER AGAIN, RIGHT?
AND IF WE DO SOMETHING STUPID NOW, WE COULD ALL GET OUR LICENSES REVOKED.

OKAY, I SEE... AND COME TO THINK OF IT, IT'S NOT LIKE THIS IS THE END, HUH?

I MEAN, SHE CAN COME TO EARTH AGAIN LATER.

YES, SHE CAN.

BUT...

...DEPENDING ON THE WILL OF THE ALMIGHTY, THAT COULD BE A HUNDRED OR EVEN A *THOUSAND* YEARS FROM NOW.

tik

tok

NO WAY!

YOU MEAN I'LL NEVER SEE URD'S... UH... FACE AGAIN?

THAT URD... ALWAYS OUT OF CONTROL...

SELFISH AND SELF-CENTERED...

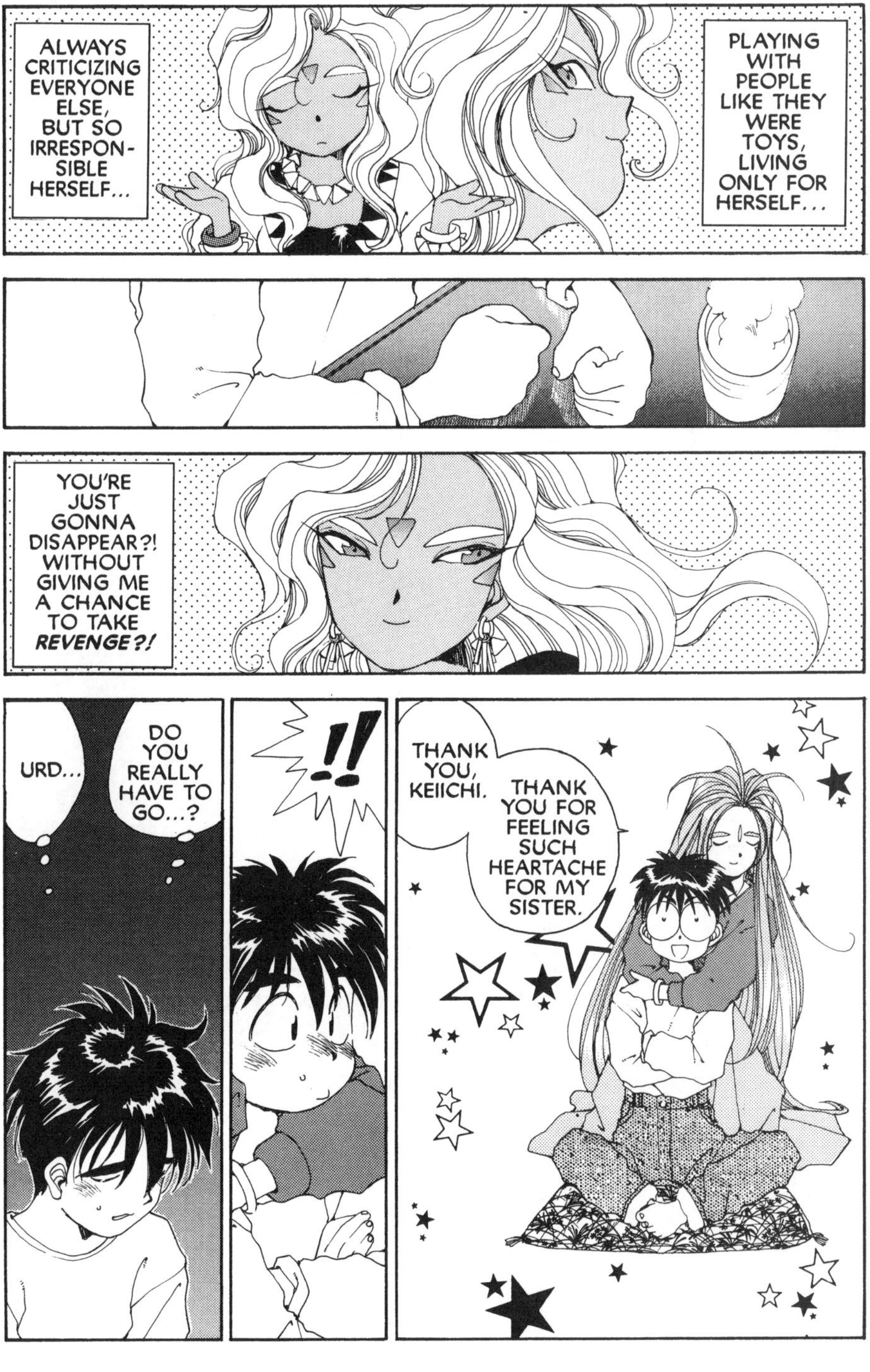
ALWAYS CRITICIZING EVERYONE ELSE, BUT SO IRRESPONSIBLE HERSELF...
PLAYING WITH PEOPLE LIKE THEY WERE TOYS, LIVING ONLY FOR HERSELF...
YOU'RE JUST GONNA DISAPPEAR?! WITHOUT GIVING ME A CHANCE TO TAKE *REVENGE?!*
URD...
DO YOU REALLY HAVE TO GO...?
!!
THANK YOU, KEIICHI.
THANK YOU FOR FEELING SUCH HEARTACHE FOR MY SISTER.

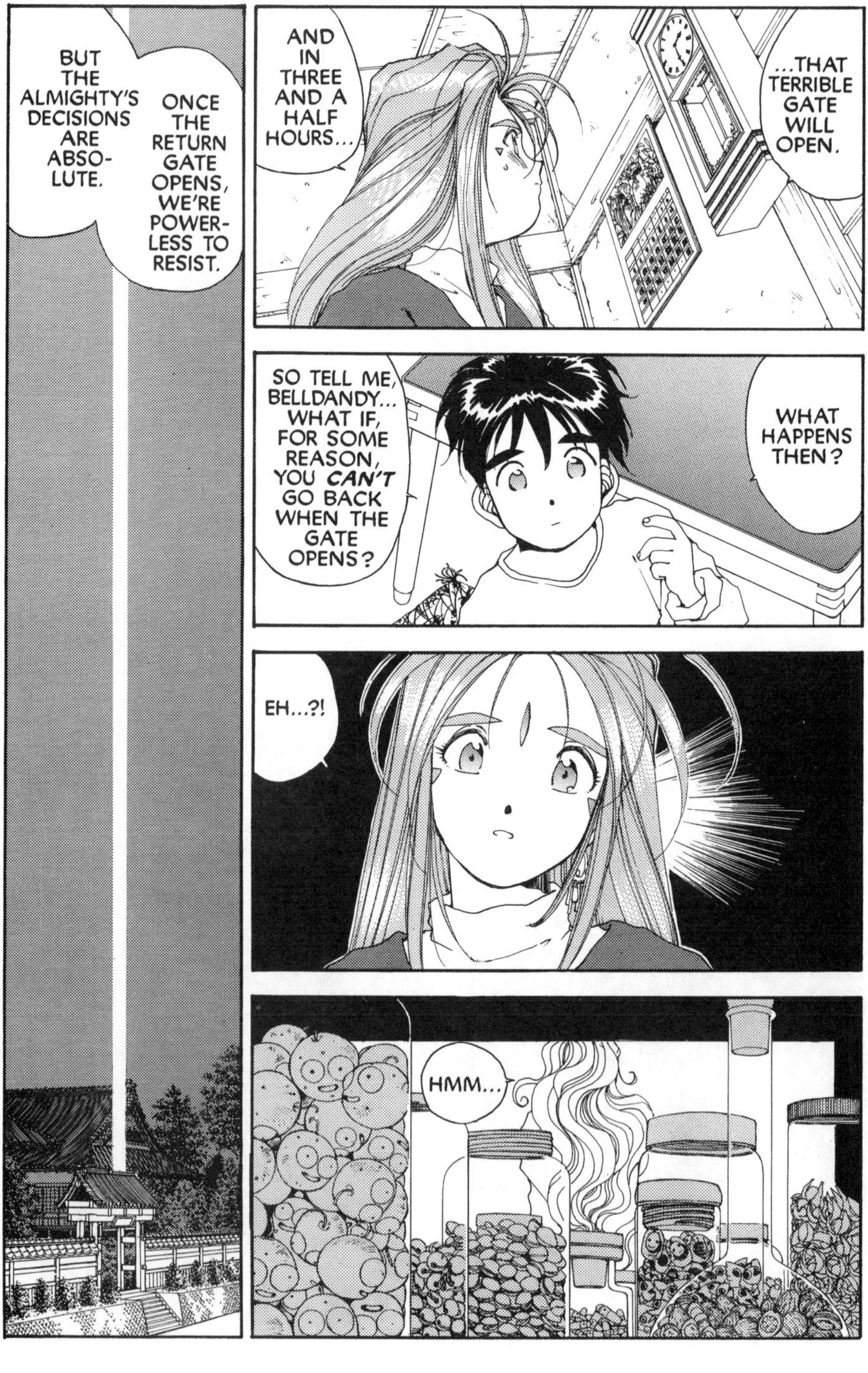
BUT THE ALMIGHTY'S DECISIONS ARE ABSO-LUTE.
ONCE THE RETURN GATE OPENS, WE'RE POWER-LESS TO RESIST.
AND IN THREE AND A HALF HOURS...
...THAT TERRIBLE GATE WILL OPEN.
SO TELL ME, BELLDANDY... WHAT IF, FOR SOME REASON, YOU *CAN'T* GO BACK WHEN THE GATE OPENS?
WHAT HAPPENS THEN?
EH...?!
HMM...

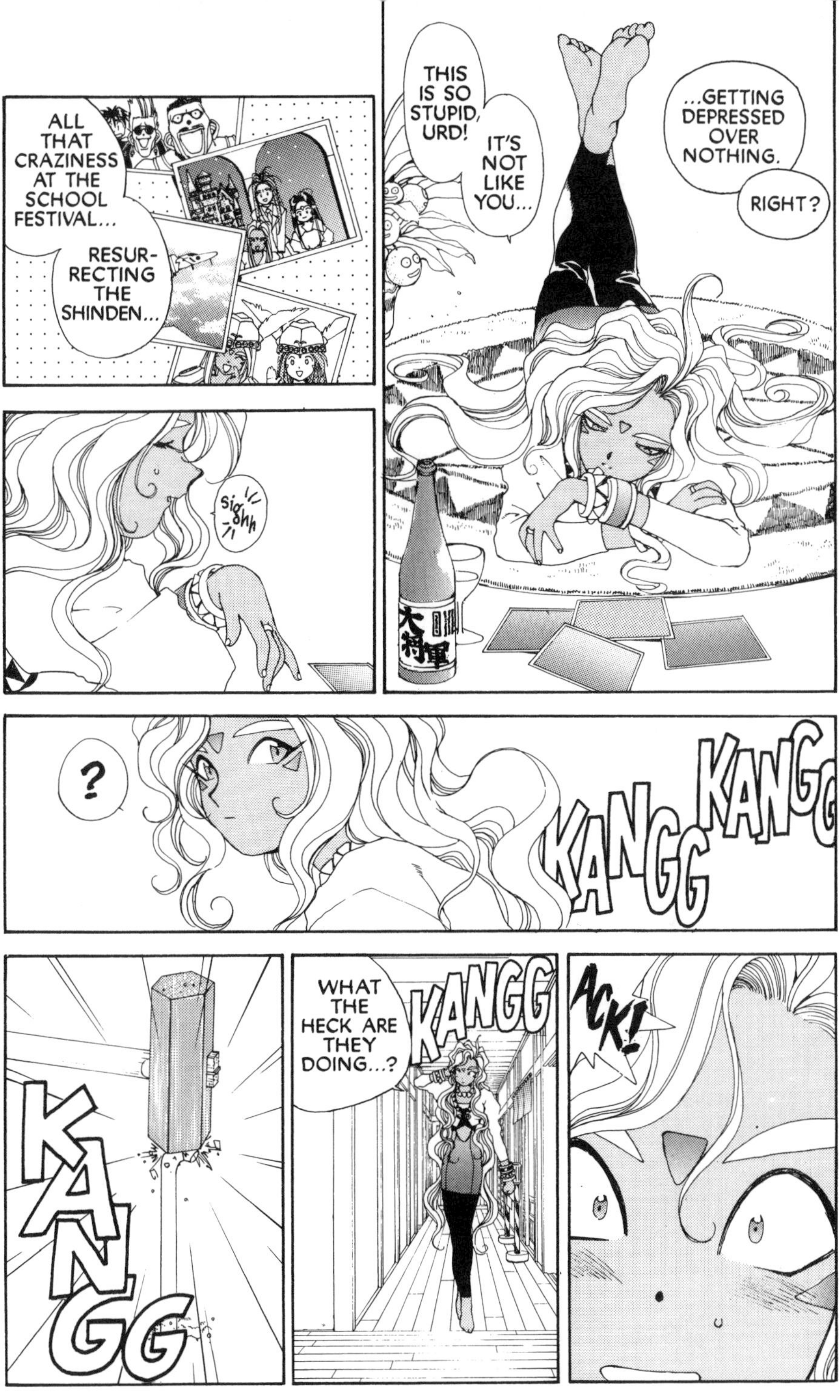
ALL THAT CRAZINESS AT THE SCHOOL FESTIVAL...
RESUR-RECTING THE SHINDEN...
sighh
THIS IS SO STUPID, URD!
IT'S NOT LIKE YOU...
...GETTING DEPRESSED OVER NOTHING.
RIGHT?
大将軍
?
KANGG
KANGG
KANGG
WHAT THE HECK ARE THEY DOING...?
KANGG
ACK!

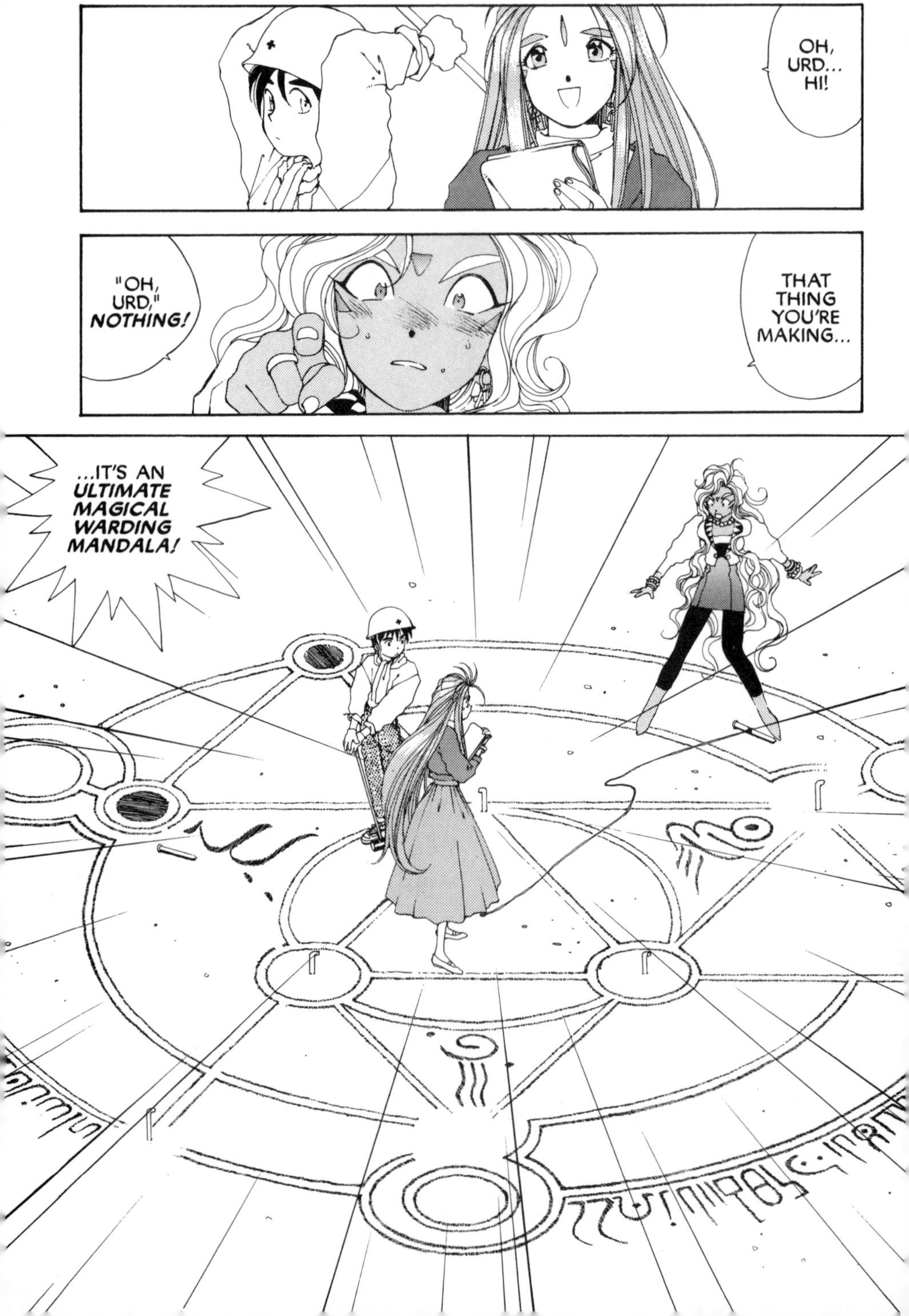
OH, URD... HI!
"OH, URD," NOTHING!
THAT THING YOU'RE MAKING...
...IT'S AN ULTIMATE MAGICAL WARDING MANDALA!

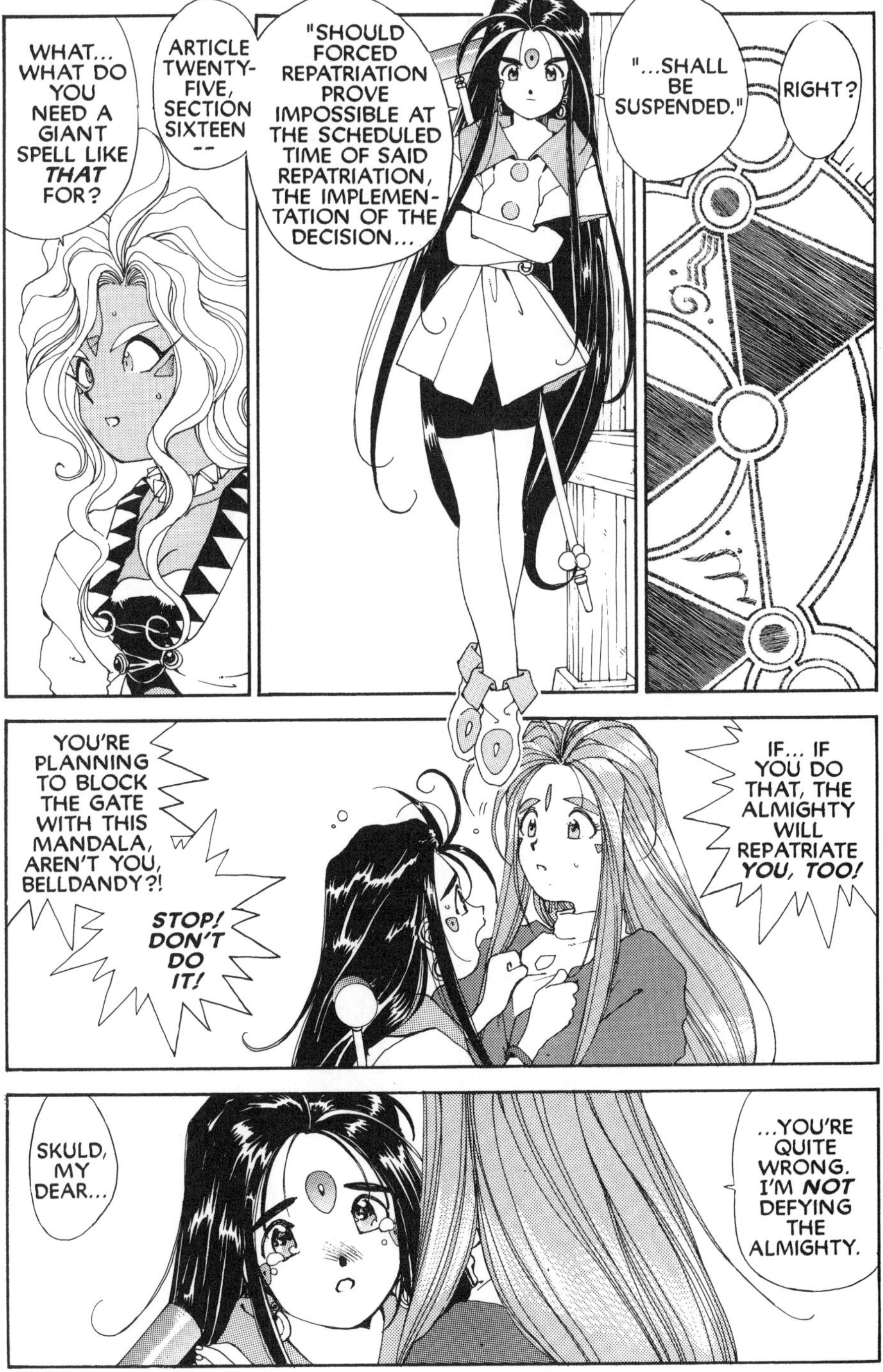
WHAT... WHAT DO YOU NEED A GIANT SPELL LIKE *THAT* FOR?
ARTICLE TWENTY-FIVE, SECTION SIXTEEN --
"SHOULD FORCED REPATRIATION PROVE IMPOSSIBLE AT THE SCHEDULED TIME OF SAID REPATRIATION, THE IMPLEMENTATION OF THE DECISION...
"...SHALL BE SUSPENDED."
RIGHT?
YOU'RE PLANNING TO BLOCK THE GATE WITH THIS MANDALA, AREN'T YOU, BELLDANDY?!
STOP! DON'T DO IT!
IF... IF YOU DO THAT, THE ALMIGHTY WILL REPATRIATE *YOU, TOO!*
SKULD, MY DEAR...
...YOU'RE QUITE WRONG. I'M *NOT* DEFYING THE ALMIGHTY.

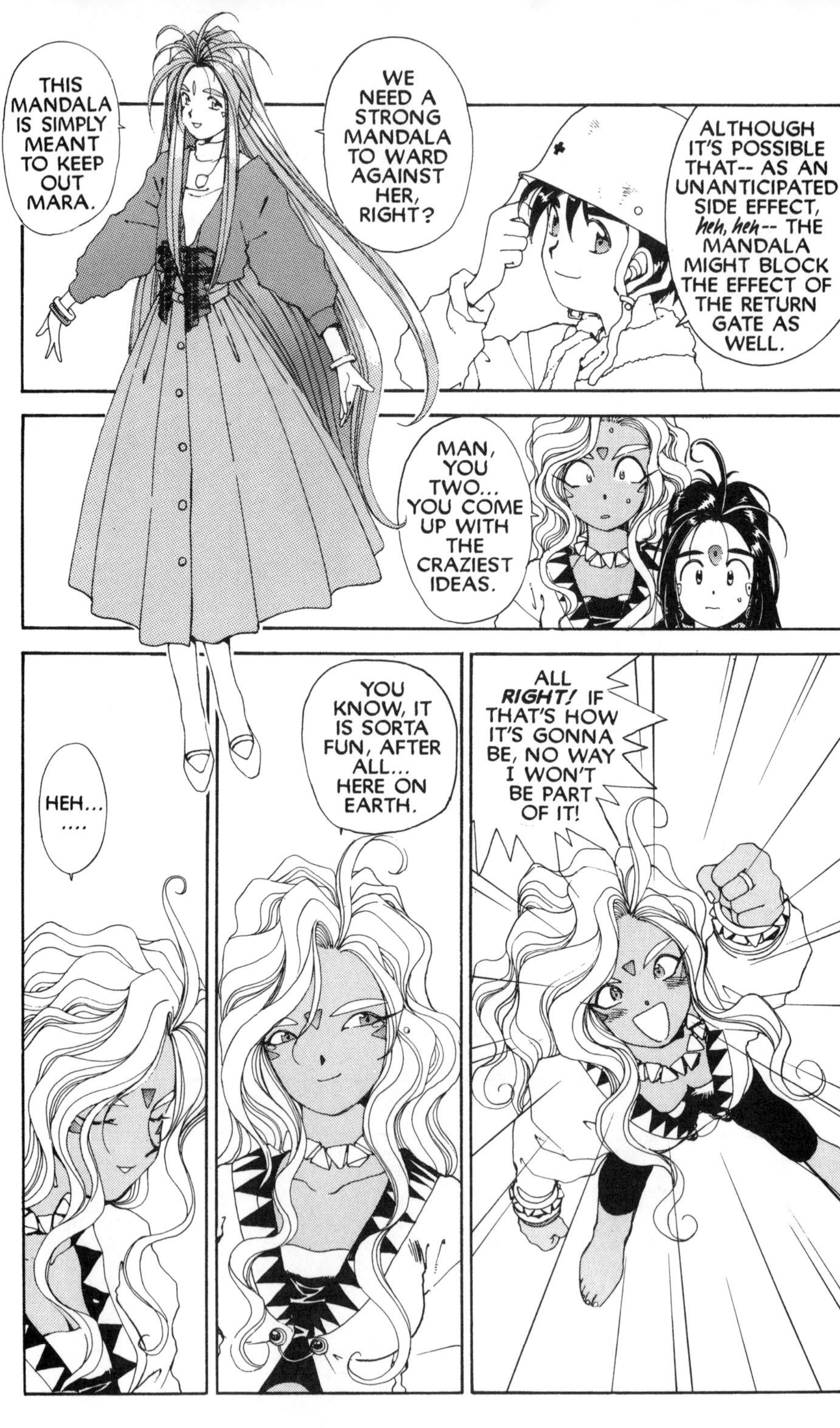

THIS MANDALA IS SIMPLY MEANT TO KEEP OUT MARA.
WE NEED A STRONG MANDALA TO WARD AGAINST HER, RIGHT?
ALTHOUGH IT'S POSSIBLE THAT-- AS AN UNANTICIPATED SIDE EFFECT, heh, heh-- THE MANDALA MIGHT BLOCK THE EFFECT OF THE RETURN GATE AS WELL.
MAN, YOU TWO... YOU COME UP WITH THE CRAZIEST IDEAS.
HEH... ....
YOU KNOW, IT IS SORTA FUN, AFTER ALL... HERE ON EARTH.
ALL RIGHT! IF THAT'S HOW IT'S GONNA BE, NO WAY I WON'T BE PART OF IT!

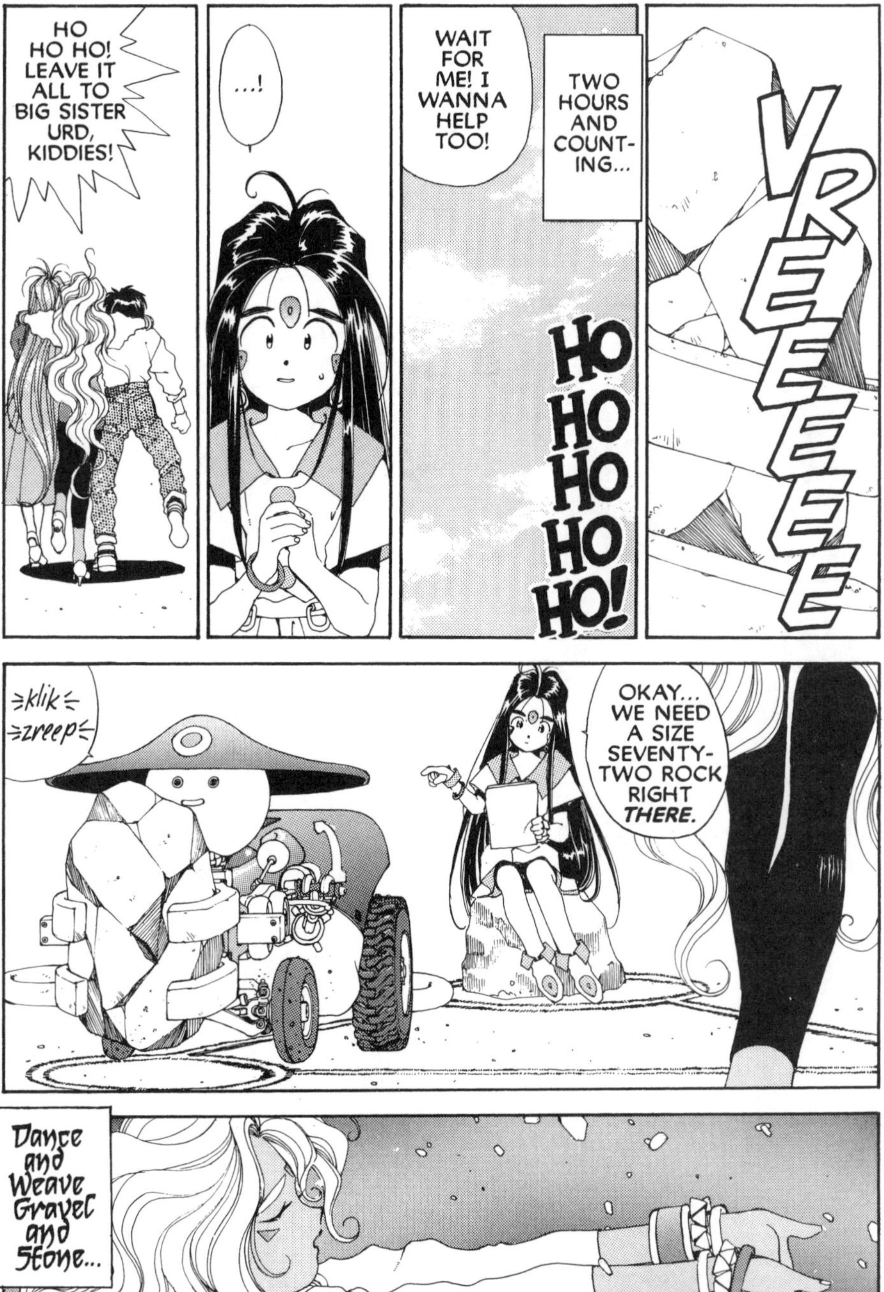
HO HO HO! LEAVE IT ALL TO BIG SISTER URD, KIDDIES!
...!
WAIT FOR ME! I WANNA HELP TOO!
TWO HOURS AND COUNTING...
HO HO HO HO HO HO!
VREEEEEE
klik
zreep
OKAY... WE NEED A SIZE SEVENTY-TWO ROCK RIGHT *THERE.*
Dance and Weave Gravel and Stone...

Obey
We
Goddesses
Three
Past,
Present
and
Future...

Hark
to the
Covenant
of
Urd,
Belldandy,
and
Skuld...

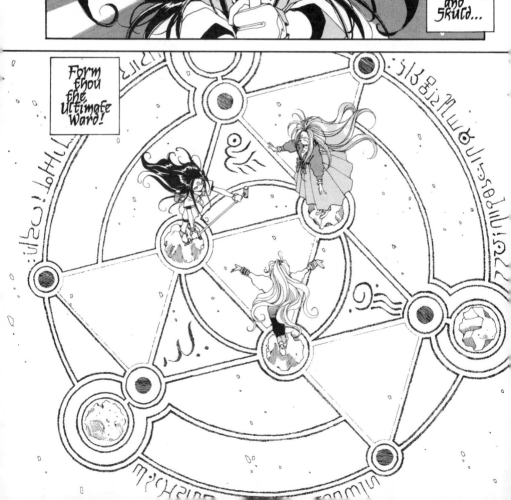

Form
thou
the
Ultimate
Ward!

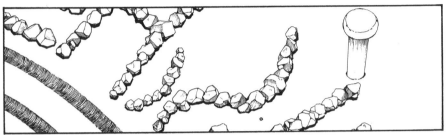

PHEW!

IN THE NICK OF TIME!

WE DID IT!!

LET ME GUESS... IT'S A FIRST?

THE FIRST TIME YOU THREE ALL COOPER- ATED?

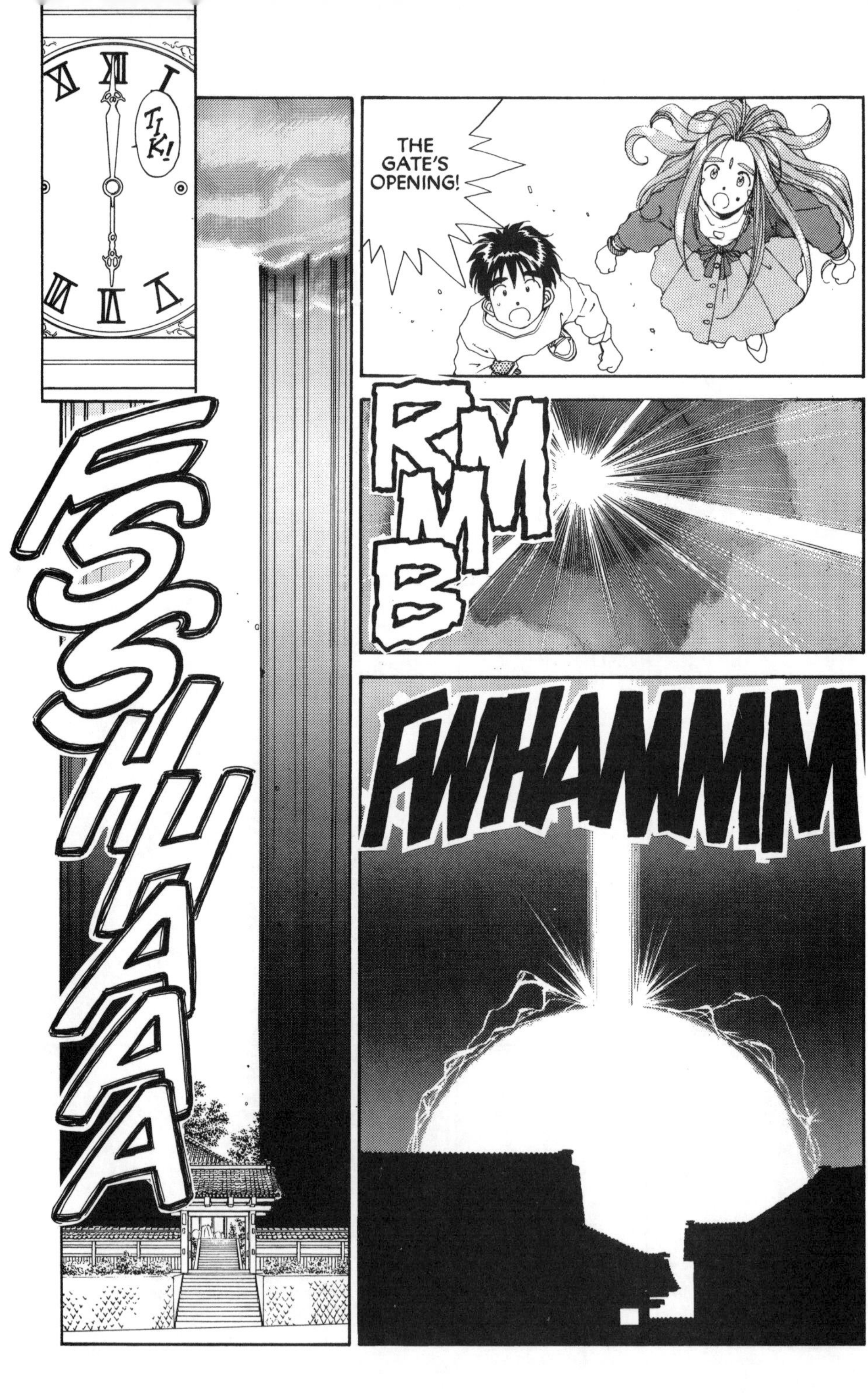
TIK!
FSSHHAAAA
THE GATE'S OPENING!
RMMB
FWHAMMM

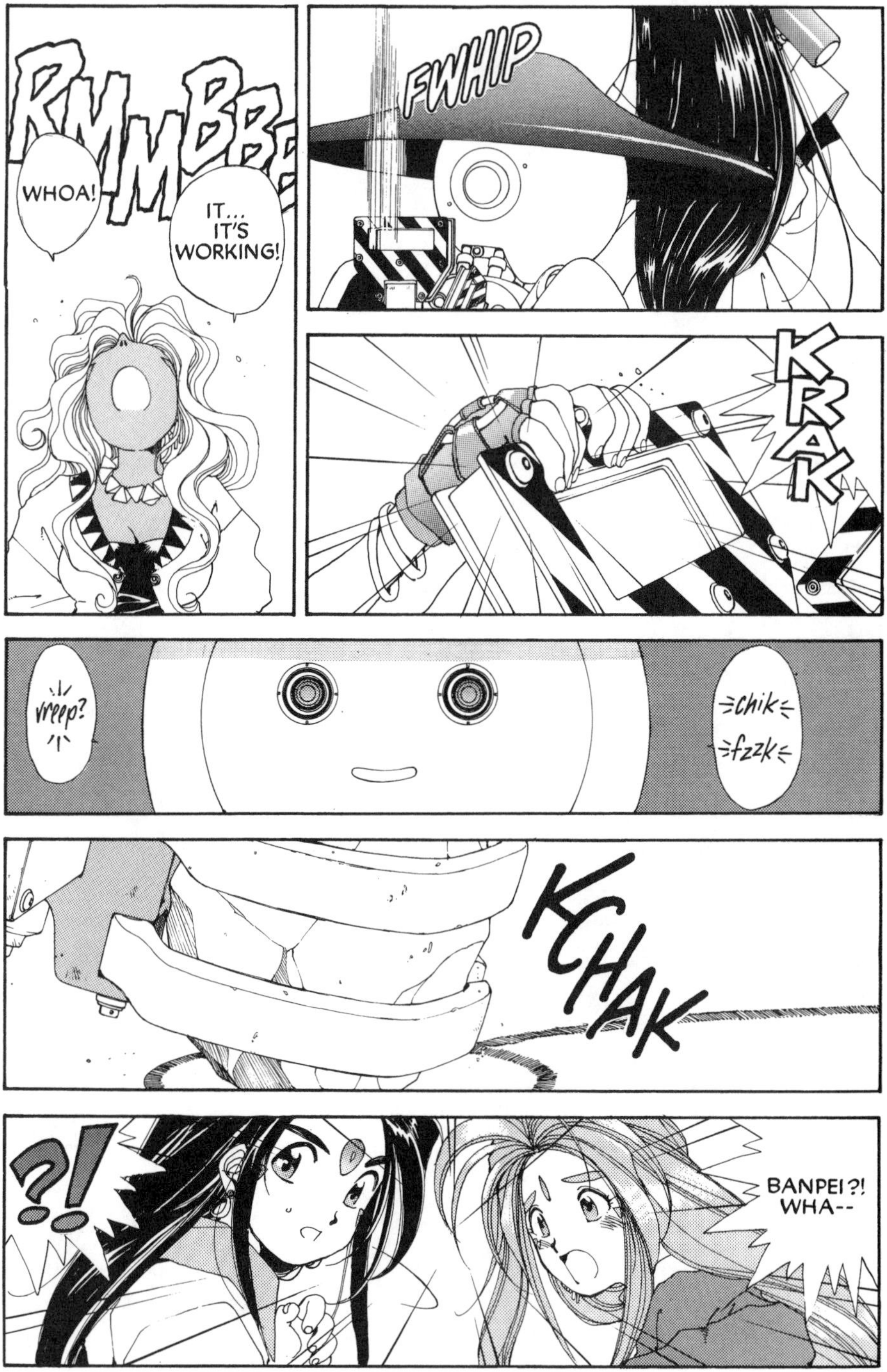
RMMBBB
WHOA!
IT... IT'S WORKING!
FWHIP
KRAK
vreep?
chik
fzzk
KCHAK
?!
BANPEI?! WHA--

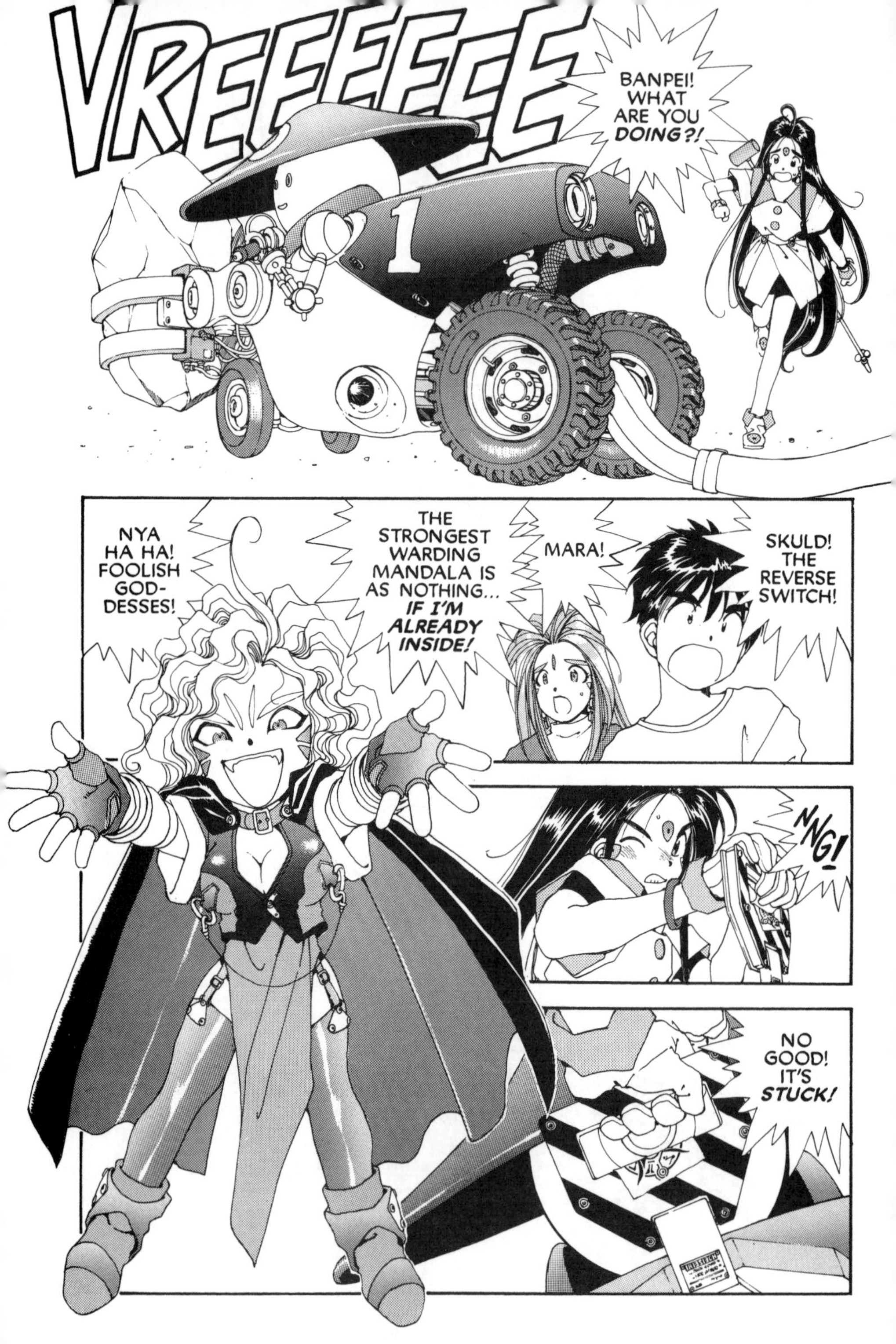
VREEEEEE
BANPEI! WHAT ARE YOU DOING?!
NYA HA HA! FOOLISH GOD-DESSES!
THE STRONGEST WARDING MANDALA IS AS NOTHING... IF I'M ALREADY INSIDE!
MARA!
SKULD! THE REVERSE SWITCH!
NNG!
NO GOOD! IT'S STUCK!

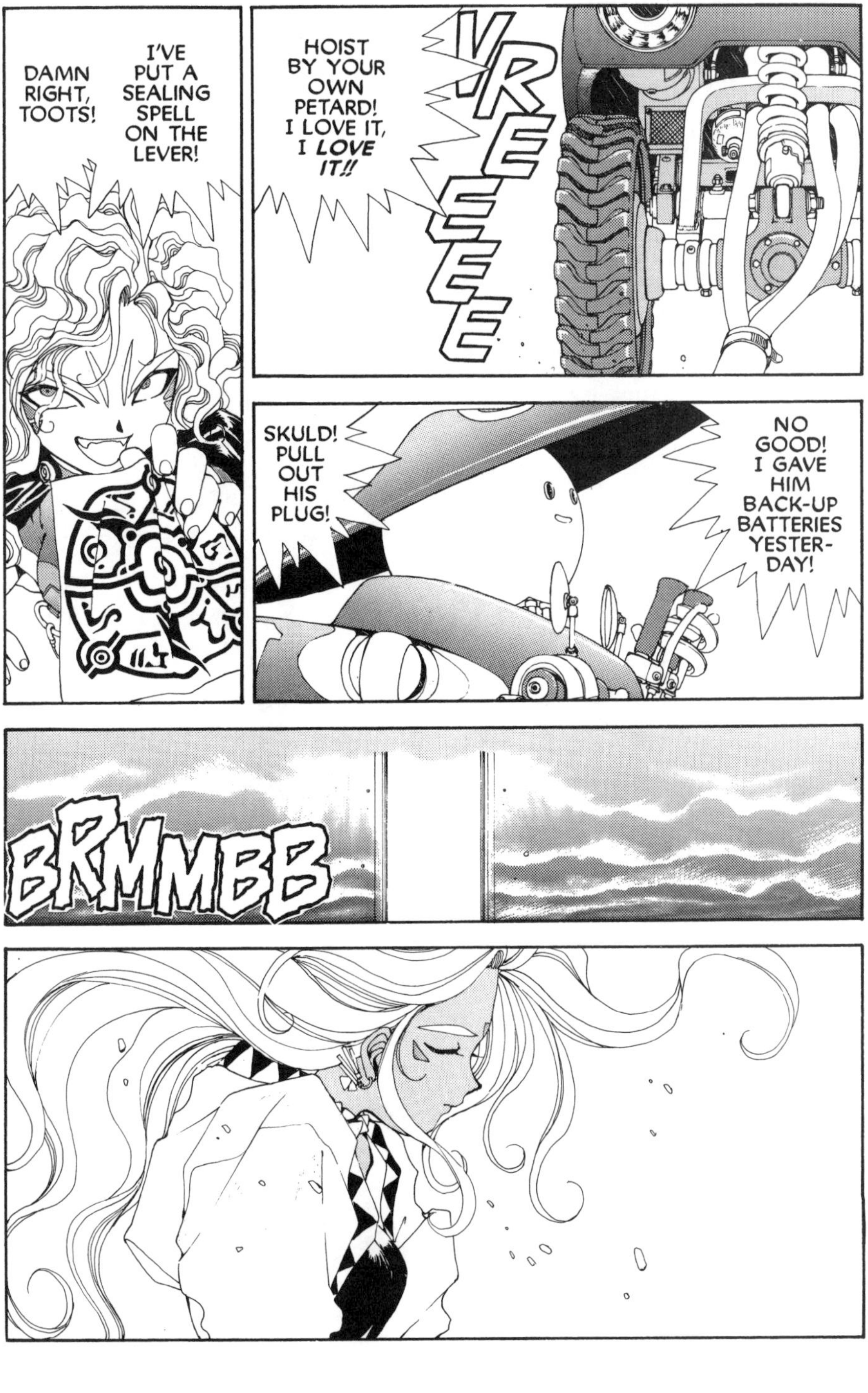
DAMN RIGHT, TOOTS!
I'VE PUT A SEALING SPELL ON THE LEVER!
HOIST BY YOUR OWN PETARD! I LOVE IT, I *LOVE IT!!*
VREEEE
SKULD! PULL OUT HIS PLUG!
NO GOOD! I GAVE HIM BACK-UP BATTERIES YESTER-DAY!
BRMMBB

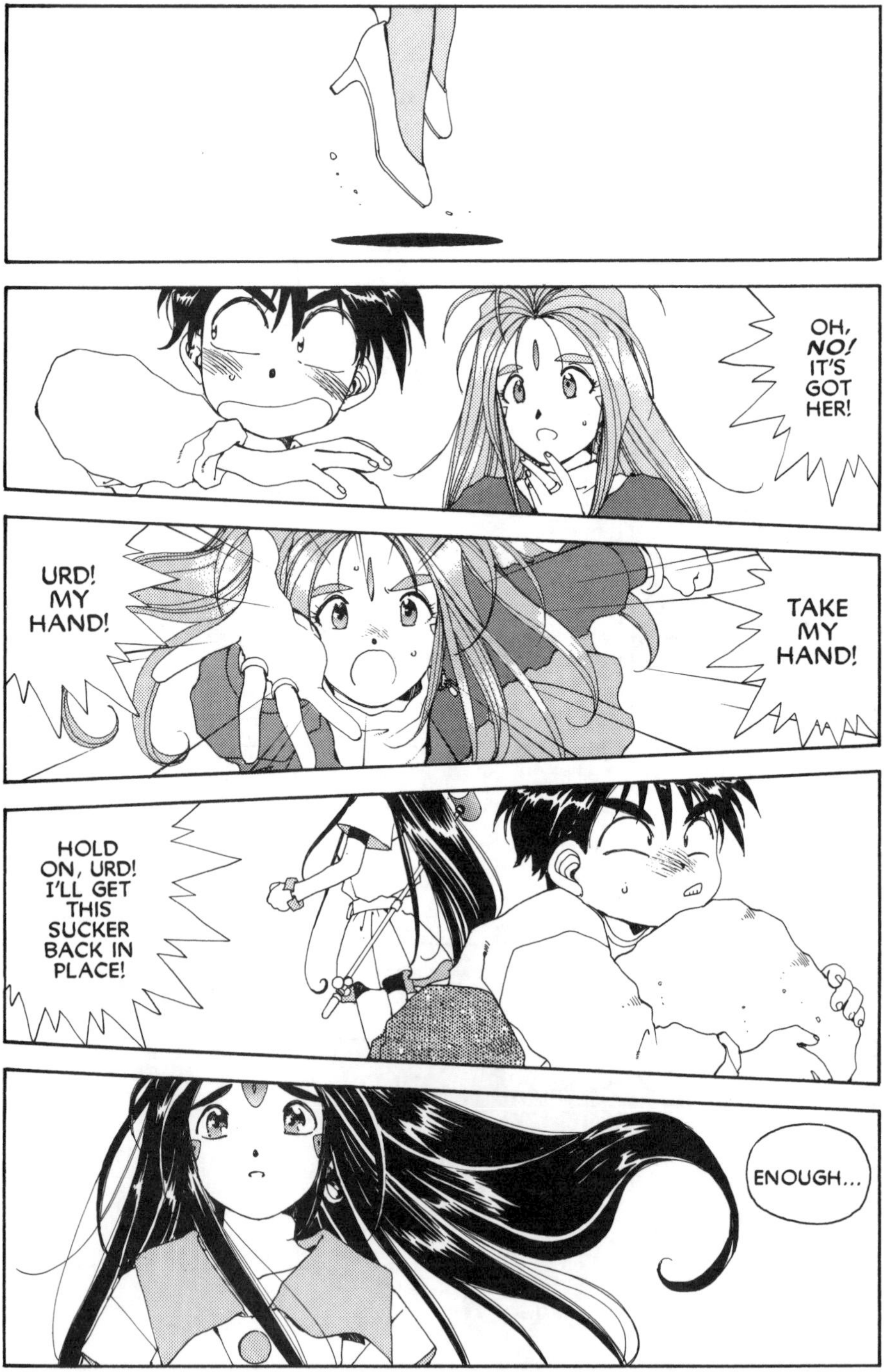
OH, NO! IT'S GOT HER!
TAKE MY HAND!
URD! MY HAND!
HOLD ON, URD! I'LL GET THIS SUCKER BACK IN PLACE!
ENOUGH...

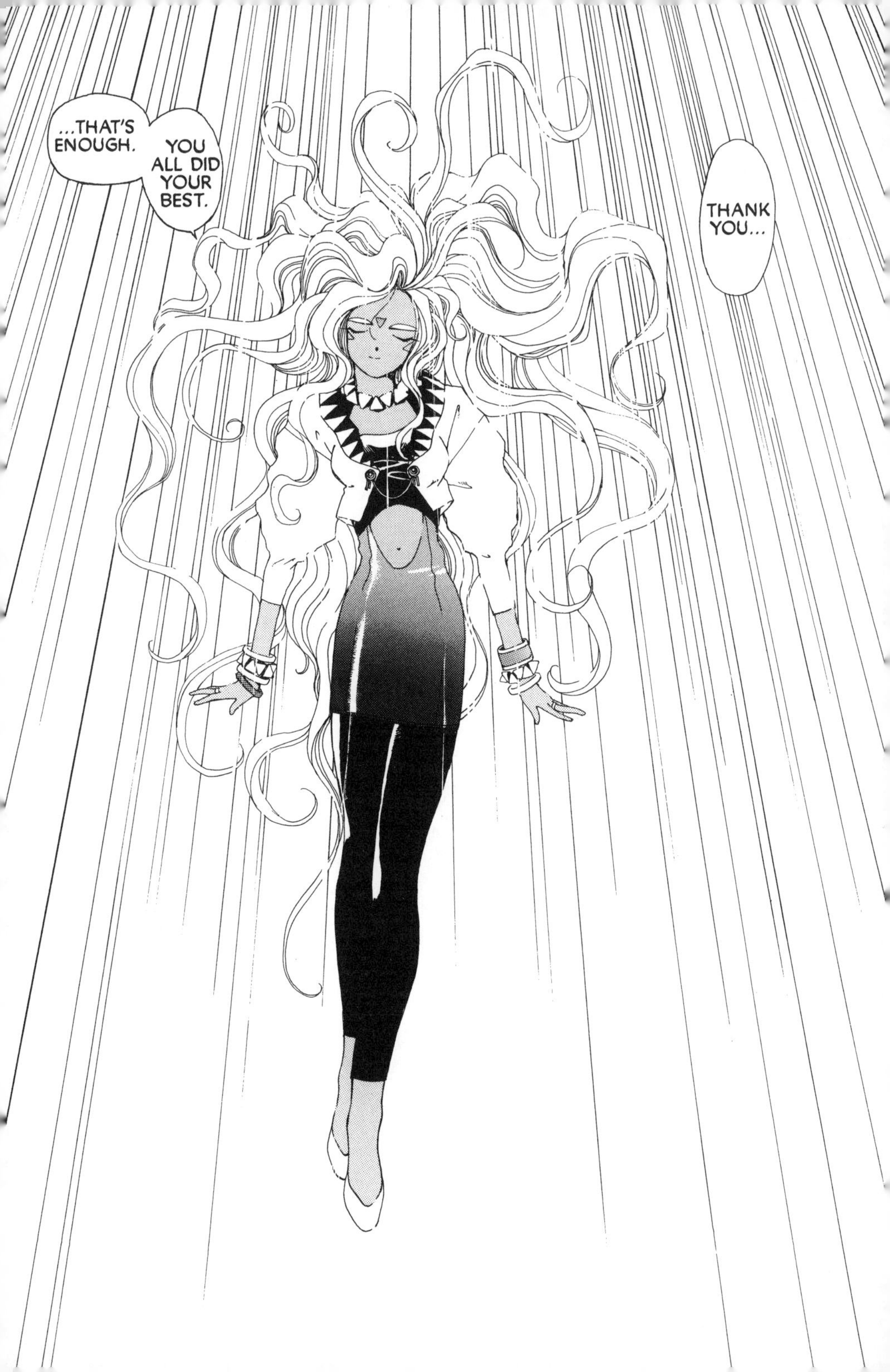
...THAT'S ENOUGH.
YOU ALL DID YOUR BEST.
THANK YOU...

URD!

YOU **CAN'T** GIVE UP!

WHDD

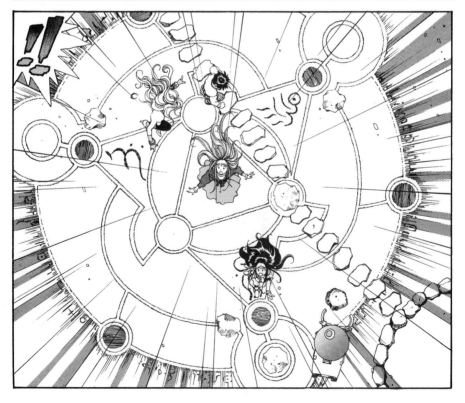

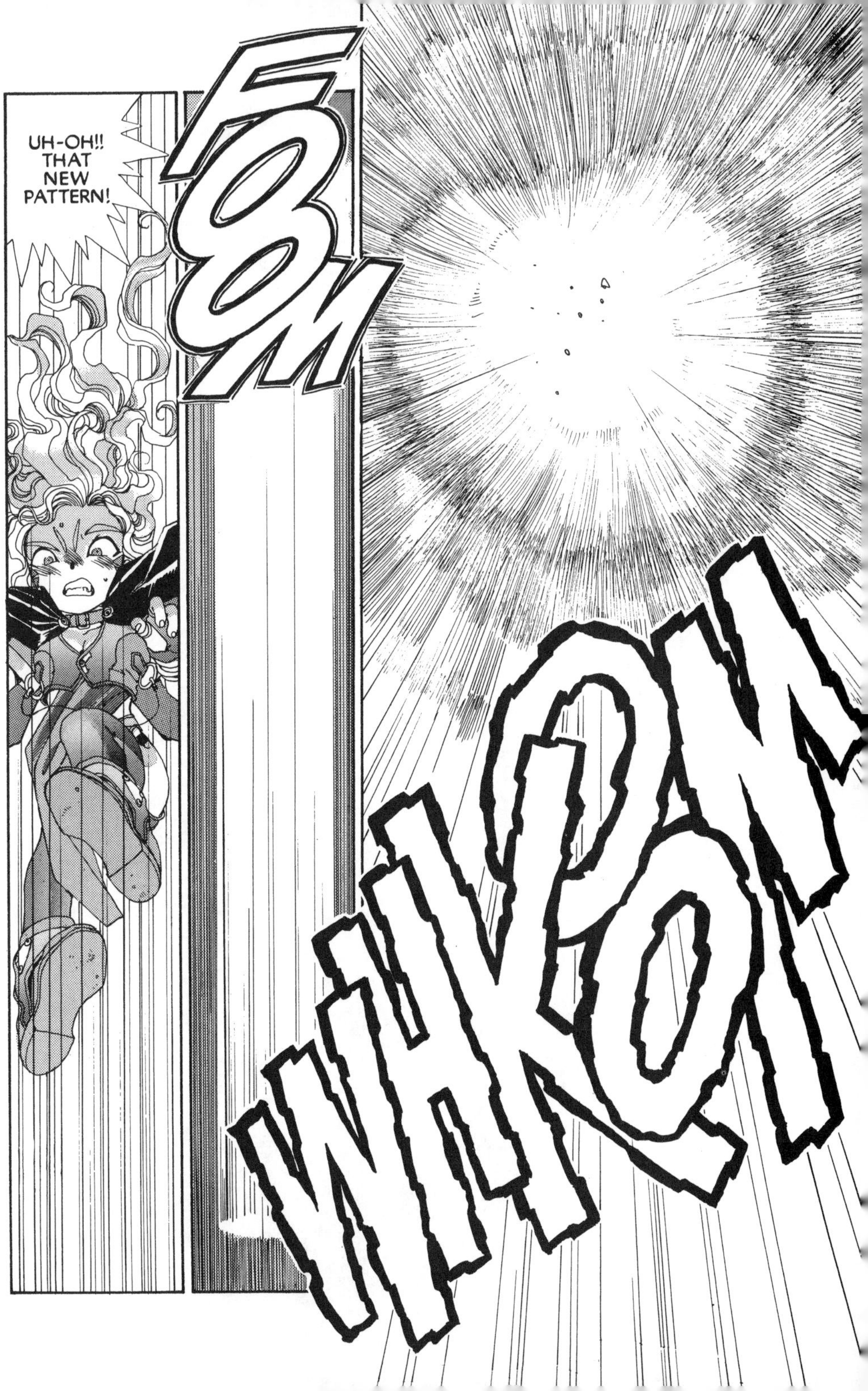
UH-OH!! THAT NEW PATTERN!
FWOM
WHOOM

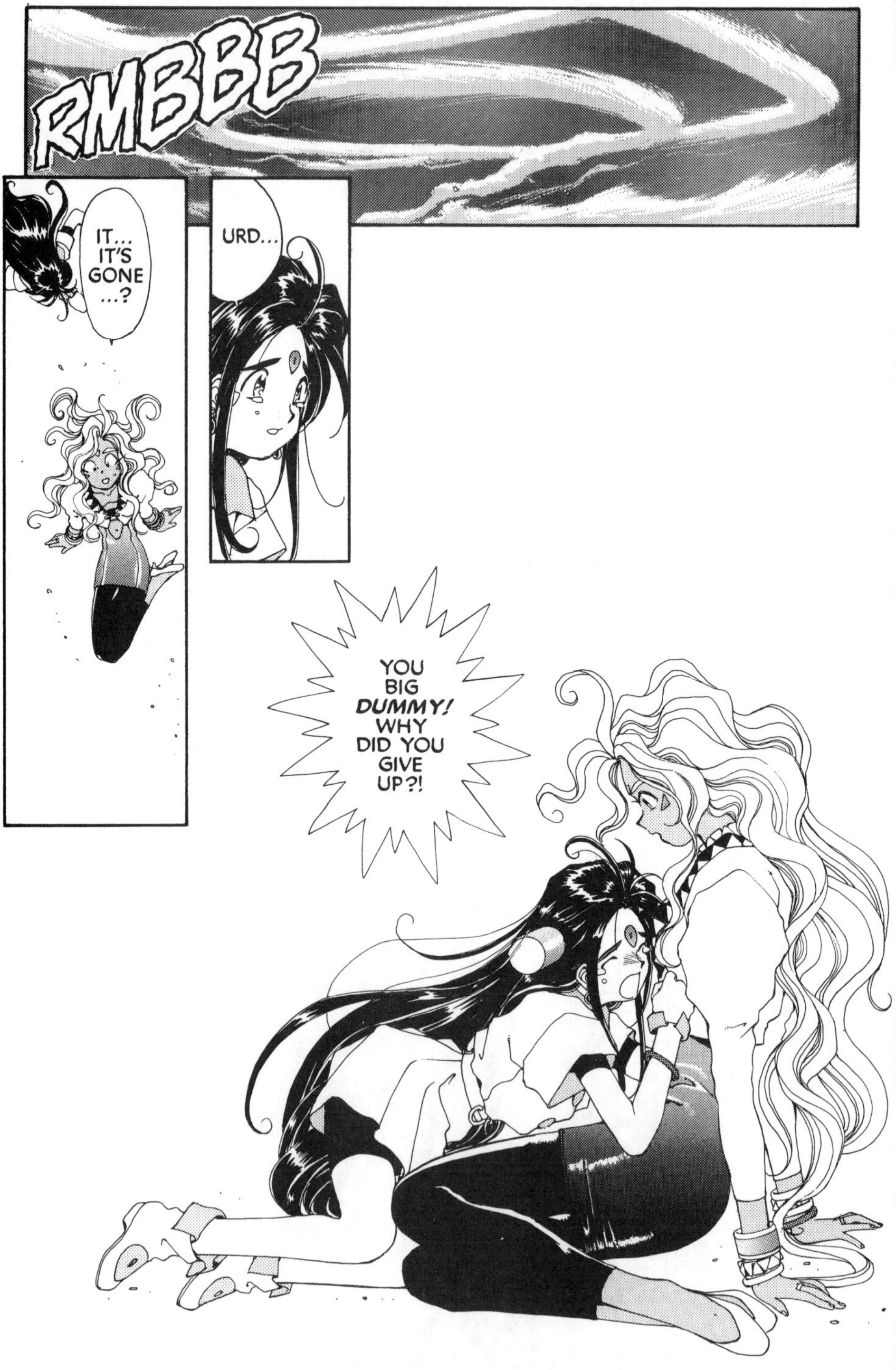
RMBBB
IT... IT'S GONE ...?
URD...
YOU BIG *DUMMY!* WHY DID YOU GIVE UP?!

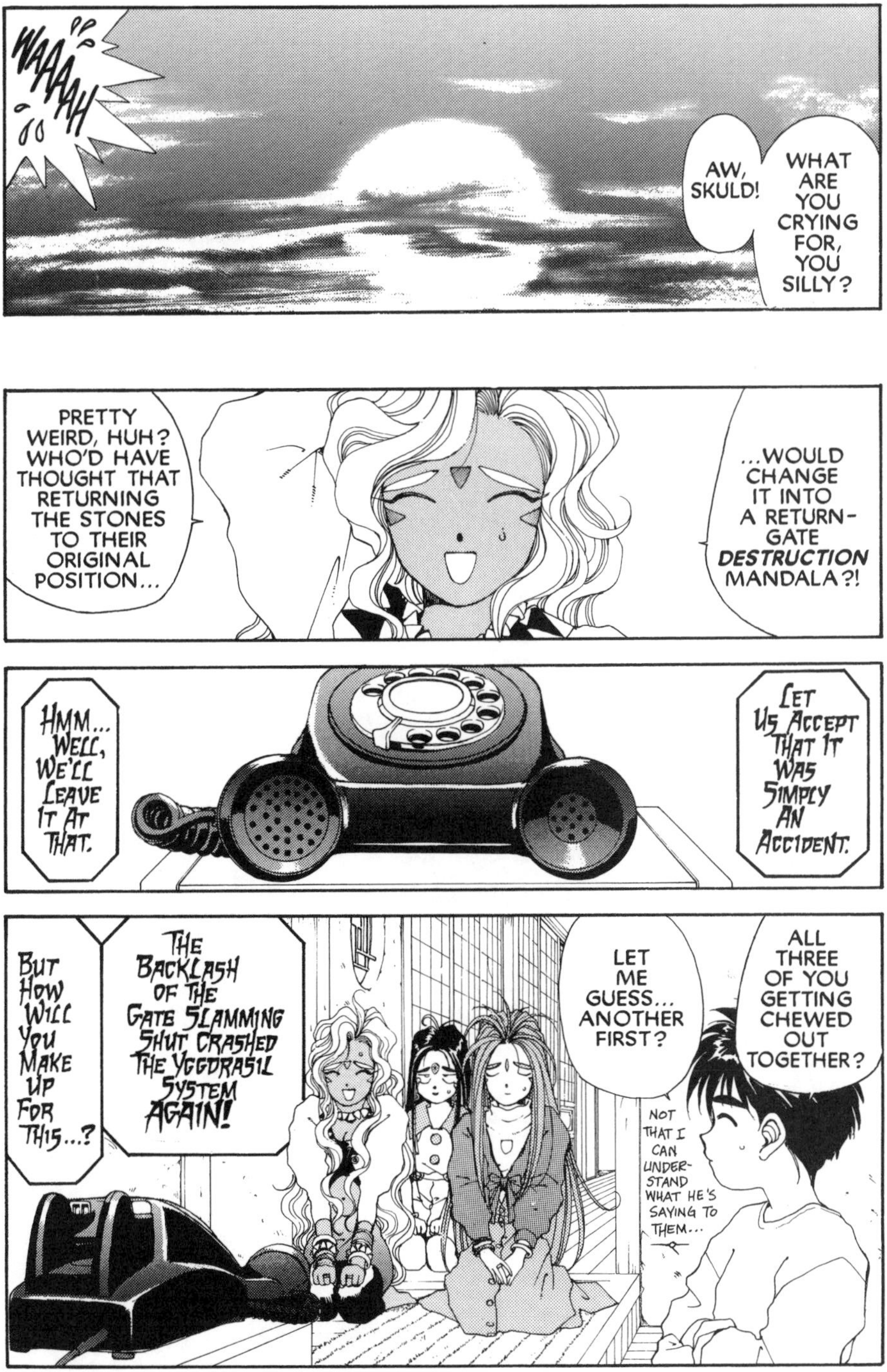
WAAAAAH
AW, SKULD!
WHAT ARE YOU CRYING FOR, YOU SILLY?
PRETTY WEIRD, HUH? WHO'D HAVE THOUGHT THAT RETURNING THE STONES TO THEIR ORIGINAL POSITION...
...WOULD CHANGE IT INTO A RETURN-GATE DESTRUCTION MANDALA?!
HMM... WELL, WE'LL LEAVE IT AT THAT.
LET US ACCEPT THAT IT WAS SIMPLY AN ACCIDENT.
BUT HOW WILL YOU MAKE UP FOR THIS...?
THE BACKLASH OF THE GATE SLAMMING SHUT CRASHED THE YGGDRASIL SYSTEM AGAIN!
LET ME GUESS... ANOTHER FIRST?
ALL THREE OF YOU GETTING CHEWED OUT TOGETHER?
NOT THAT I CAN UNDER-STAND WHAT HE'S SAYING TO THEM...

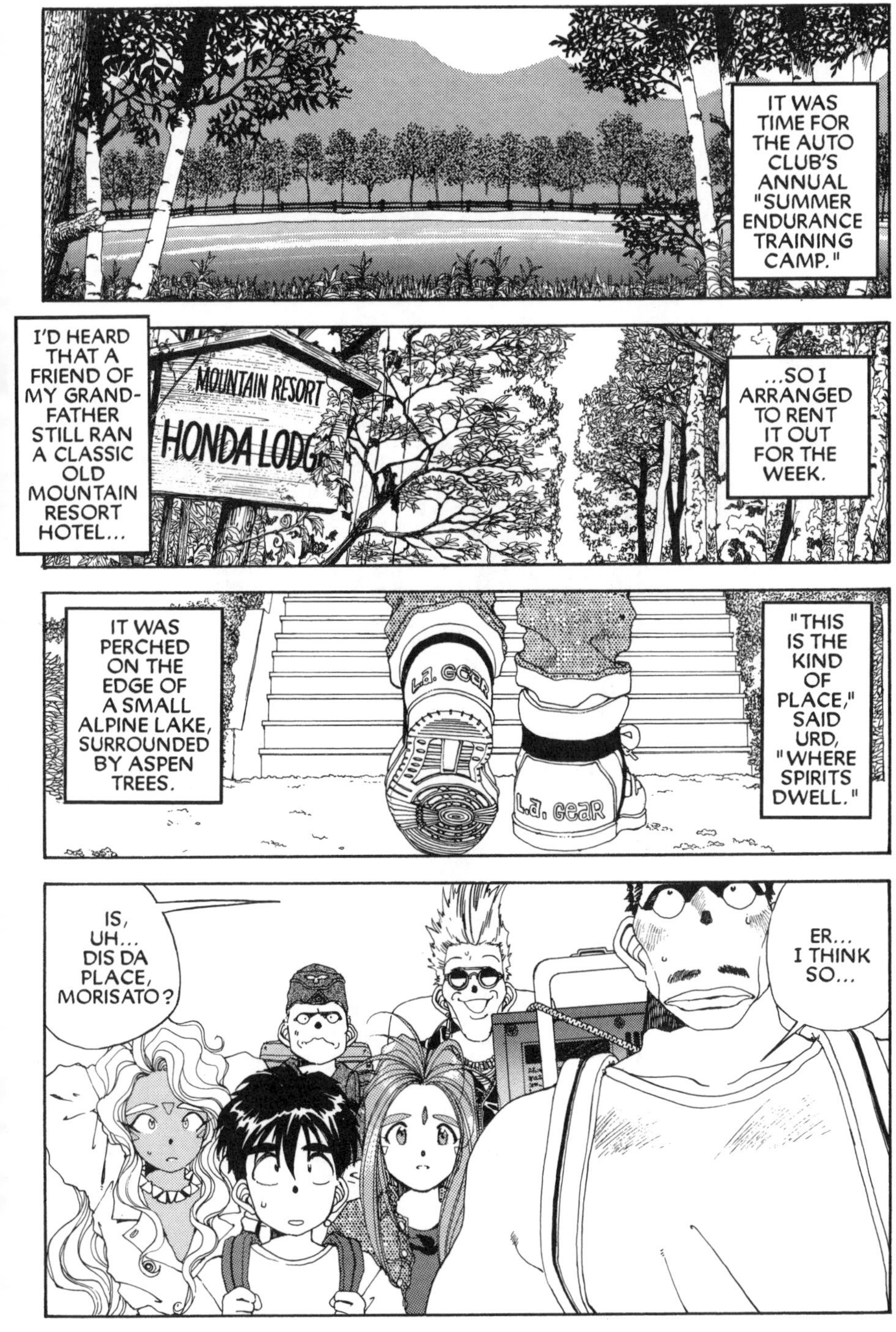
IT WAS TIME FOR THE AUTO CLUB'S ANNUAL "SUMMER ENDURANCE TRAINING CAMP."
I'D HEARD THAT A FRIEND OF MY GRAND-FATHER STILL RAN A CLASSIC OLD MOUNTAIN RESORT HOTEL...
MOUNTAIN RESORT
HONDA LODG
...SO I ARRANGED TO RENT IT OUT FOR THE WEEK.
IT WAS PERCHED ON THE EDGE OF A SMALL ALPINE LAKE, SURROUNDED BY ASPEN TREES.
L.a. GeaR
L.a. GeaR
"THIS IS THE KIND OF PLACE," SAID URD, "WHERE SPIRITS DWELL."
IS, UH... DIS DA PLACE, MORISATO?
ER... I THINK SO...

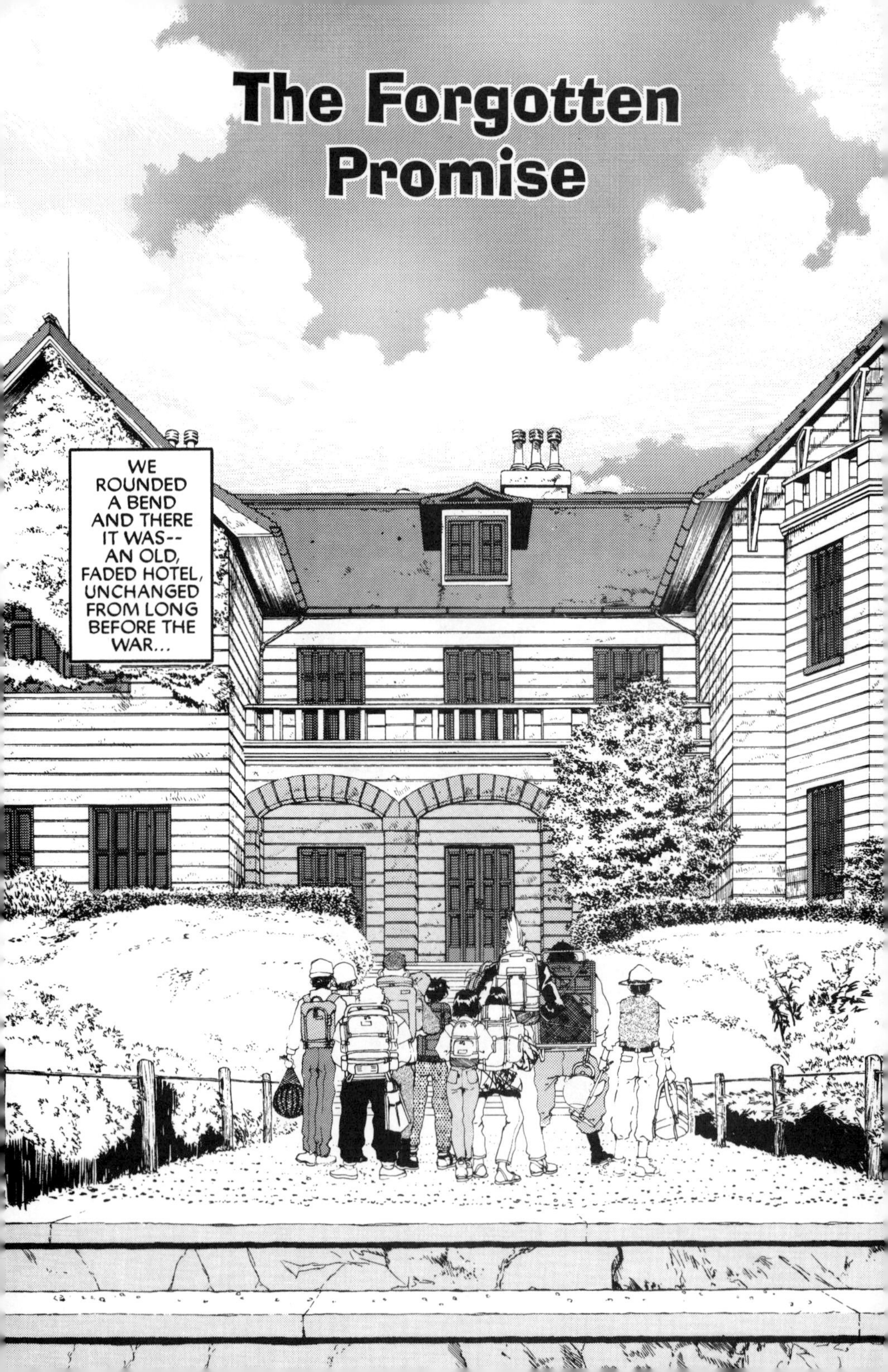
The Forgotten Promise
WE ROUNDED A BEND AND THERE IT WAS-- AN OLD, FADED HOTEL, UNCHANGED FROM LONG BEFORE THE WAR...

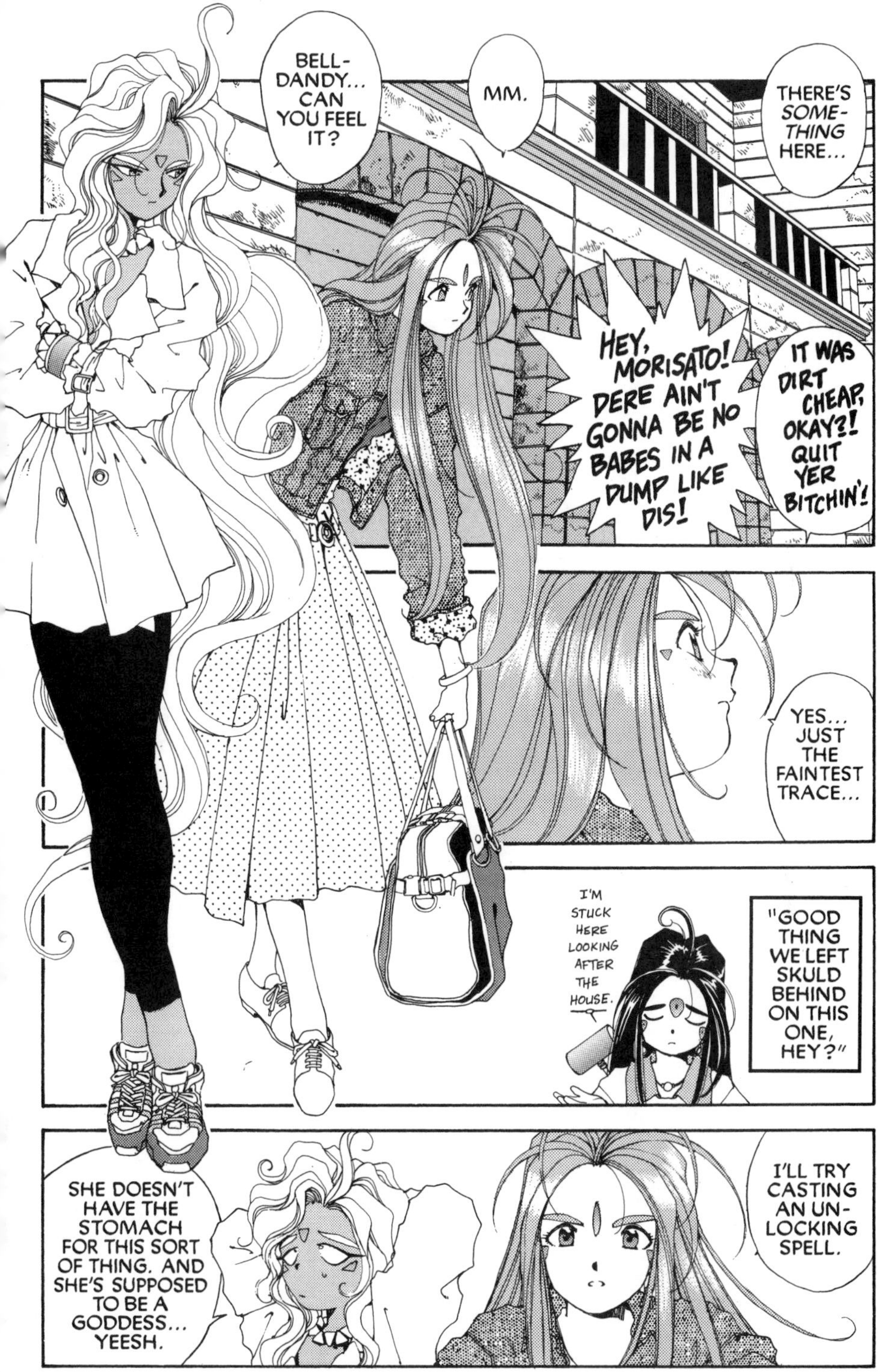
BELL-DANDY... CAN YOU FEEL IT?
MM.
THERE'S SOME-THING HERE...
HEY, MORISATO! DERE AIN'T GONNA BE NO BABES IN A DUMP LIKE DIS!
IT WAS DIRT CHEAP, OKAY?! QUIT YER BITCHIN'!
YES... JUST THE FAINTEST TRACE...
I'M STUCK HERE LOOKING AFTER THE HOUSE.
"GOOD THING WE LEFT SKULD BEHIND ON THIS ONE, HEY?"
SHE DOESN'T HAVE THE STOMACH FOR THIS SORT OF THING. AND SHE'S SUPPOSED TO BE A GODDESS... YEESH.
I'LL TRY CASTING AN UN-LOCKING SPELL.

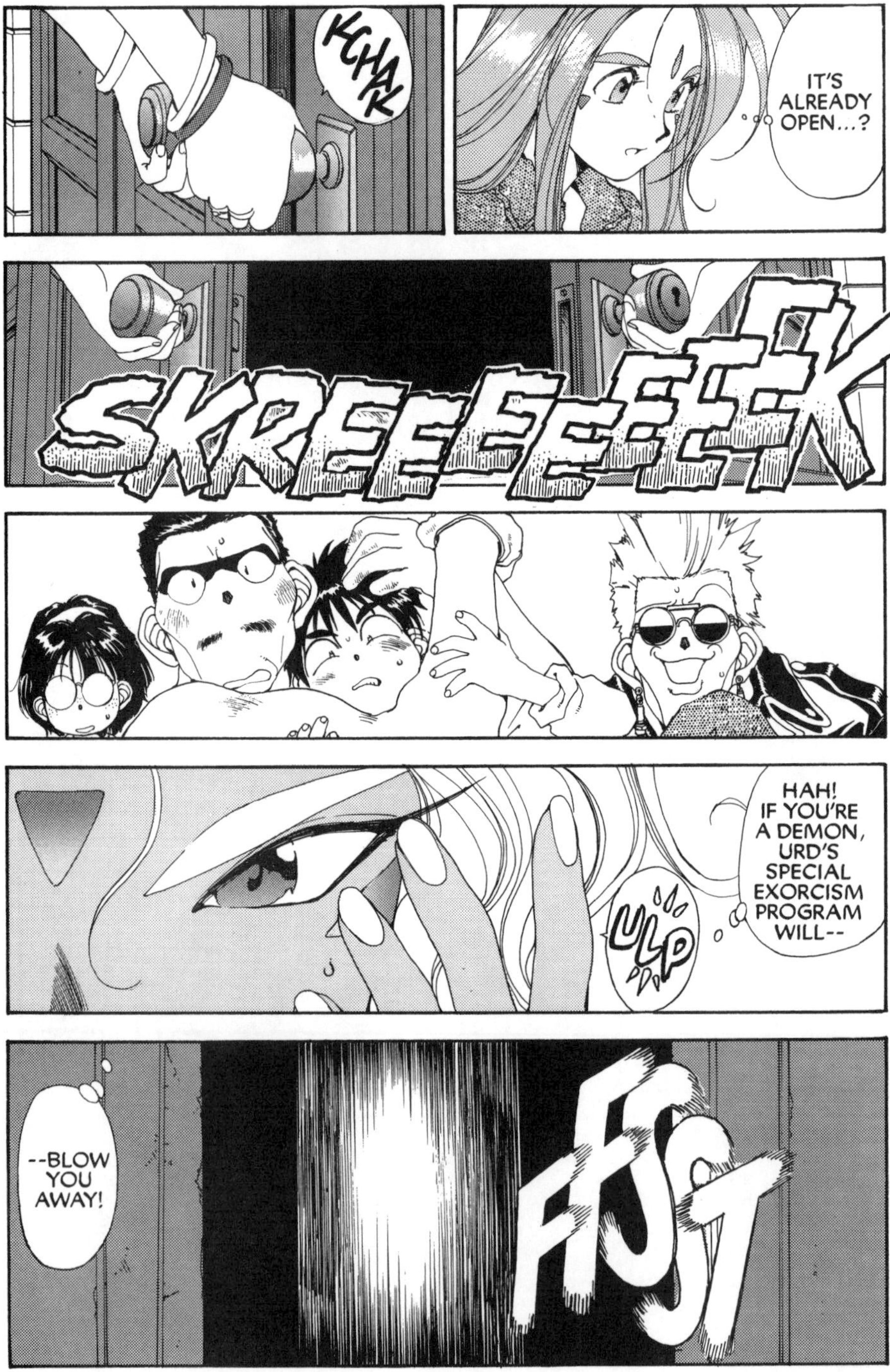
KCHAK
IT'S ALREADY OPEN...?
SKREEEEEEEK
HAH! IF YOU'RE A DEMON, URD'S SPECIAL EXORCISM PROGRAM WILL--
ULP
--BLOW YOU AWAY!
FSST

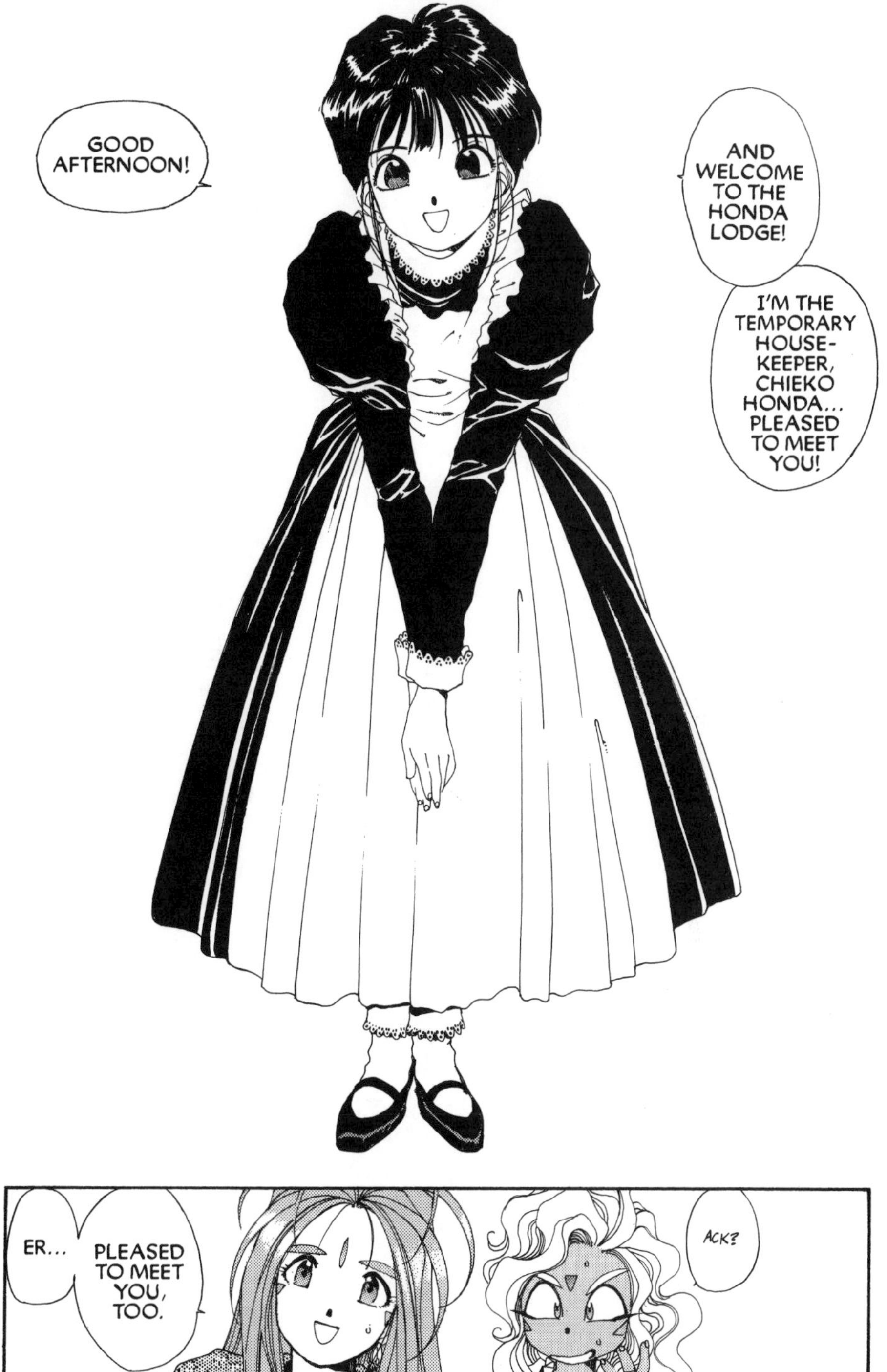
GOOD AFTERNOON!
AND WELCOME TO THE HONDA LODGE!
I'M THE TEMPORARY HOUSE-KEEPER, CHIEKO HONDA... PLEASED TO MEET YOU!
ER...
PLEASED TO MEET YOU, TOO.
ACK?

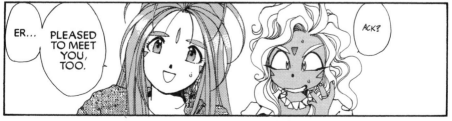

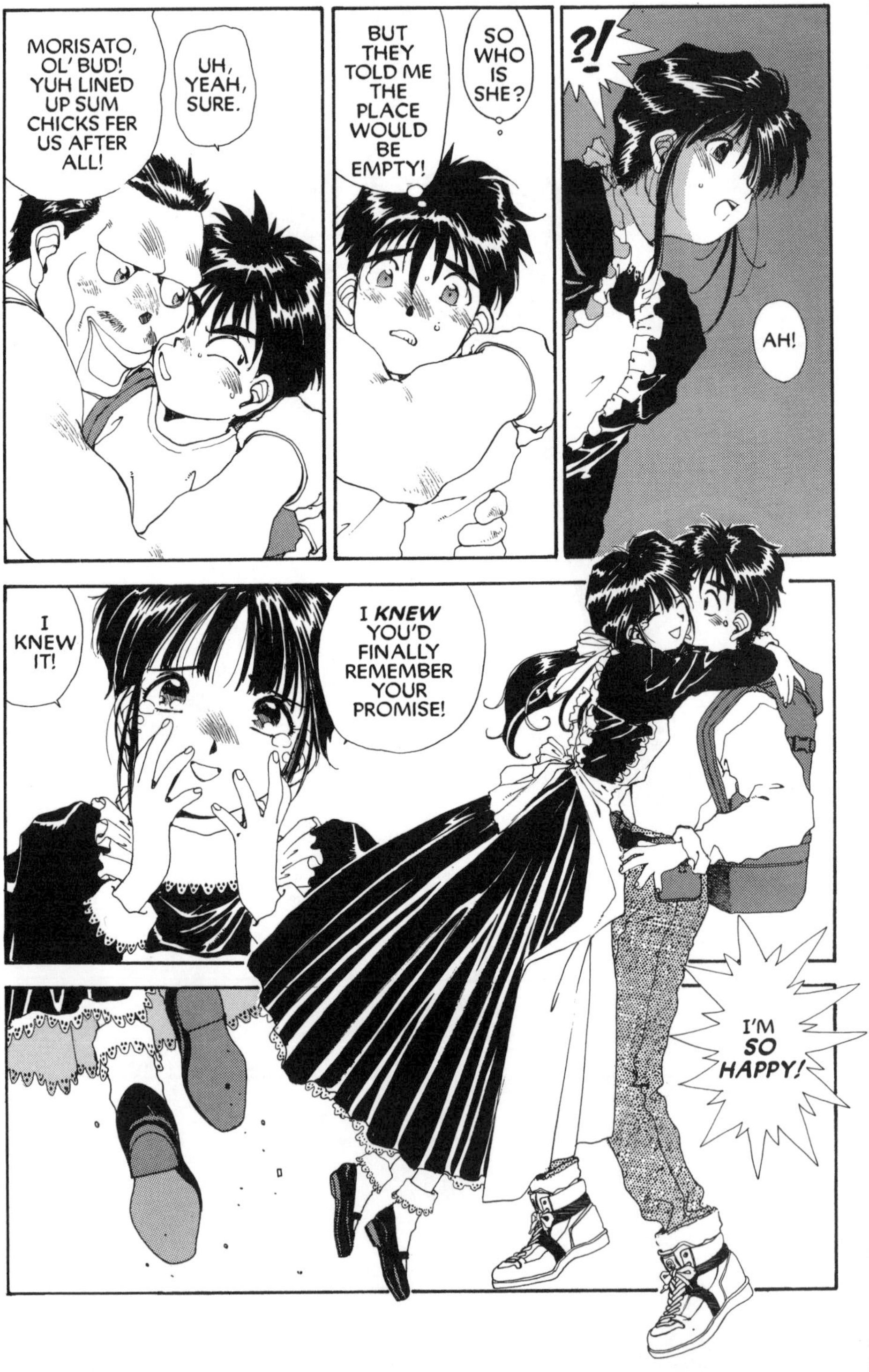
MORISATO, OL' BUD! YUH LINED UP SUM CHICKS FER US AFTER ALL!
UH, YEAH, SURE.
BUT THEY TOLD ME THE PLACE WOULD BE EMPTY!
SO WHO IS SHE?
?!
AH!
I KNEW IT!
I *KNEW* YOU'D FINALLY REMEMBER YOUR PROMISE!
I'M *SO HAPPY!*

MORISATO, YOU SCUM PUPPY!

I... AH... ER?

ALWAYS KEEPIN' DA GOOD STUFF FER YERSELF!

OWW! BUT I DIDN'T-- YEOW!

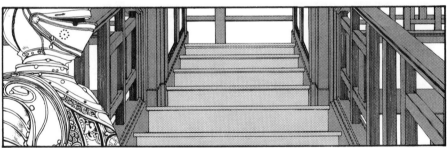

REALLY ...?

YOU REALLY DON'T REMEMBER YOUR PROMISE?

UM...
IT'S NOT
LIKE I'VE
FORGOTTEN.
THAT'S NOT
THE CASE
AT ALL.

OW!

AND
YOU'VE
EVEN F-
FORGOTTEN
ME?

UM...
I HATE TO
TELL YOU
THIS, BUT...
I'VE NEVER
EVEN *HEARD*
OF YOU
BEFORE.

OW!
WATCH IT
BELLDANDY--
THAT
STUFF
STINGS!

OH!
I'M
SORRY,
DEAR.

I'VE
HEARD
ENOUGH!

WELL, WELL--
AREN'T YOU
SOMETHING,
LOVER BOY!
I NEVER
DREAMED YOU
HAD IT IN YOU
TO KEEP TWO
BABES ON A
STRING.

WHO,
ME?
BUT--

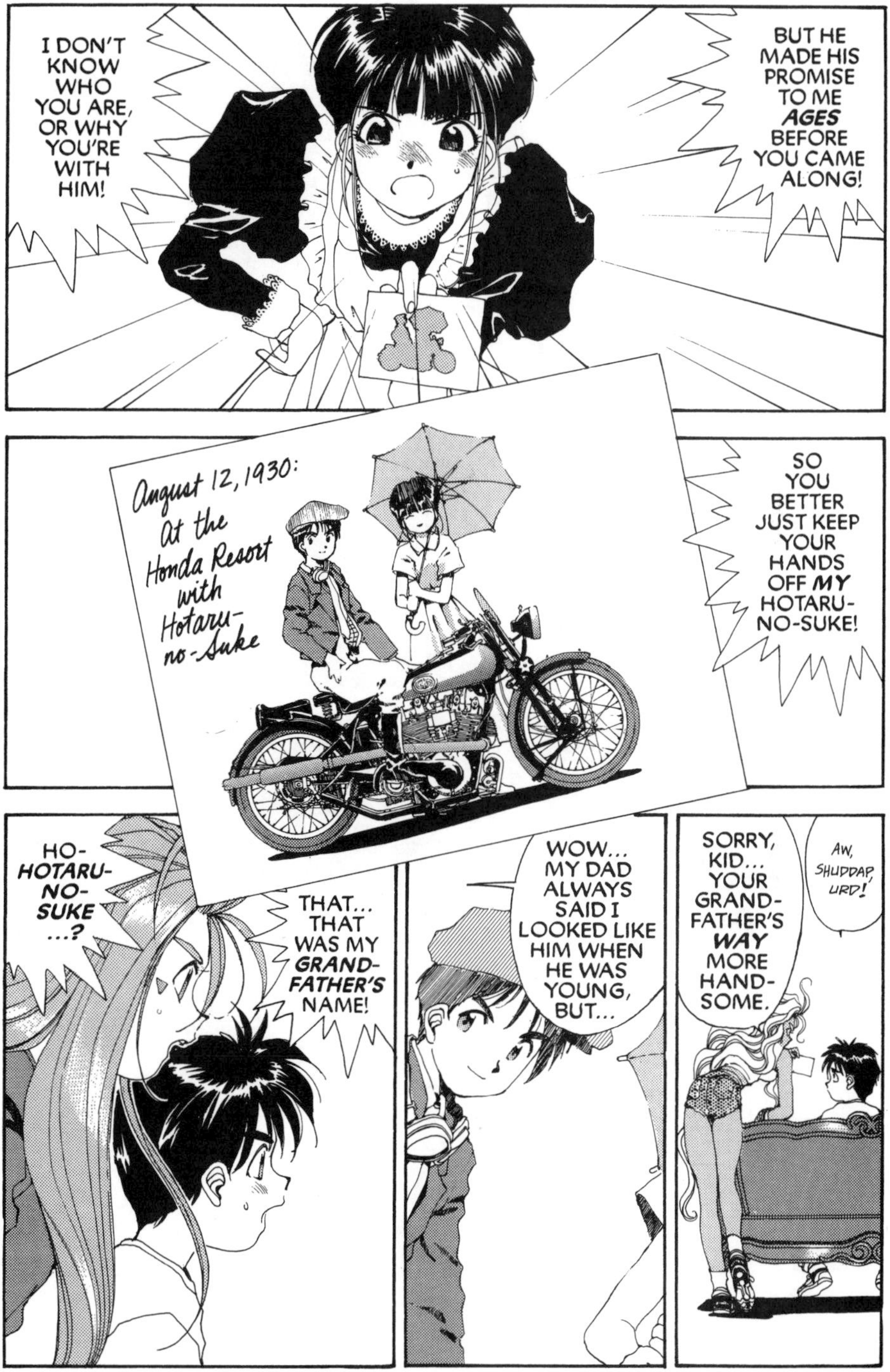
I DON'T KNOW WHO YOU ARE, OR WHY YOU'RE WITH HIM!
BUT HE MADE HIS PROMISE TO ME AGES BEFORE YOU CAME ALONG!
August 12, 1930: At the Honda Resort with Hotaru-no-Suke
SO YOU BETTER JUST KEEP YOUR HANDS OFF MY HOTARU-NO-SUKE!
HO-HOTARU-NO-SUKE...?
THAT... THAT WAS MY GRAND-FATHER'S NAME!
WOW... MY DAD ALWAYS SAID I LOOKED LIKE HIM WHEN HE WAS YOUNG, BUT...
SORRY, KID... YOUR GRAND-FATHER'S WAY MORE HAND-SOME.
AW, SHUDDAP, URD!

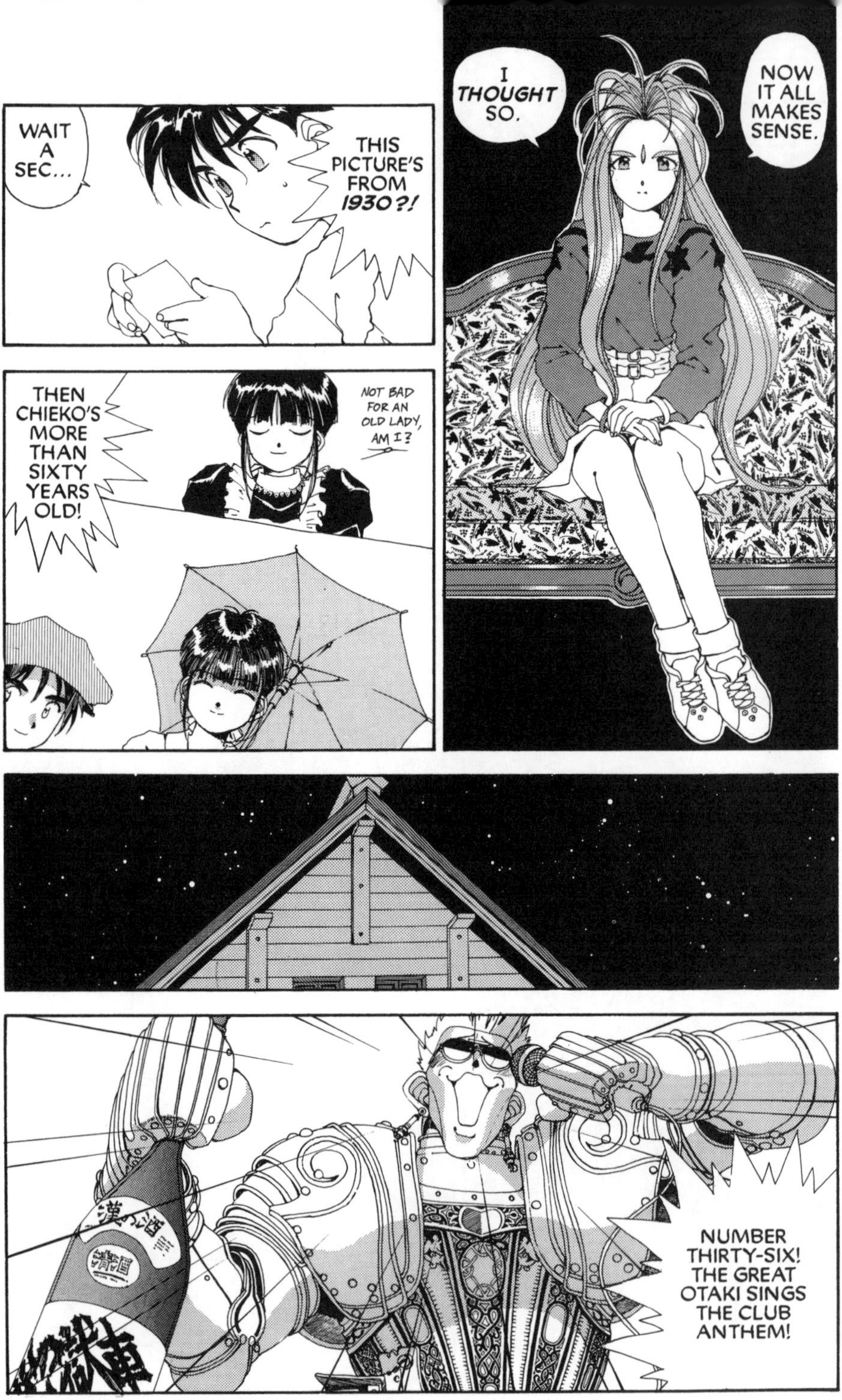
WAIT A SEC...
THIS PICTURE'S FROM *1930?!*
THEN CHIEKO'S MORE THAN SIXTY YEARS OLD!
NOT BAD FOR AN OLD LADY, AM I?
I *THOUGHT* SO.
NOW IT ALL MAKES SENSE.
NUMBER THIRTY-SIX! THE GREAT OTAKI SINGS THE CLUB ANTHEM!

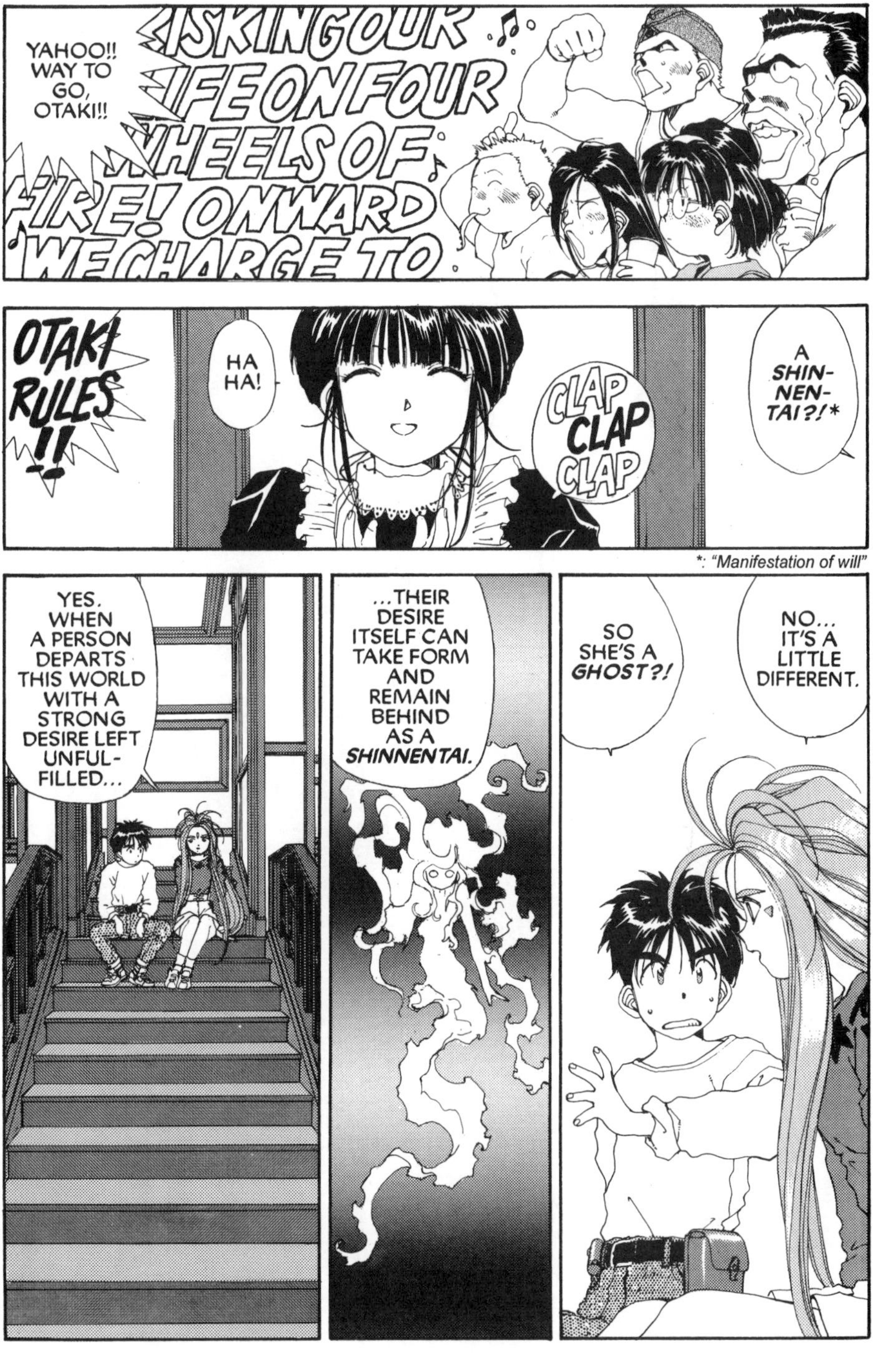
YAHOO!! WAY TO GO, OTAKI!!
RISKING OUR LIFE ON FOUR WHEELS OF FIRE! ONWARD WE CHARGE TO
OTAKI RULES!!
HA HA!
CLAP CLAP CLAP
A SHINNENTAI?!*
*: "Manifestation of will"
YES. WHEN A PERSON DEPARTS THIS WORLD WITH A STRONG DESIRE LEFT UNFULFILLED...
...THEIR DESIRE ITSELF CAN TAKE FORM AND REMAIN BEHIND AS A SHINNENTAI.
SO SHE'S A GHOST?!
NO... IT'S A LITTLE DIFFERENT.

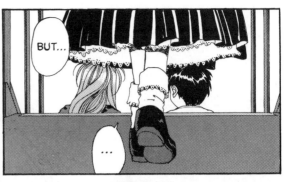

"A GHOST IS JUST THE LINGERING WILL ITSELF, PROJECTED INTO OUR PSYCHES.

"BUT A *SHINNENTAI* MANIFESTS AS AN ACTUAL PHYSICAL PRESENCE."

BUT...

...

THAT'S WHY YOU SEE ME IN THE MIRROR!

HA! FOUND YOU!

!!

WHAT ARE YOU DOING OUT HERE?

EVERY- ONE'S BEEN ASKING FOR YOU!

ER... I...

NYAA!

AW, HEY!

I'VE NEVER HEARD OF A *SHINNENTAI* PRESERVING ITS FORM FOR SO MANY YEARS.

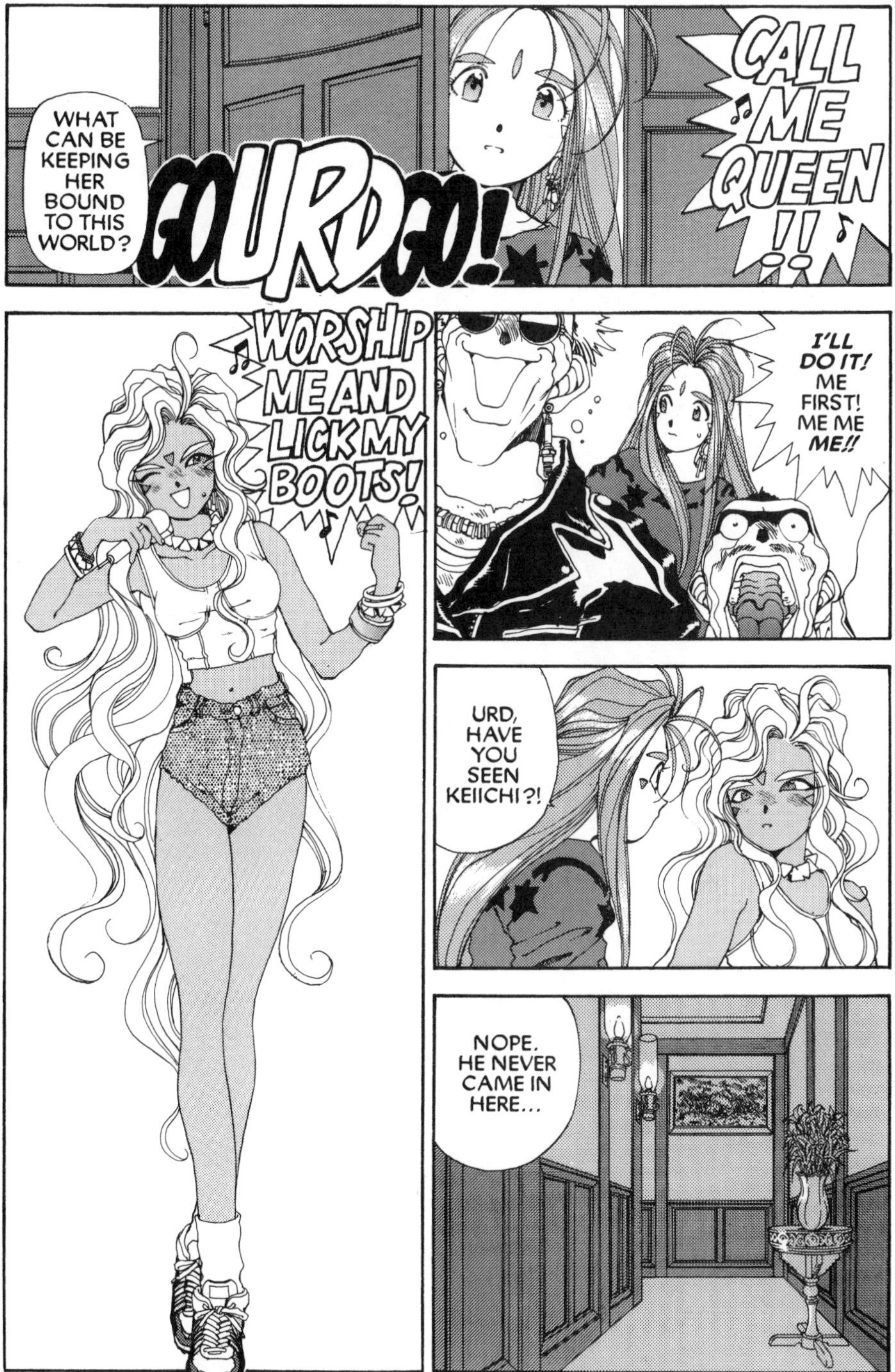
WHAT CAN BE KEEPING HER BOUND TO THIS WORLD?
GOURDGO!
CALL ME QUEEN!!
WORSHIP ME AND LICK MY BOOTS!
I'LL DO IT! ME FIRST! ME ME ME!!
URD, HAVE YOU SEEN KEIICHI?!
NOPE. HE NEVER CAME IN HERE...

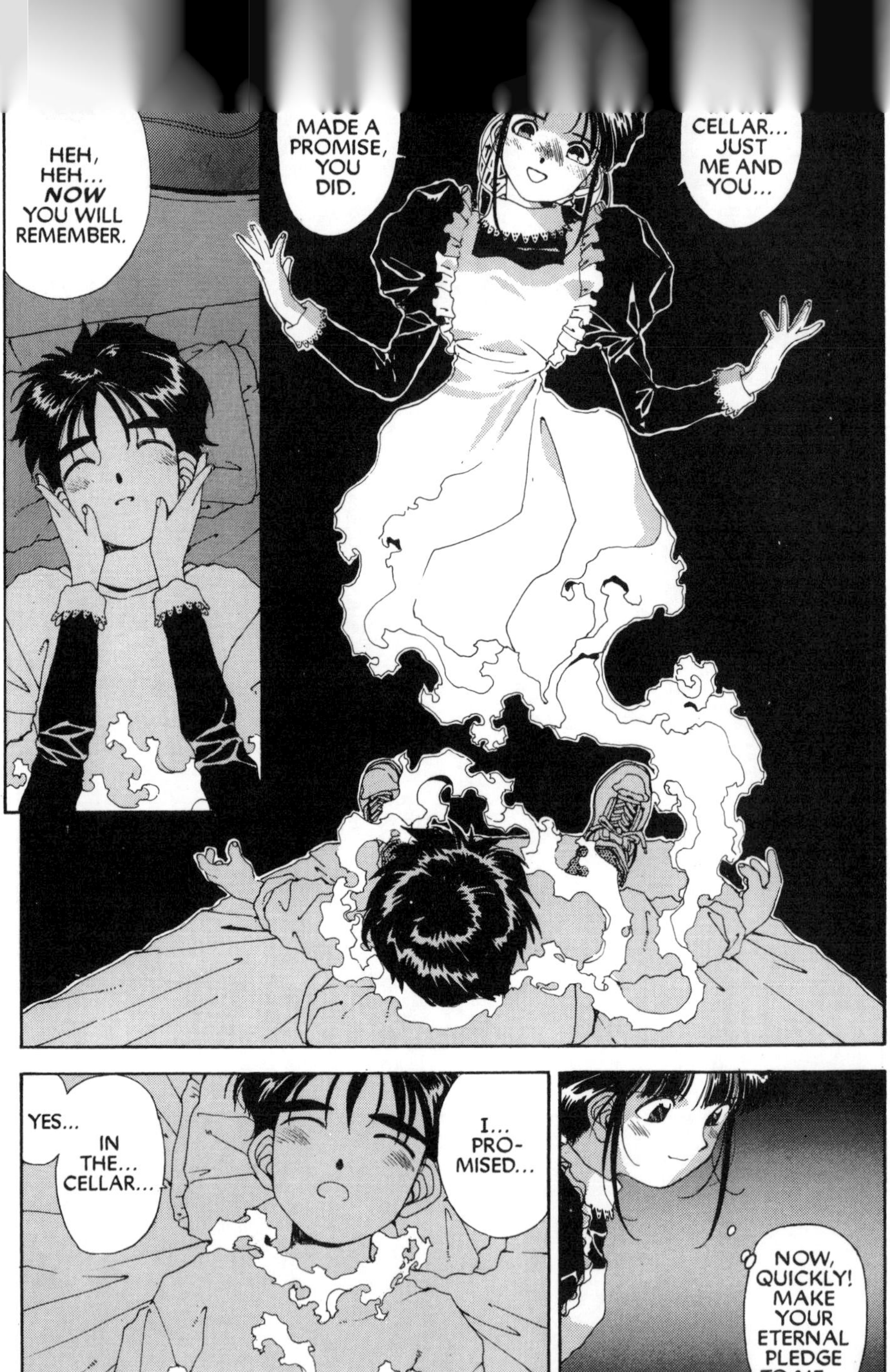
HEH, HEH... NOW YOU WILL REMEMBER.
MADE A PROMISE, YOU DID.
CELLAR... JUST ME AND YOU...
YES... IN THE... CELLAR...
I... PRO-MISED...
NOW, QUICKLY! MAKE YOUR ETERNAL PLEDGE TO ME...

AH?!

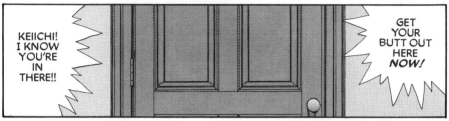

KEIICHI! I KNOW YOU'RE IN THERE!!

GET YOUR BUTT OUT HERE *NOW!*

HEH HEH ...

YOU'RE TOO LATE! THOSE DOORS SHALL NEVER OPEN AGAIN!

NOW... KEEP YOUR PROMISE...

GRR! SHE'S PLANNING TO POSSESS KEIICHI, I BET!

NO! SHE WOULDN'T!

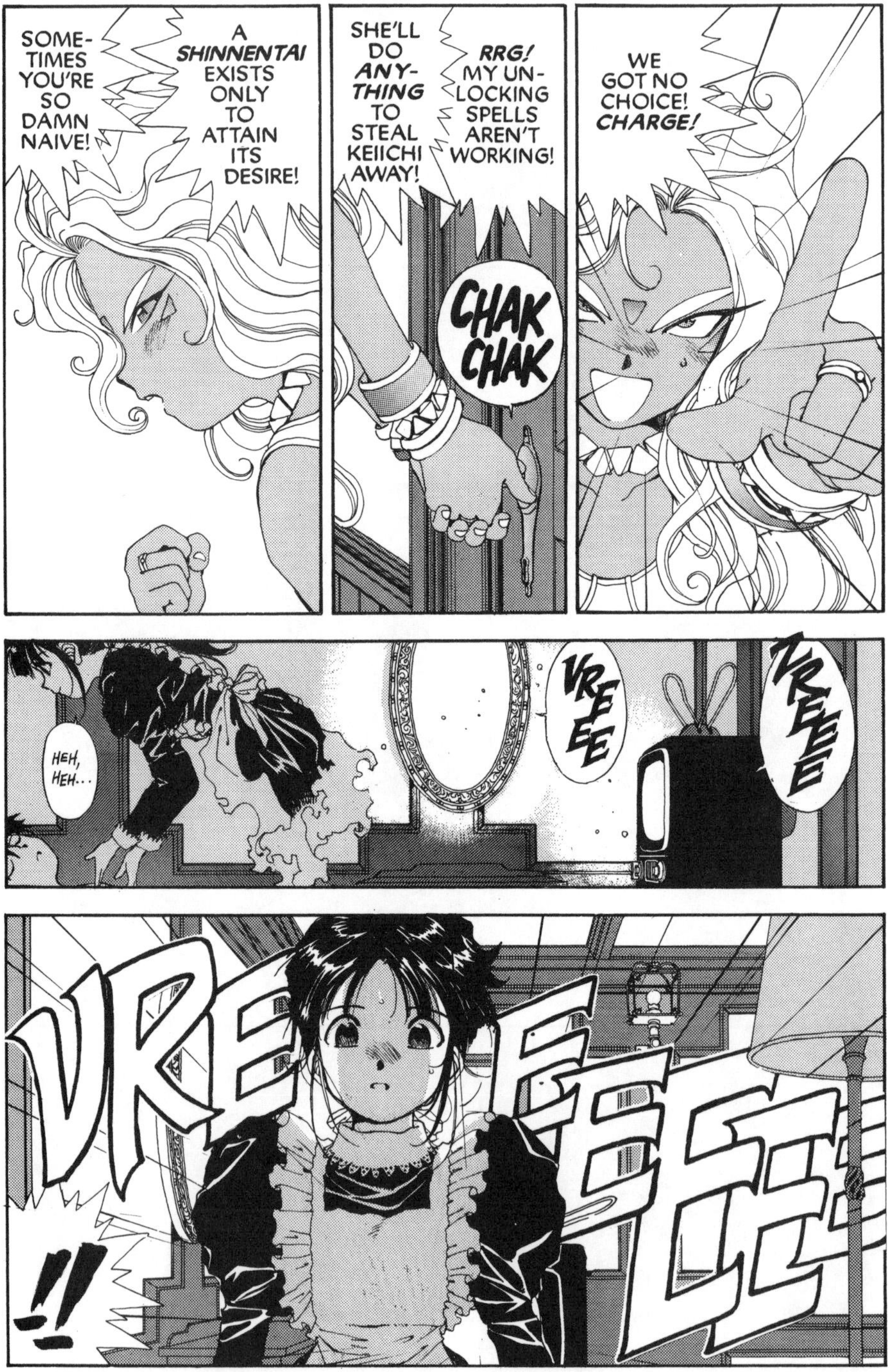
SOME-TIMES YOU'RE SO DAMN NAIVE!
A *SHINNENTAI* EXISTS ONLY TO ATTAIN ITS DESIRE!
SHE'LL DO *ANYTHING* TO STEAL KEIICHI AWAY!
RRG! MY UN-LOCKING SPELLS AREN'T WORKING!
CHAK CHAK
WE GOT NO CHOICE! *CHARGE!*
HEH, HEH...
VREEEE
VREEEE
VREEEEEEE
!!

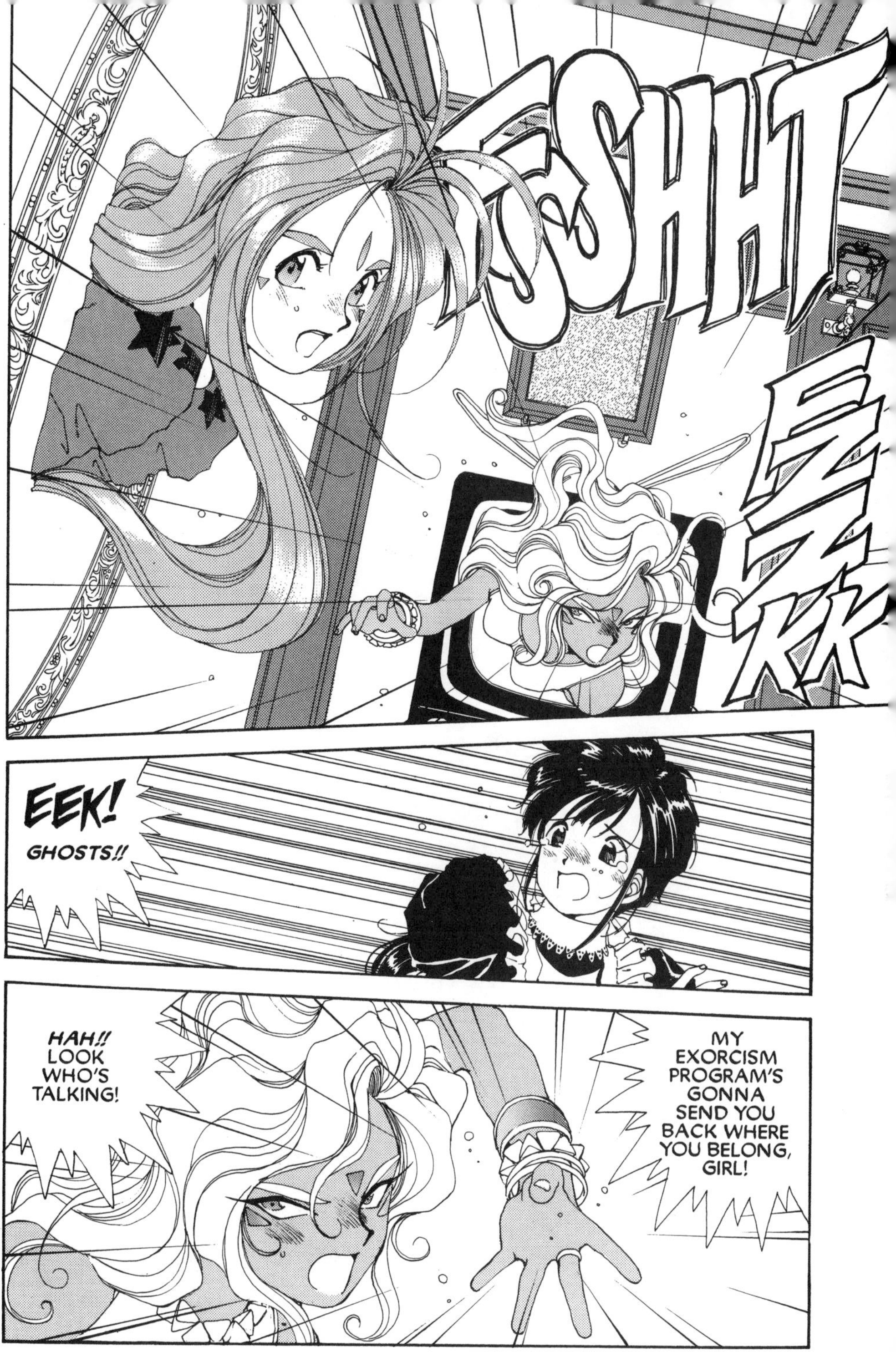
SHHT
EEK!
GHOSTS!!
HAH!! LOOK WHO'S TALKING!
MY EXORCISM PROGRAM'S GONNA SEND YOU BACK WHERE YOU BELONG, GIRL!

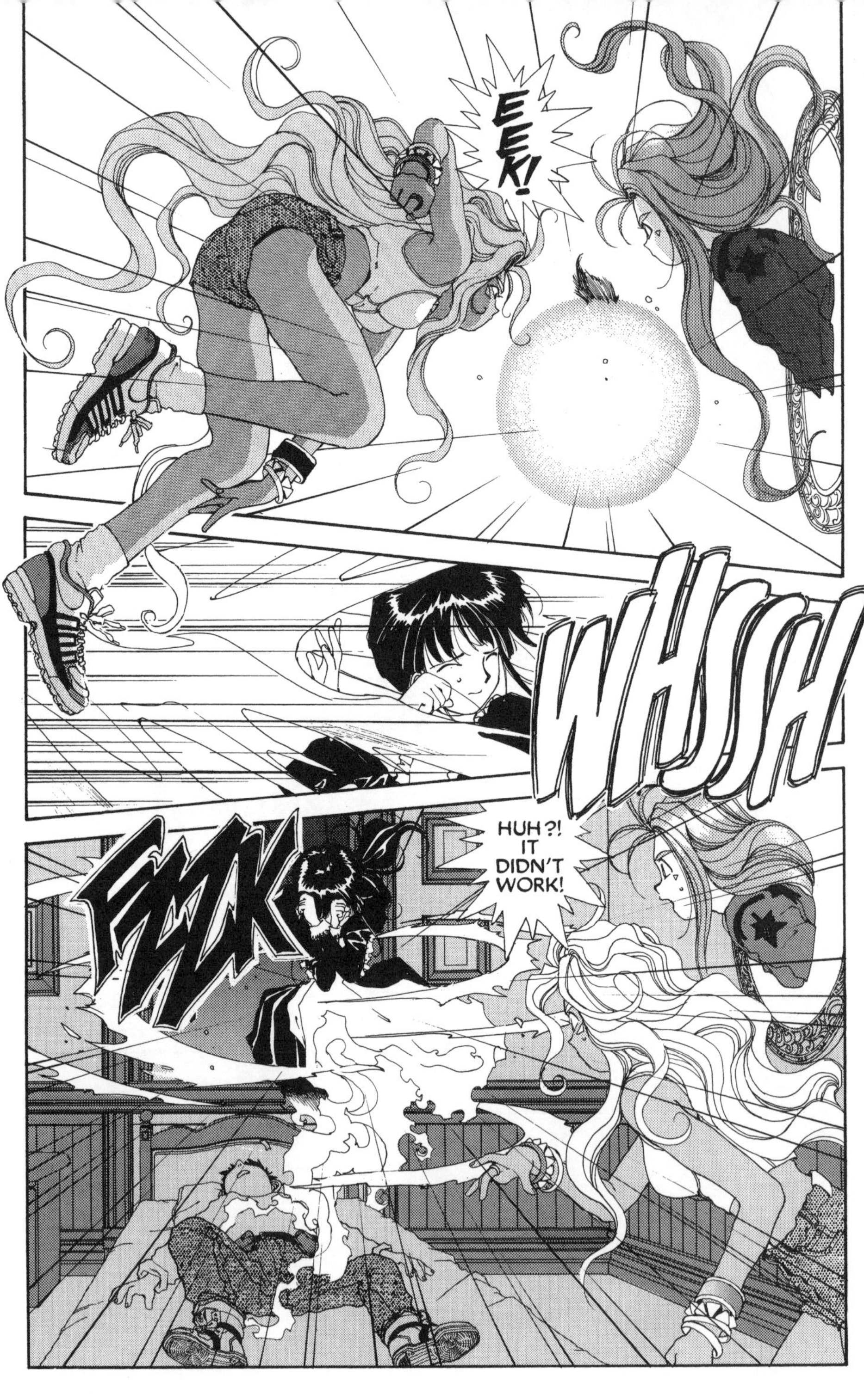
EEK!
WHSH
FWK
HUH?! IT DIDN'T WORK!

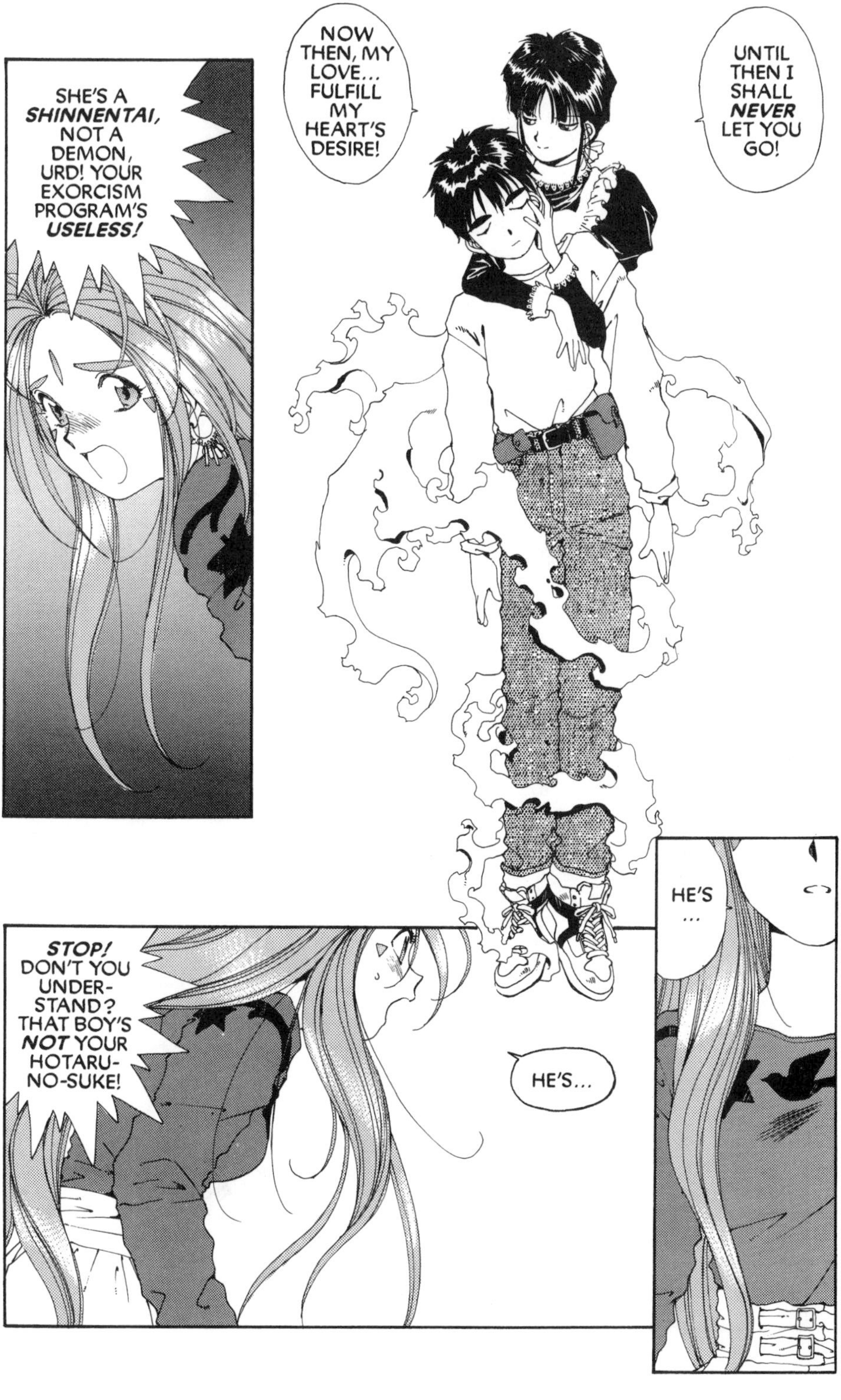
SHE'S A *SHINNENTAI,* NOT A DEMON, URD! YOUR EXORCISM PROGRAM'S *USELESS!*
NOW THEN, MY LOVE... FULFILL MY HEART'S DESIRE!
UNTIL THEN I SHALL *NEVER* LET YOU GO!
STOP! DON'T YOU UNDER-STAND? THAT BOY'S *NOT* YOUR HOTARU-NO-SUKE!
HE'S...
HE'S ...

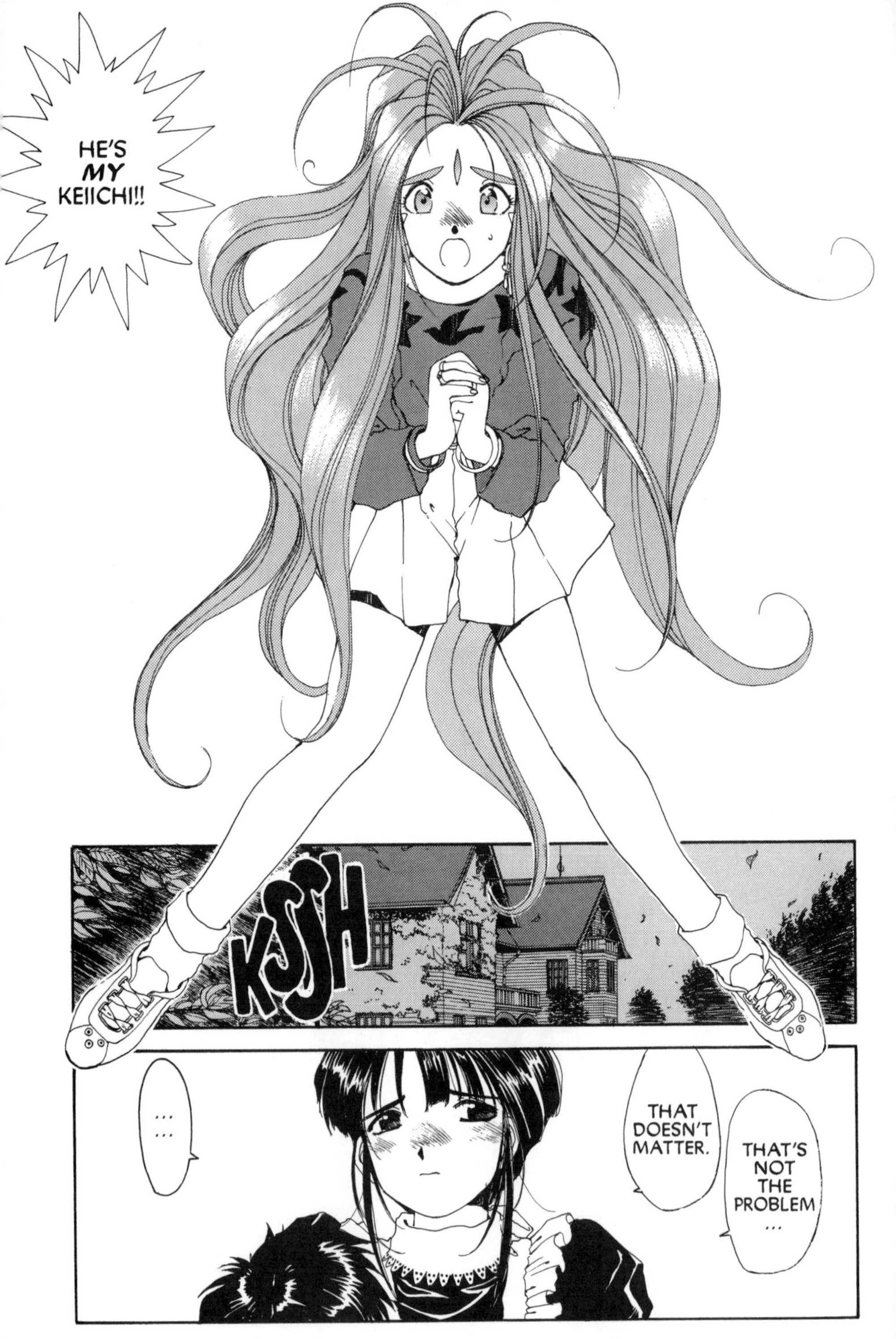
HE'S **MY** KEIICHI!!
KSH
... ...
THAT DOESN'T MATTER.
THAT'S NOT THE PROBLEM ...

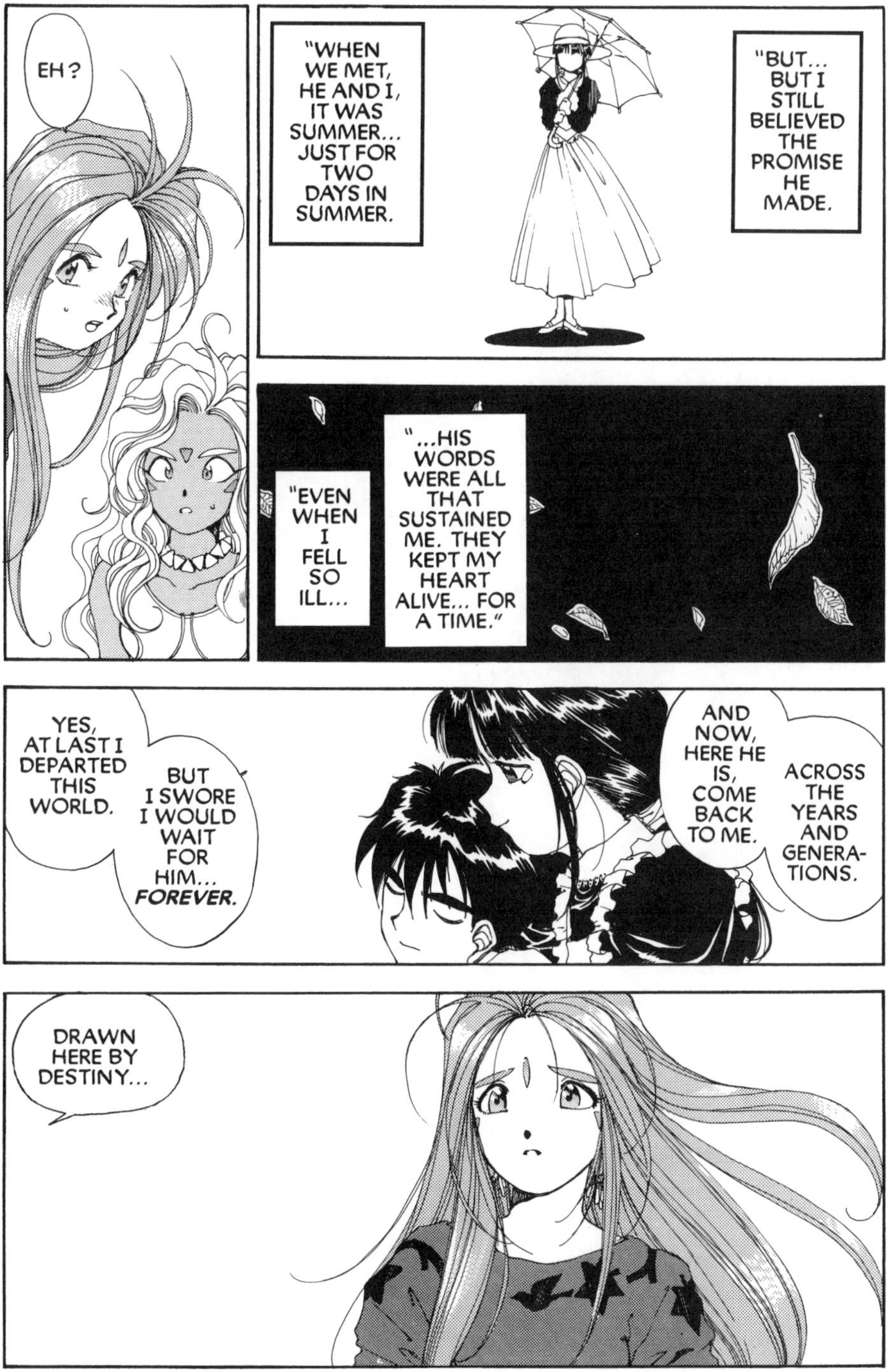
EH ?
"WHEN WE MET, HE AND I, IT WAS SUMMER... JUST FOR TWO DAYS IN SUMMER.
"BUT... BUT I STILL BELIEVED THE PROMISE HE MADE.
"EVEN WHEN I FELL SO ILL...
"...HIS WORDS WERE ALL THAT SUSTAINED ME. THEY KEPT MY HEART ALIVE... FOR A TIME."
YES, AT LAST I DEPARTED THIS WORLD.
BUT I SWORE I WOULD WAIT FOR HIM... ***FOREVER.***
AND NOW, HERE HE IS, COME BACK TO ME.
ACROSS THE YEARS AND GENERATIONS.
DRAWN HERE BY DESTINY...

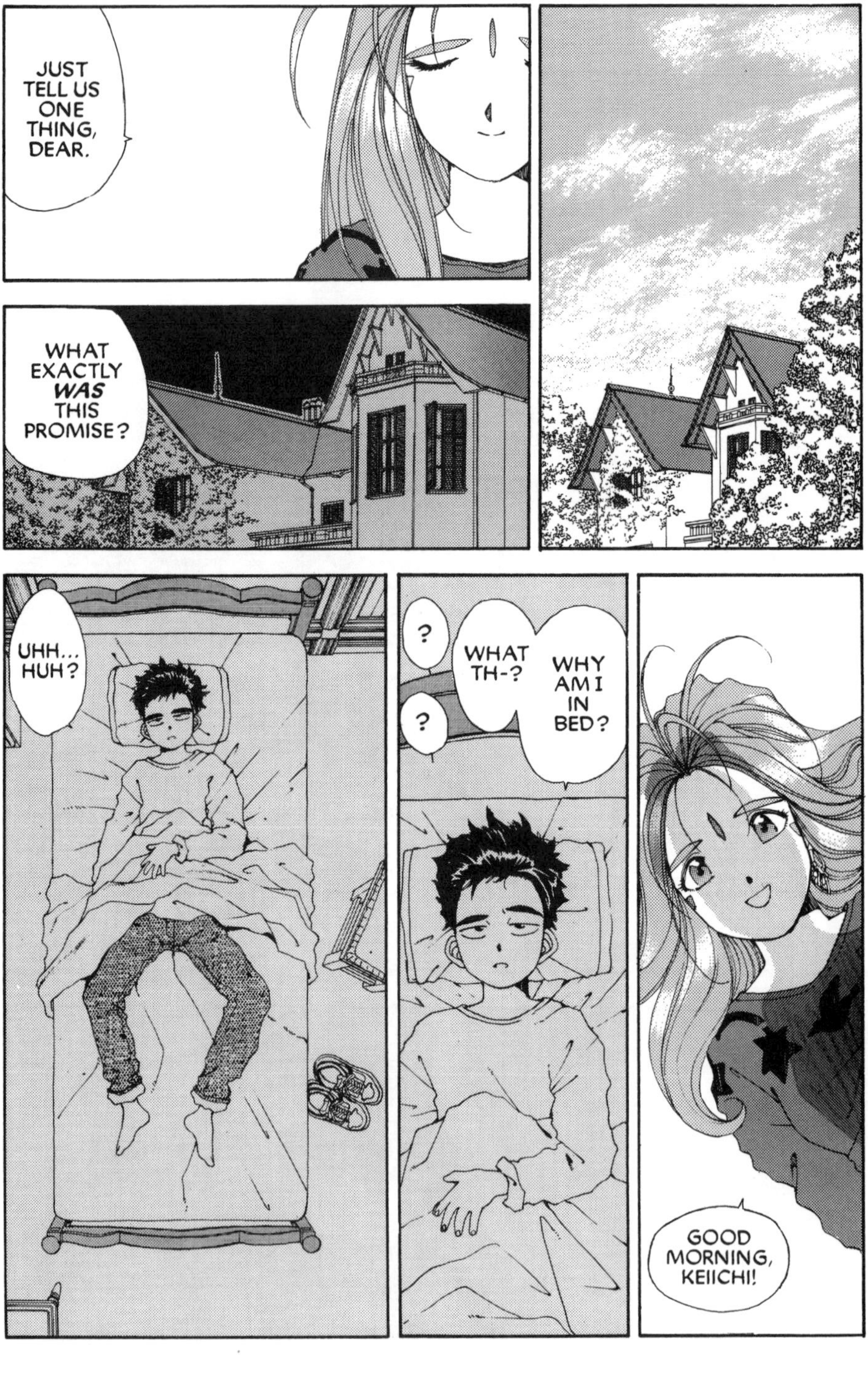
JUST TELL US ONE THING, DEAR.
WHAT EXACTLY **WAS** THIS PROMISE?
UHH... HUH?
?
?
WHAT TH-?
WHY AM I IN BED?
GOOD MORNING, KEIICHI!

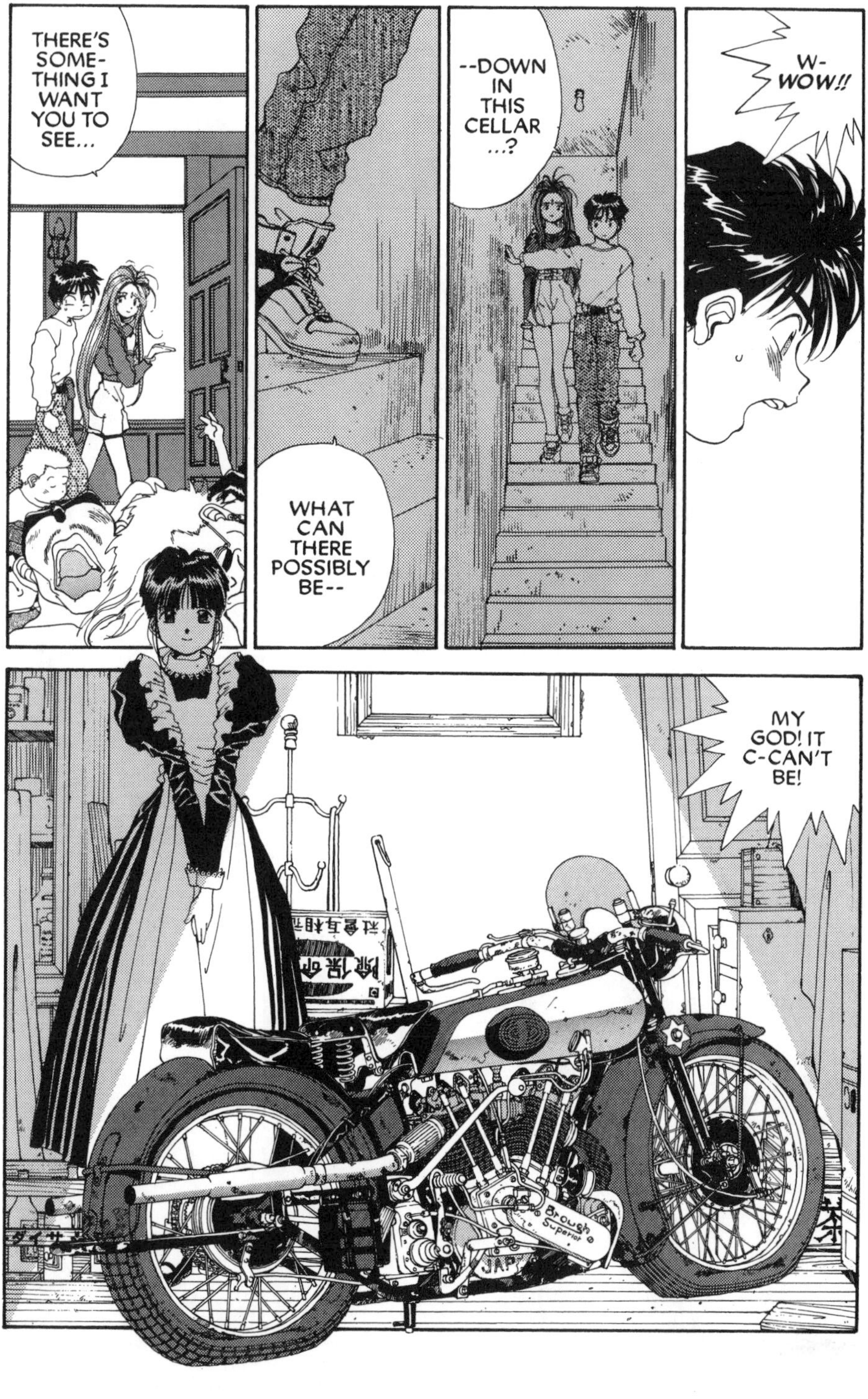
THERE'S SOME-THING I WANT YOU TO SEE...
WHAT CAN THERE POSSIBLY BE--
--DOWN IN THIS CELLAR ...?
W- WOW!!
MY GOD! IT C-CAN'T BE!
Brough Superior
JAP

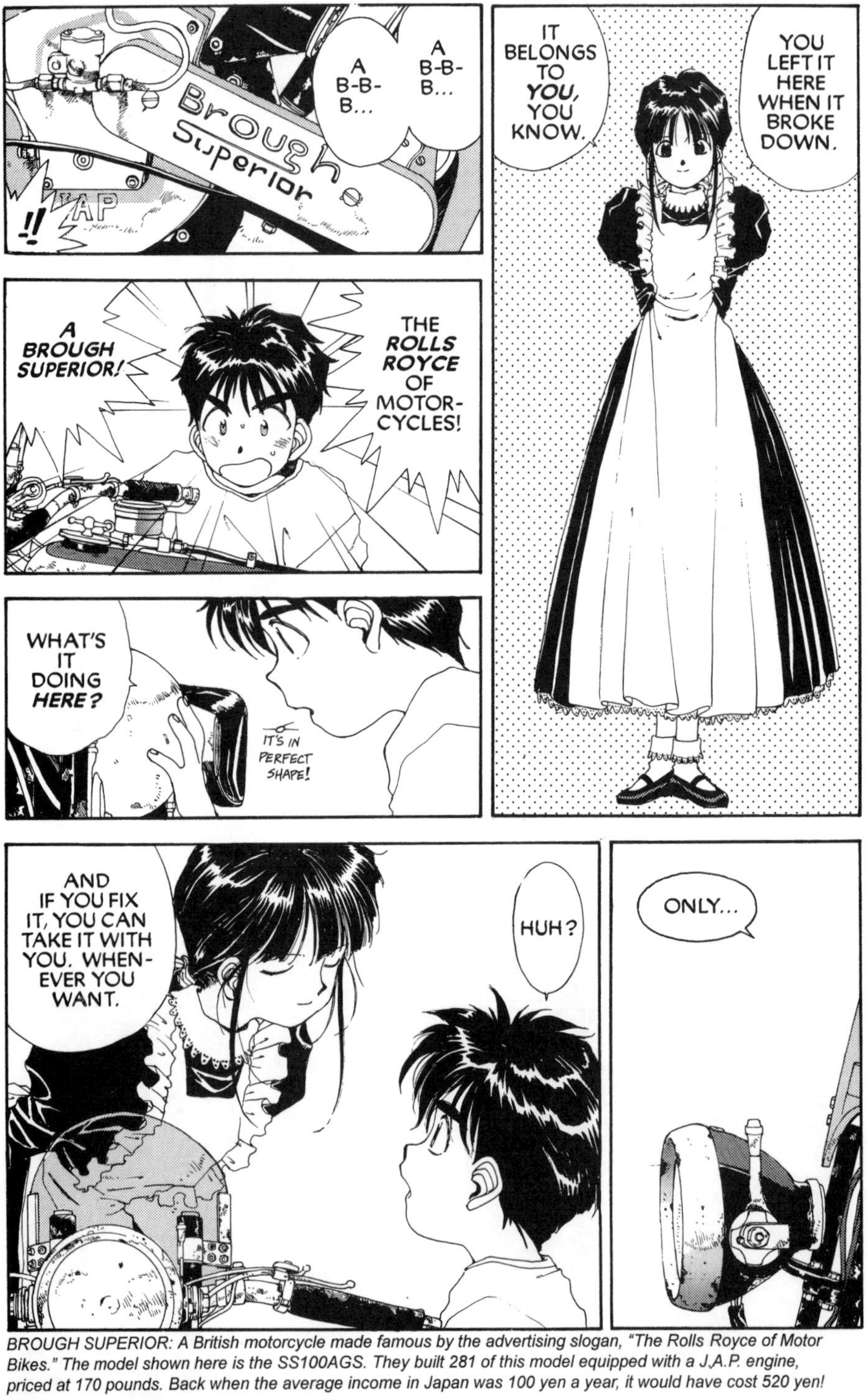
Brough Superior
A B-B-B...
A B-B-B...
!!
AP
A BROUGH SUPERIOR!
THE ROLLS ROYCE OF MOTOR-CYCLES!
WHAT'S IT DOING HERE?
IT'S IN PERFECT SHAPE!
IT BELONGS TO YOU, YOU KNOW.
YOU LEFT IT HERE WHEN IT BROKE DOWN.
AND IF YOU FIX IT, YOU CAN TAKE IT WITH YOU. WHEN-EVER YOU WANT.
HUH?
ONLY...

BROUGH SUPERIOR: A British motorcycle made famous by the advertising slogan, "The Rolls Royce of Motor Bikes." The model shown here is the SS100AGS. They built 281 of this model equipped with a J.A.P. engine, priced at 170 pounds. Back when the average income in Japan was 100 yen a year, it would have cost 520 yen!

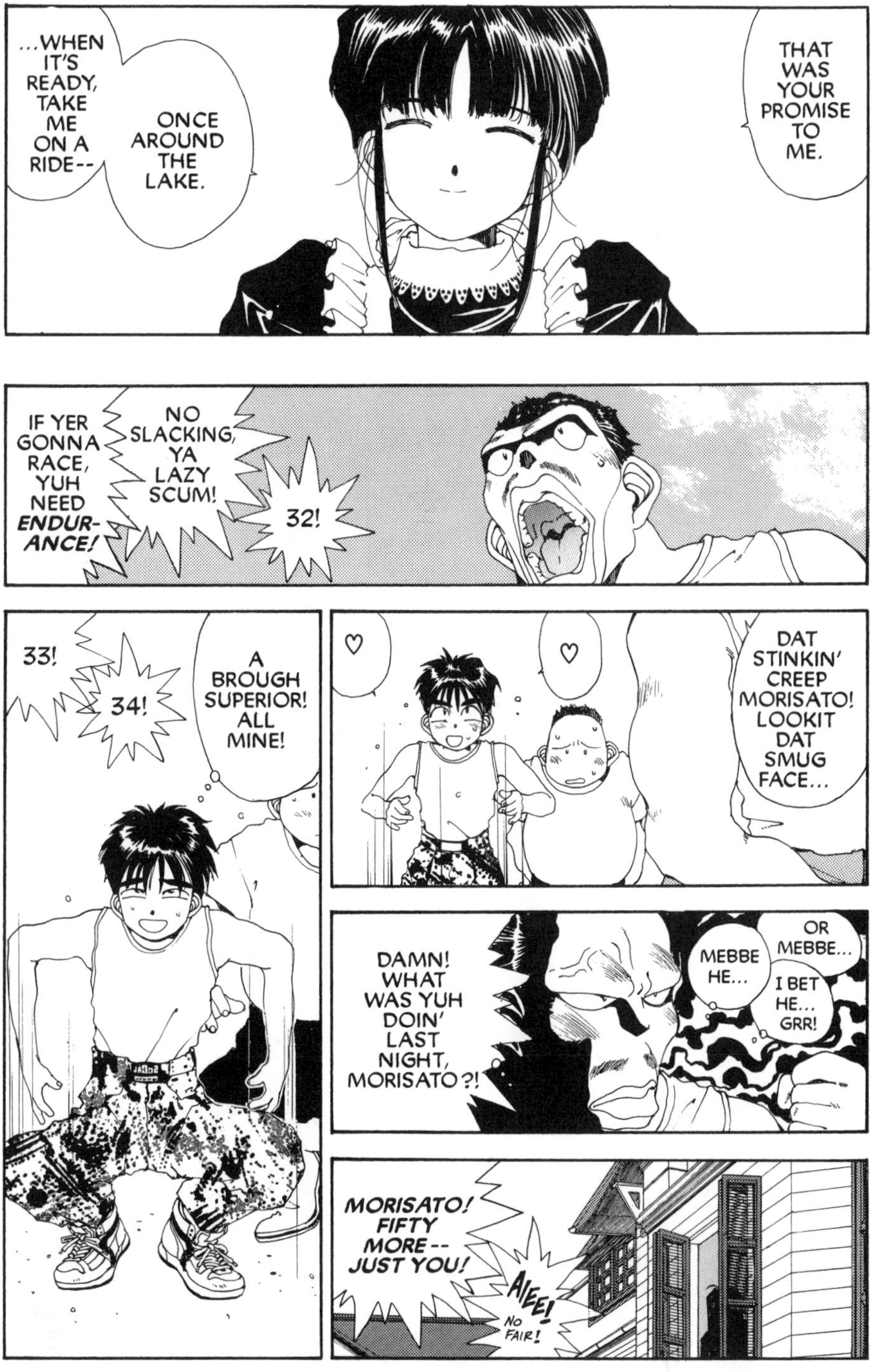
...WHEN IT'S READY, TAKE ME ON A RIDE--
ONCE AROUND THE LAKE.
THAT WAS YOUR PROMISE TO ME.
IF YER GONNA RACE, YUH NEED *ENDURANCE!*
NO SLACKING, YA LAZY SCUM!
32!
33!
34!
A BROUGH SUPERIOR! ALL MINE!
♡
♡
DAT STINKIN' CREEP MORISATO! LOOKIT DAT SMUG FACE...
DAMN! WHAT WAS YUH DOIN' LAST NIGHT, MORISATO?!
MEBBE HE...
OR MEBBE...
I BET HE... GRR!
MORISATO! FIFTY MORE-- JUST YOU!
AIEE!
NO FAIR!

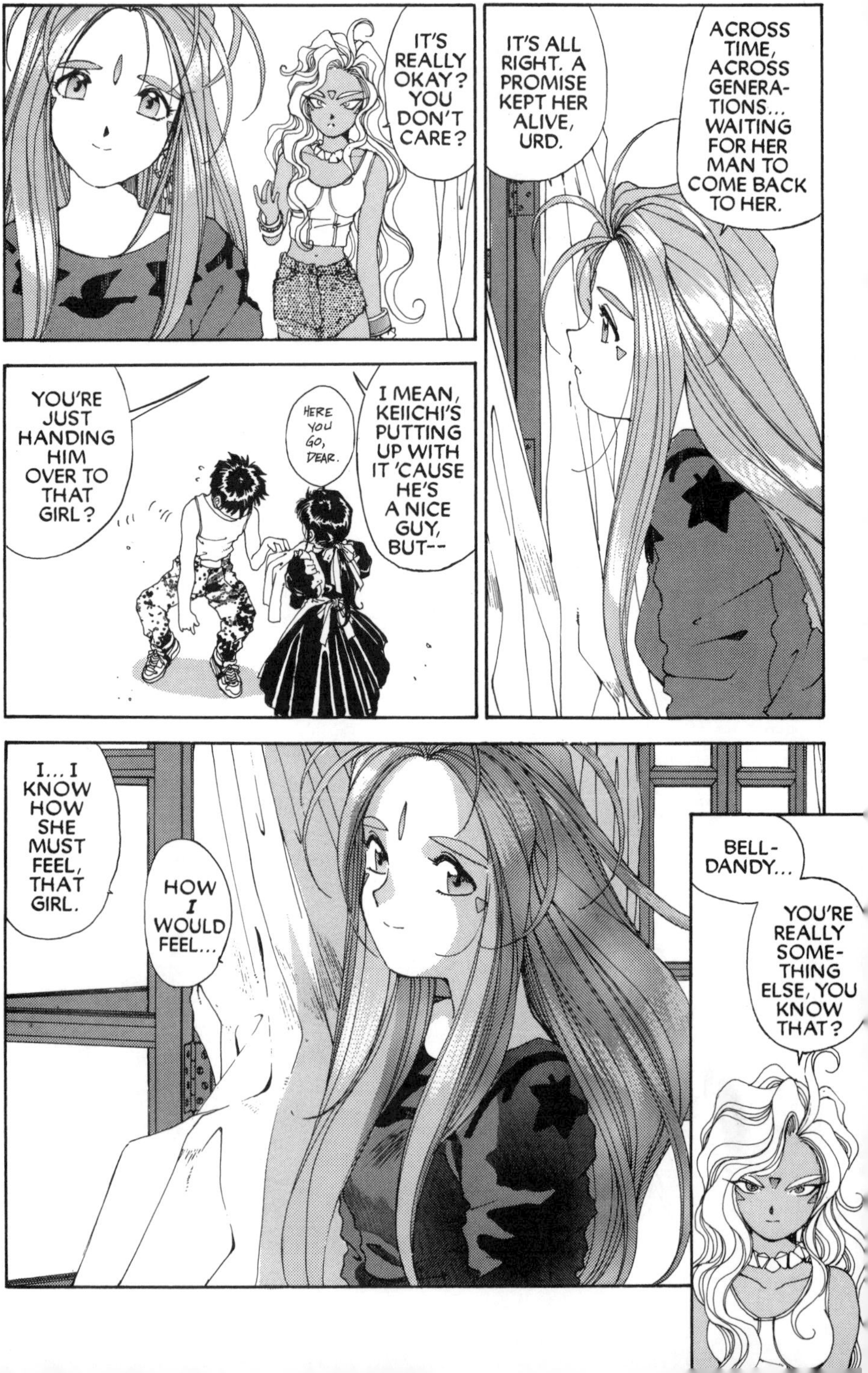
IT'S REALLY OKAY? YOU DON'T CARE?
YOU'RE JUST HANDING HIM OVER TO THAT GIRL?
HERE YOU GO, DEAR.
I MEAN, KEIICHI'S PUTTING UP WITH IT 'CAUSE HE'S A NICE GUY, BUT--
IT'S ALL RIGHT. A PROMISE KEPT HER ALIVE, URD.
ACROSS TIME, ACROSS GENERATIONS... WAITING FOR HER MAN TO COME BACK TO HER.
I... I KNOW HOW SHE MUST FEEL, THAT GIRL.
HOW *I* WOULD FEEL...
BELL-DANDY...
YOU'RE REALLY SOMETHING ELSE, YOU KNOW THAT?

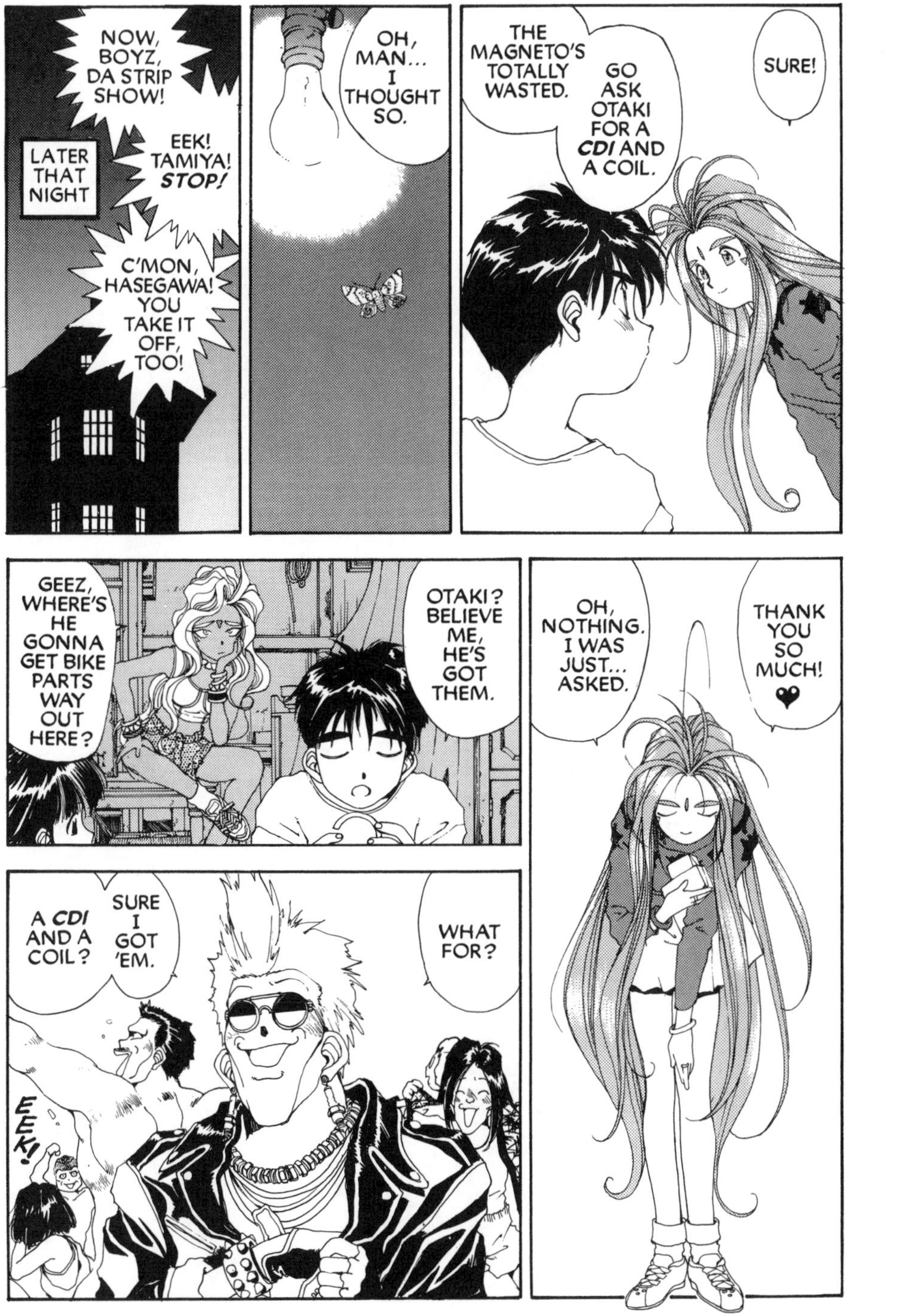
NOW, BOYZ, DA STRIP SHOW!
LATER THAT NIGHT
EEK! TAMIYA! STOP!
C'MON, HASEGAWA! YOU TAKE IT OFF, TOO!
OH, MAN... I THOUGHT SO.
THE MAGNETO'S TOTALLY WASTED.
GO ASK OTAKI FOR A CDI AND A COIL.
SURE!
GEEZ, WHERE'S HE GONNA GET BIKE PARTS WAY OUT HERE?
OTAKI? BELIEVE ME, HE'S GOT THEM.
A CDI AND A COIL?
SURE I GOT 'EM.
WHAT FOR?
EEEK!
OH, NOTHING. I WAS JUST... ASKED.
THANK YOU SO MUCH! ❤

BELL-DANDY... WHAT A BABE... WHAT A *BABE!*

MORISATO, YOU LITTLE *CREEP!*

IT'S THE "SPECIAL TREATMENT" FOR *YOU,* SONNY BOY!

YOU'LL PAY, MORISATO!

AND THUS, DURING THE DAY THE BRUTAL (OR AS TAMIYA AND OTAKI WOULD PUT IT, "REASONABLE") TRAINING DRAGGED ON...

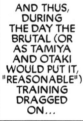

MORISATO! FIVE MORE MILES FOR YOU, YA SLACKER!

A-IEE!

...WHILE THE NIGHTS WERE DEDICATED TO REPAIRING THE BROUGH.

OH, MAN, AM I BUSHED...

UNTIL FINALLY... ON THE LAST MORNING...

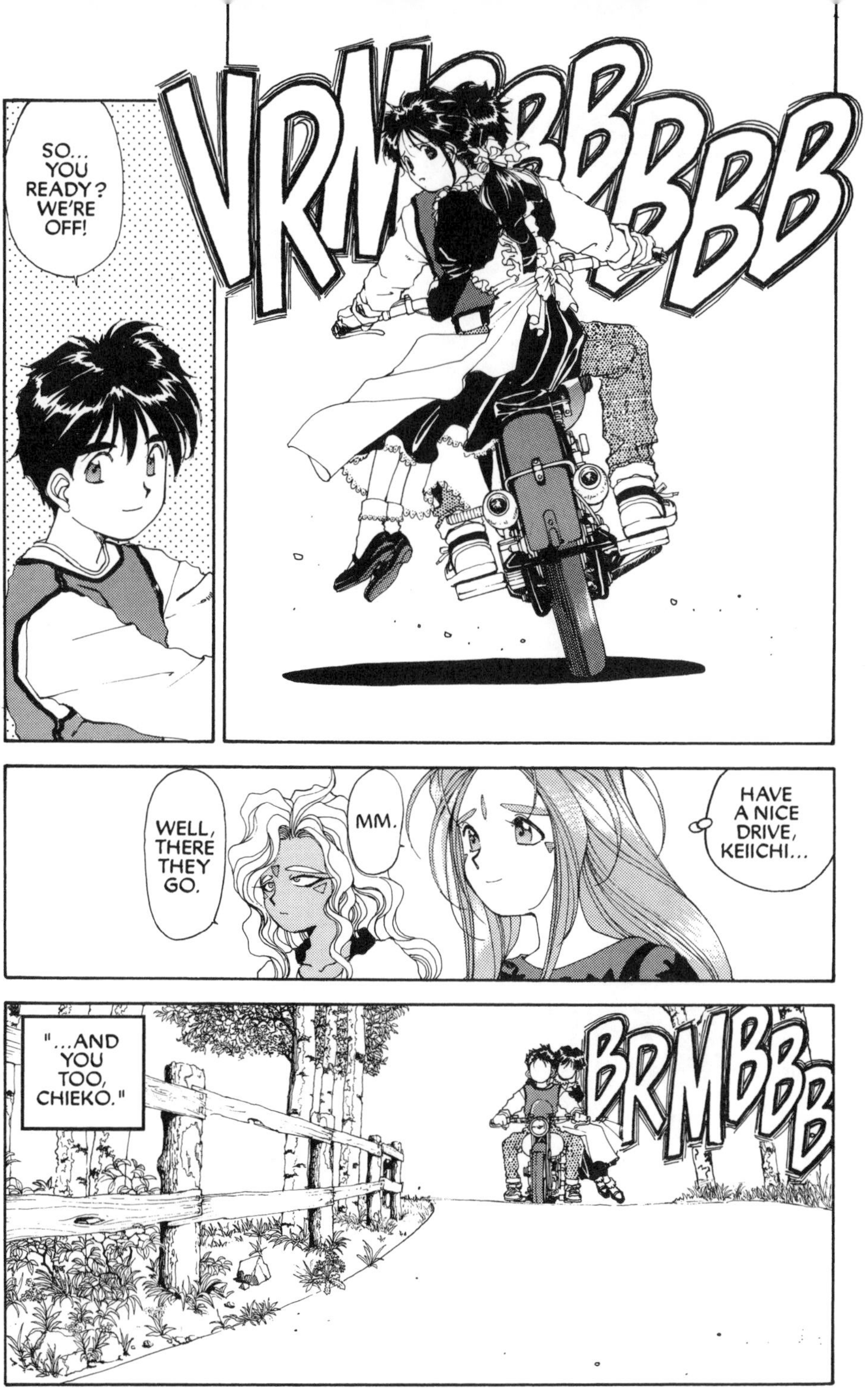
SO... YOU READY? WE'RE OFF!
VRMBBBBBB
WELL, THERE THEY GO.
MM.
HAVE A NICE DRIVE, KEIICHI...
"...AND YOU TOO, CHIEKO."
BRMBBB

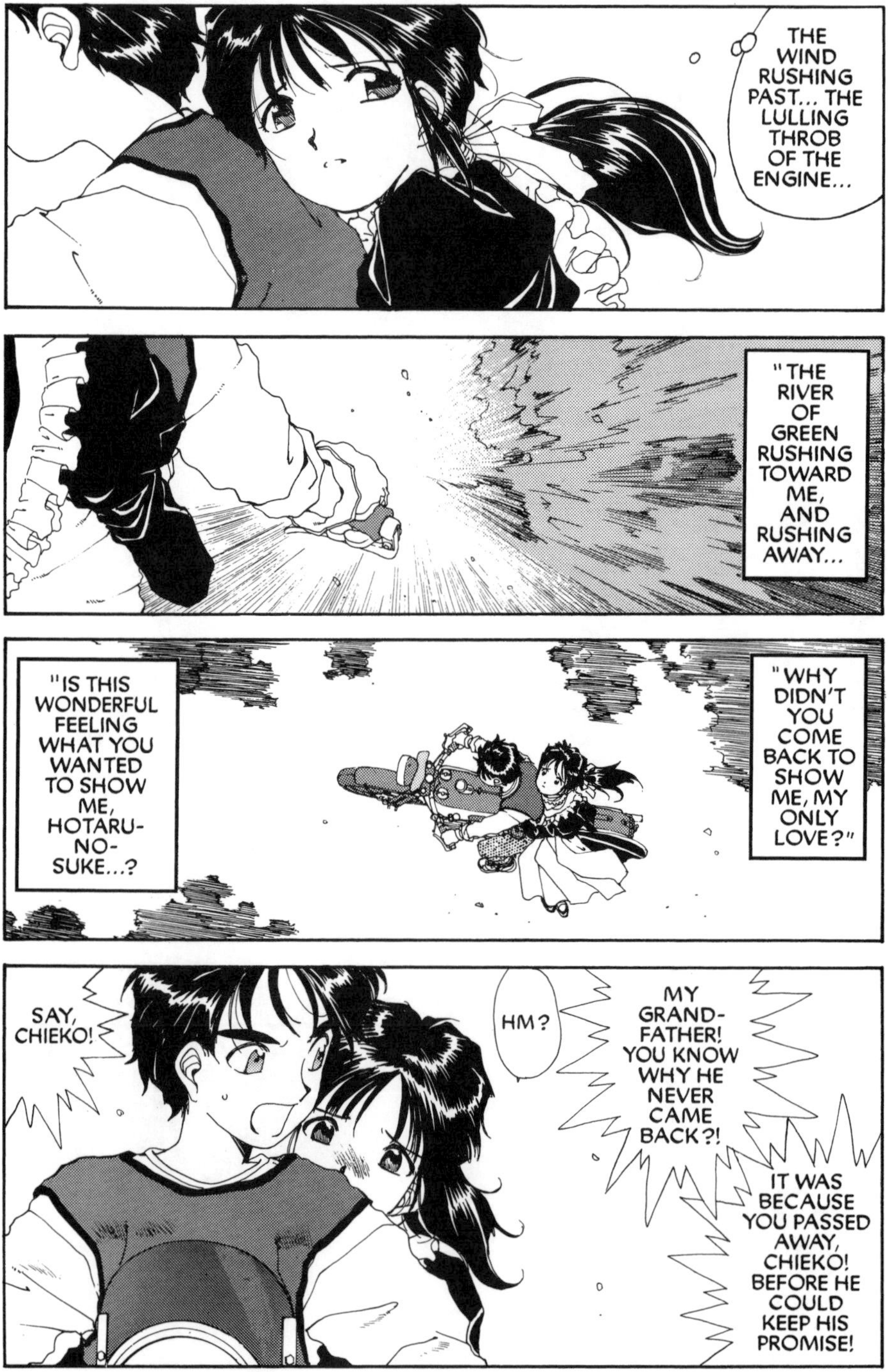
THE WIND RUSHING PAST... THE LULLING THROB OF THE ENGINE...
"THE RIVER OF GREEN RUSHING TOWARD ME, AND RUSHING AWAY...
"IS THIS WONDERFUL FEELING WHAT YOU WANTED TO SHOW ME, HOTARU-NO-SUKE...?
"WHY DIDN'T YOU COME BACK TO SHOW ME, MY ONLY LOVE?"
SAY, CHIEKO!
HM?
MY GRANDFATHER! YOU KNOW WHY HE NEVER CAME BACK?!
IT WAS BECAUSE YOU PASSED AWAY, CHIEKO! BEFORE HE COULD KEEP HIS PROMISE!

THAT'S WHY HE LEFT HIS BIKE HERE! WHY HE NEVER FIXED IT!!

YES... I SEE IT NOW...

"HOTARU-NO-SUKE... THIS BOY REALLY DOES HAVE YOUR BLOOD IN HIM.

"OTHERWISE, HOW COULD HE SO UNDERSTAND YOUR HEART...?"

HERE'S THE LAST CORNER. WE'LL BE BACK AT THE LODGE IN A MINUTE!

EH?! ALREADY?

.... SO? ONE MORE TIME AROUND?

N-NO...

ONCE IS FINE.

BUT ACTUALLY...

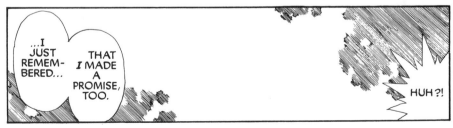

...I JUST REMEMBERED...

THAT I MADE A PROMISE, TOO.

HUH?!

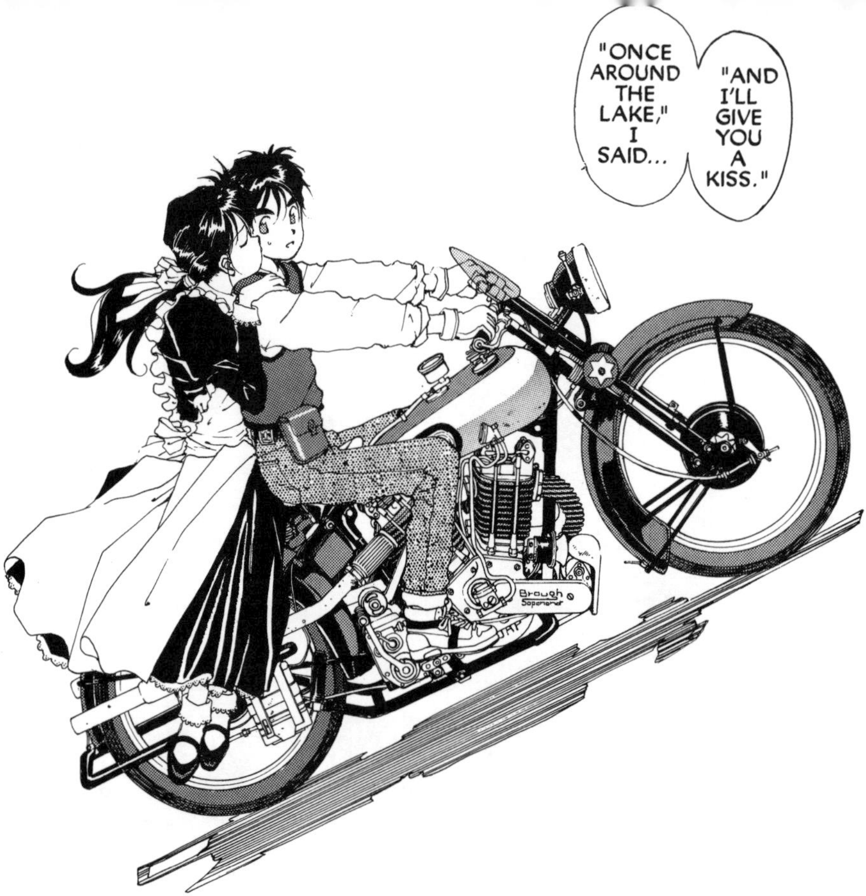
"ONCE AROUND THE LAKE," I SAID...
"AND I'LL GIVE YOU A KISS."

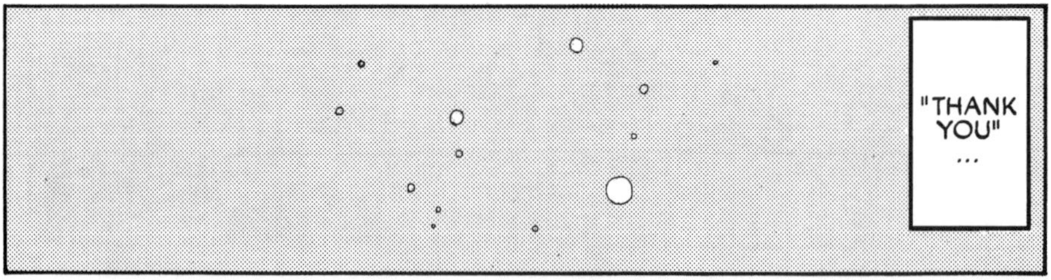
"THANK YOU" ...

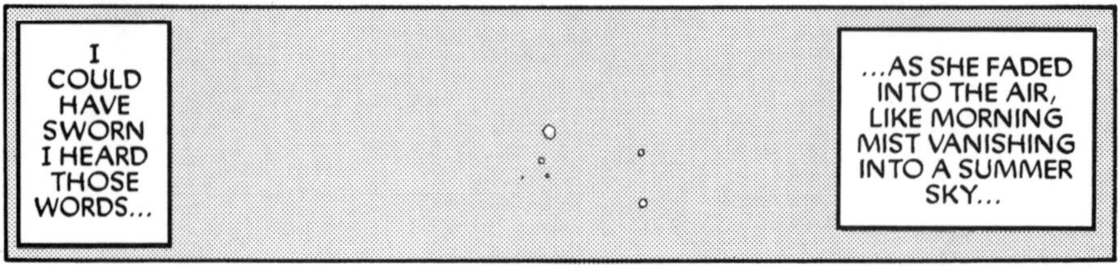
I COULD HAVE SWORN I HEARD THOSE WORDS...
...AS SHE FADED INTO THE AIR, LIKE MORNING MIST VANISHING INTO A SUMMER SKY...

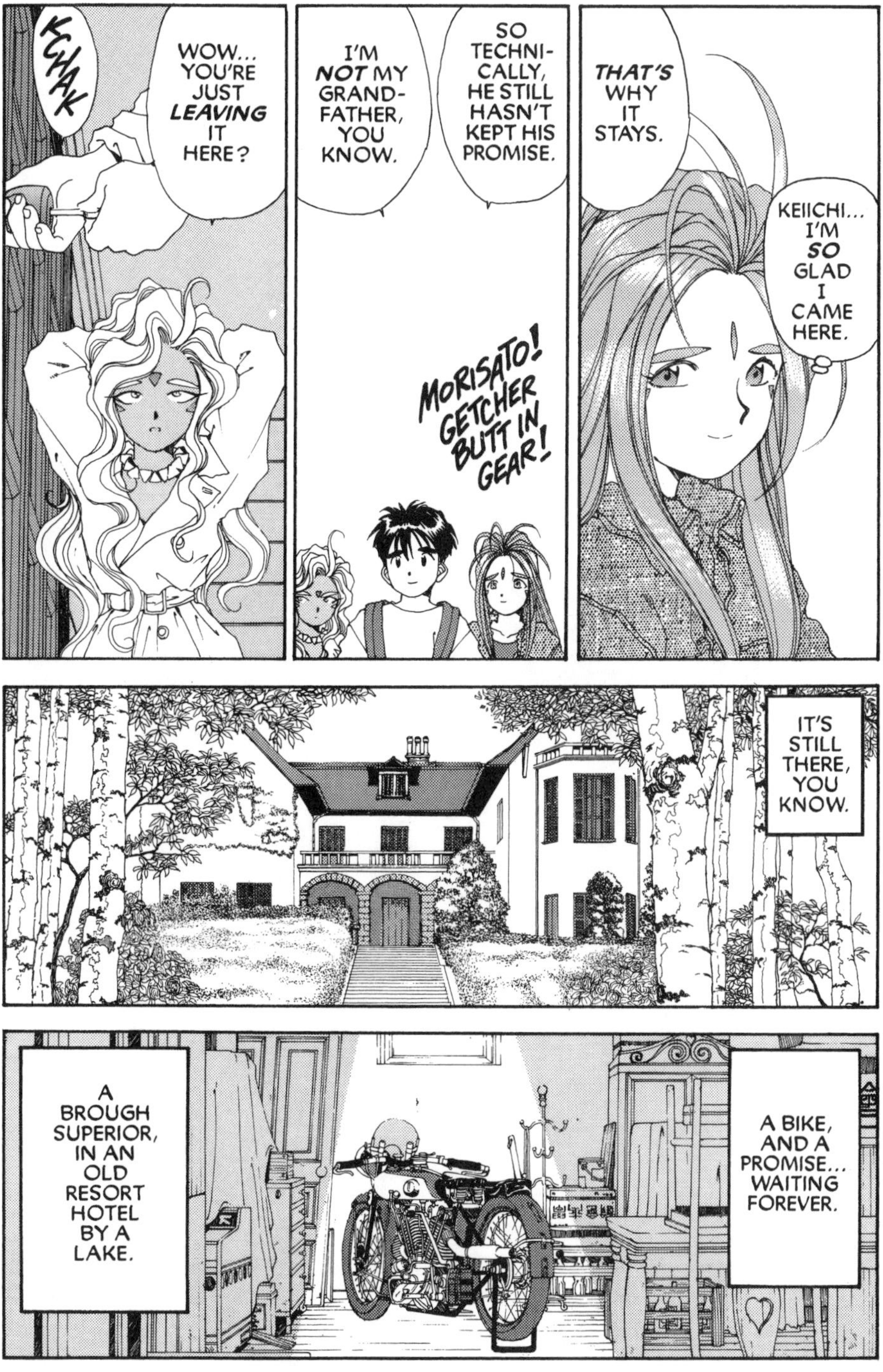
KCHAK
WOW... YOU'RE JUST *LEAVING* IT HERE?
I'M *NOT* MY GRANDFATHER, YOU KNOW.
SO TECHNICALLY, HE STILL HASN'T KEPT HIS PROMISE.
MORISATO! GETCHER BUTT IN GEAR!
THAT'S WHY IT STAYS.
KEIICHI... I'M *SO* GLAD I CAME HERE.
IT'S STILL THERE, YOU KNOW.
A BROUGH SUPERIOR, IN AN OLD RESORT HOTEL BY A LAKE.
A BIKE, AND A PROMISE... WAITING FOREVER.

The Lunchbox of Love

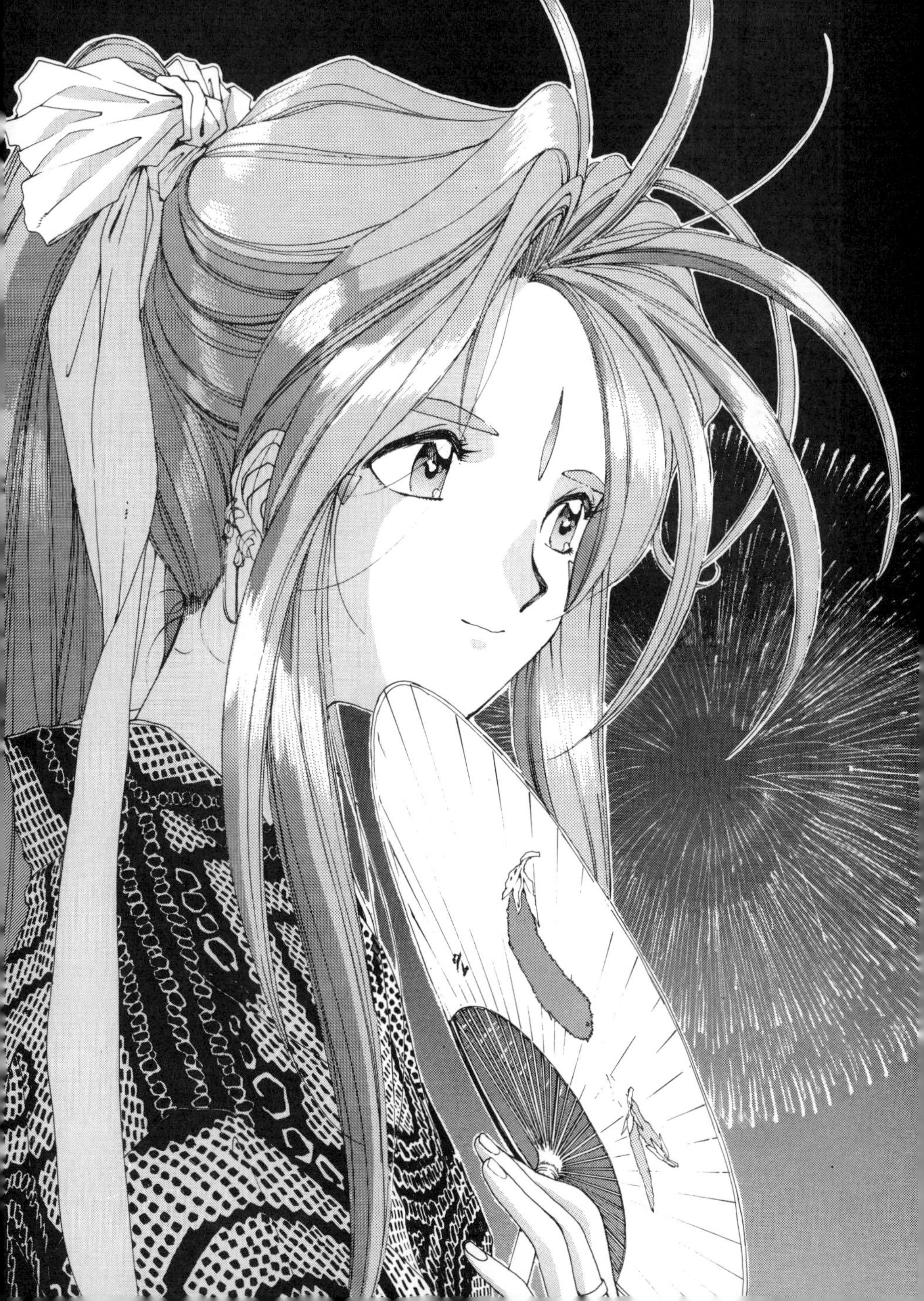

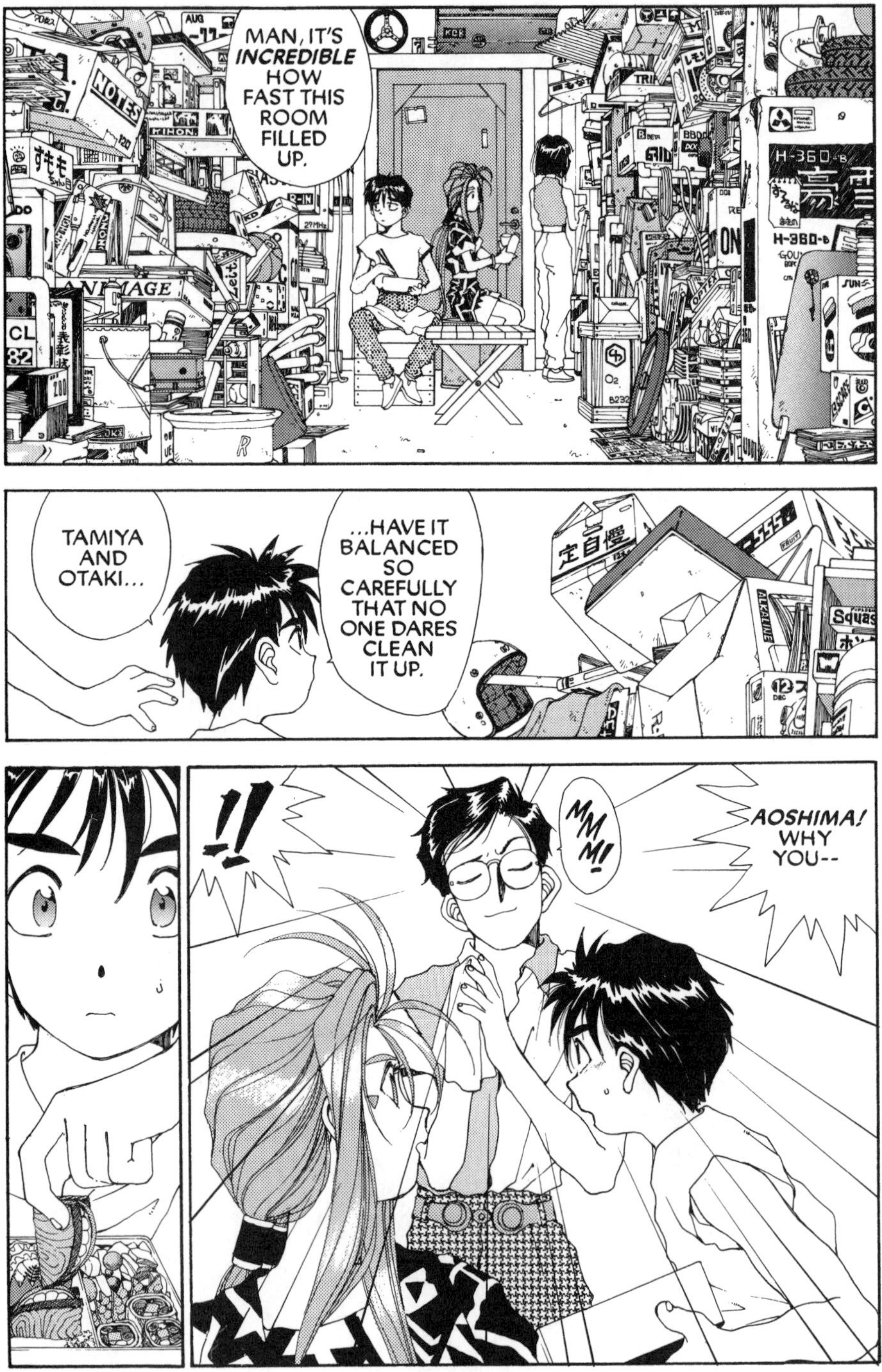
MAN, IT'S *INCREDIBLE* HOW FAST THIS ROOM FILLED UP.
TAMIYA AND OTAKI...
...HAVE IT BALANCED SO CAREFULLY THAT NO ONE DARES CLEAN IT UP.
!!
MMM!
AOSHIMA! WHY YOU--

AH!

OH MY GOD!!

IT'S SOOO DELICIOUS!!

BELLDANDY, TRULY YOUR LUNCHBOX AND YOURS ALONE IS WORTHY OF FEEDING ME!

EH?

YEESH... WHAT WOULD YOUR FOLLOWERS IN THE AOSHIMA GROUP THINK IF THEY SAW YOU NOW?!

HEY! ARE YOU LISTENING TO ME, AOSHIMA?! I--

FWIP

--HUH?

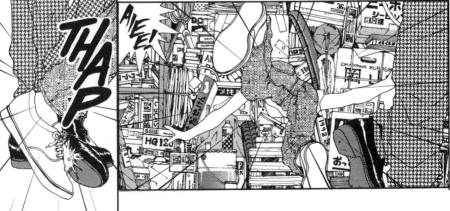

THAP!

AIEE!

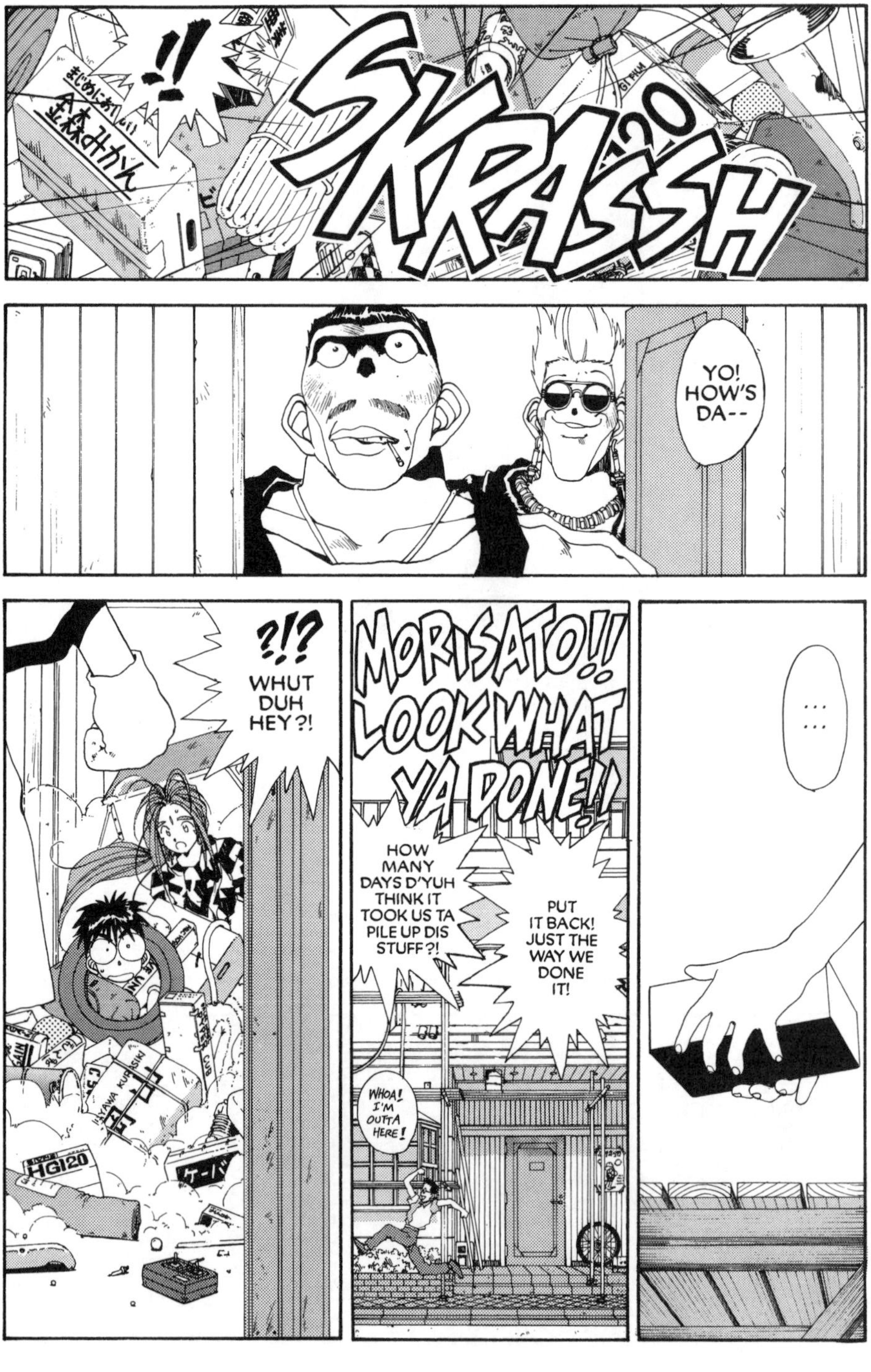
!!
SKRASSH
YO! HOW'S DA--
?!? WHUT DUH HEY?!
MORISATO!! LOOK WHAT YA DONE!!
HOW MANY DAYS D'YUH THINK IT TOOK US TA PILE UP DIS STUFF?!
PUT IT BACK! JUST THE WAY WE DONE IT!
WHOA! I'M OUTTA HERE!
... ...

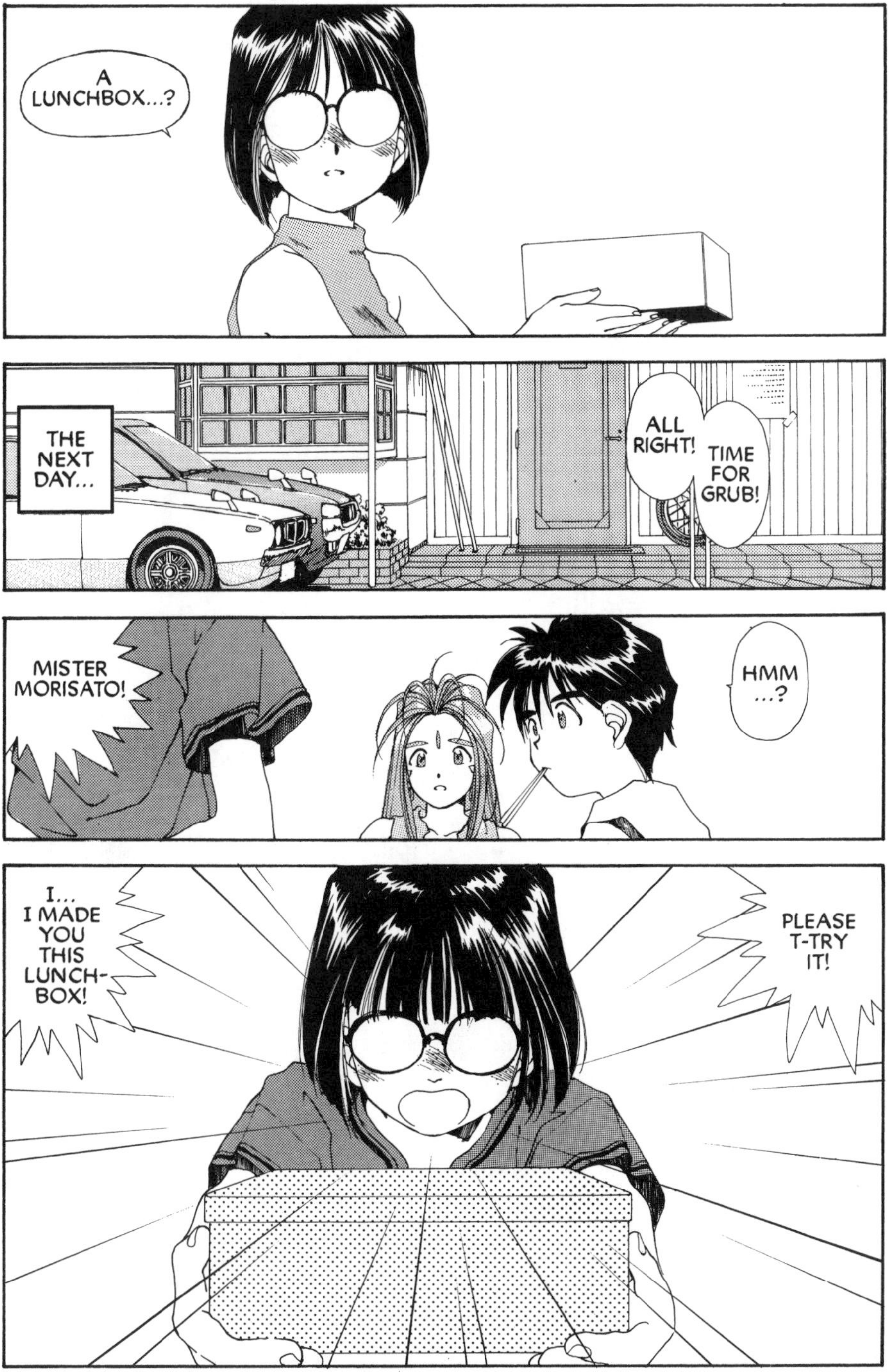
A LUNCHBOX...?
THE NEXT DAY...
ALL RIGHT!
TIME FOR GRUB!
MISTER MORISATO!
HMM ...?
I... I MADE YOU THIS LUNCH-BOX!
PLEASE T-TRY IT!

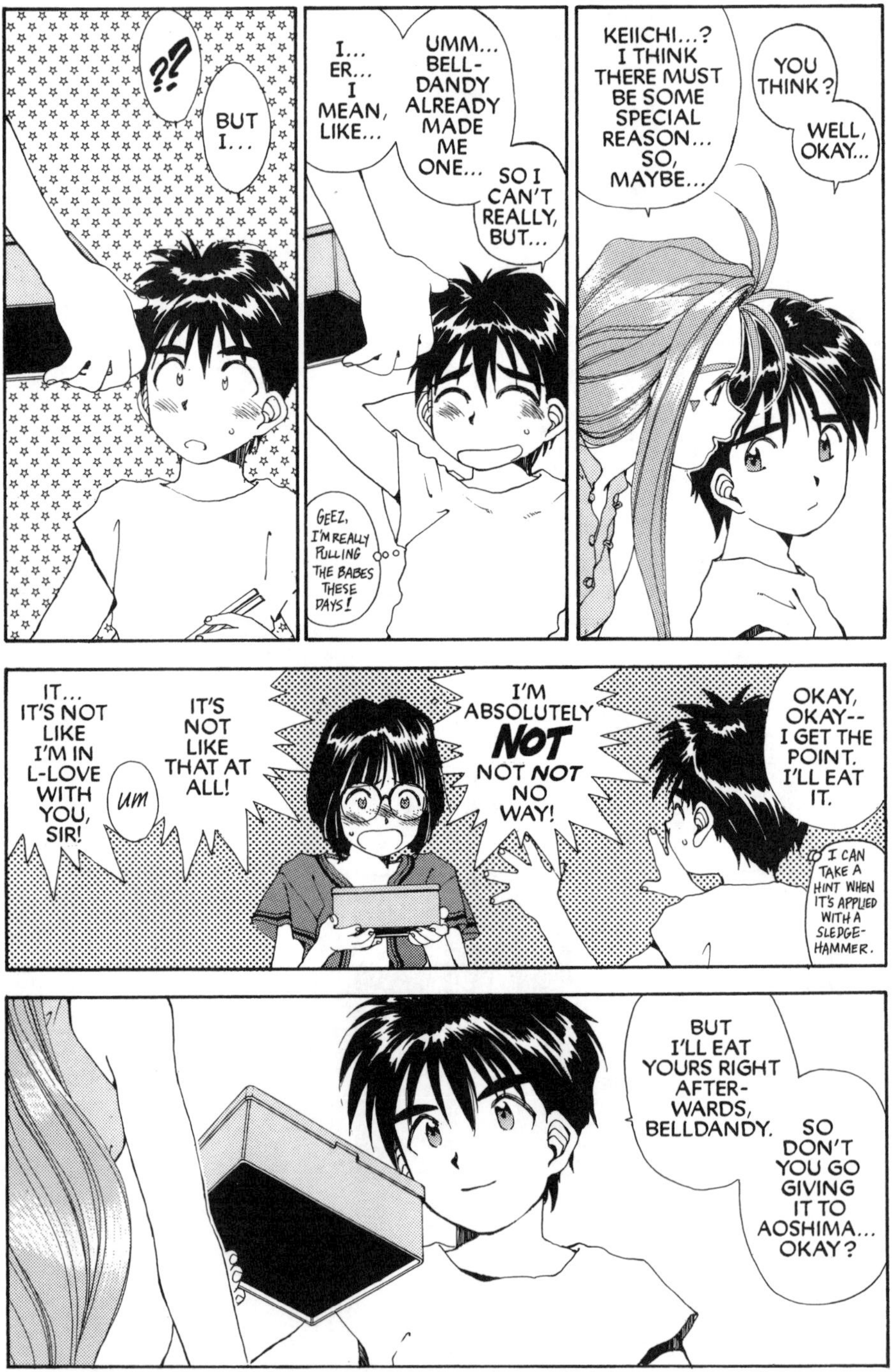
??
BUT I...
I... ER... I MEAN, LIKE...
UMM... BELL-DANDY ALREADY MADE ME ONE...
SO I CAN'T REALLY, BUT...
GEEZ, I'M REALLY PULLING THE BABES THESE DAYS!
KEIICHI...? I THINK THERE MUST BE SOME SPECIAL REASON... SO, MAYBE...
YOU THINK?
WELL, OKAY...
IT... IT'S NOT LIKE I'M IN L-LOVE WITH YOU, SIR!
UM
IT'S NOT LIKE THAT AT ALL!
I'M ABSOLUTELY NOT NOT NOT NO WAY!
OKAY, OKAY-- I GET THE POINT. I'LL EAT IT.
I CAN TAKE A HINT WHEN IT'S APPLIED WITH A SLEDGE-HAMMER.
BUT I'LL EAT YOURS RIGHT AFTER-WARDS, BELLDANDY.
SO DON'T YOU GO GIVING IT TO AOSHIMA... OKAY?

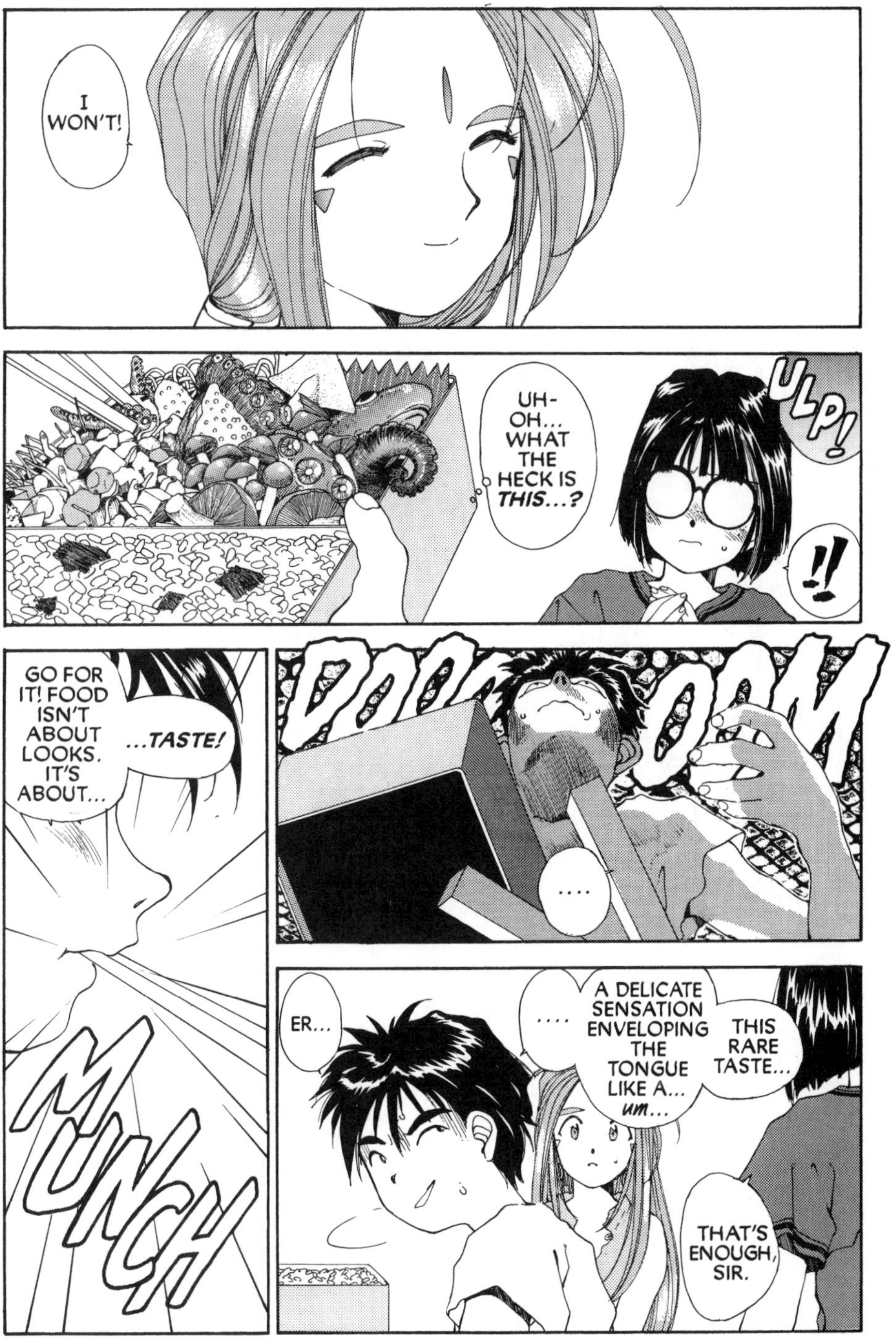
I WON'T!
UH-OH... WHAT THE HECK IS *THIS...?*
ULP!
!!
GO FOR IT! FOOD ISN'T ABOUT LOOKS. IT'S ABOUT...
...TASTE!
MUNCH
....
ER...
....
A DELICATE SENSATION ENVELOPING THE TONGUE LIKE A... *um...*
THIS RARE TASTE...
THAT'S ENOUGH, SIR.

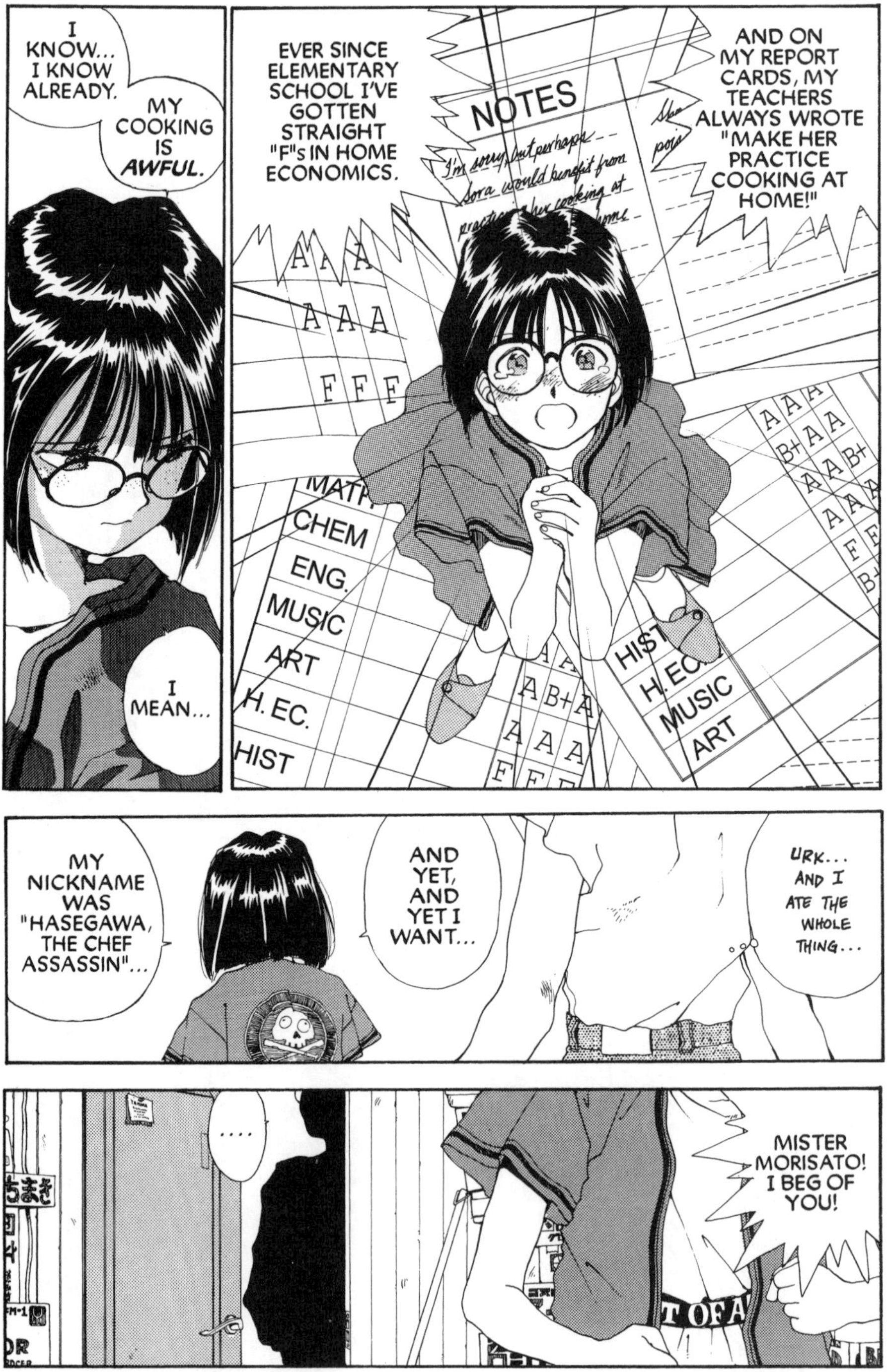
I KNOW... I KNOW ALREADY.
MY COOKING IS ***AWFUL.***
I MEAN...
EVER SINCE ELEMENTARY SCHOOL I'VE GOTTEN STRAIGHT "F"s IN HOME ECONOMICS.
NOTES
I'm sorry, but perhaps Sora would benefit from
AND ON MY REPORT CARDS, MY TEACHERS ALWAYS WROTE "MAKE HER PRACTICE COOKING AT HOME!"
CHEM
ENG.
MUSIC
ART
H. EC.
HIST
HIST
H. EC.
MUSIC
ART
MY NICKNAME WAS "HASEGAWA, THE CHEF ASSASSIN"...
AND YET, AND YET I WANT...
URK... AND I ATE THE WHOLE THING...
....
MISTER MORISATO! I BEG OF YOU!

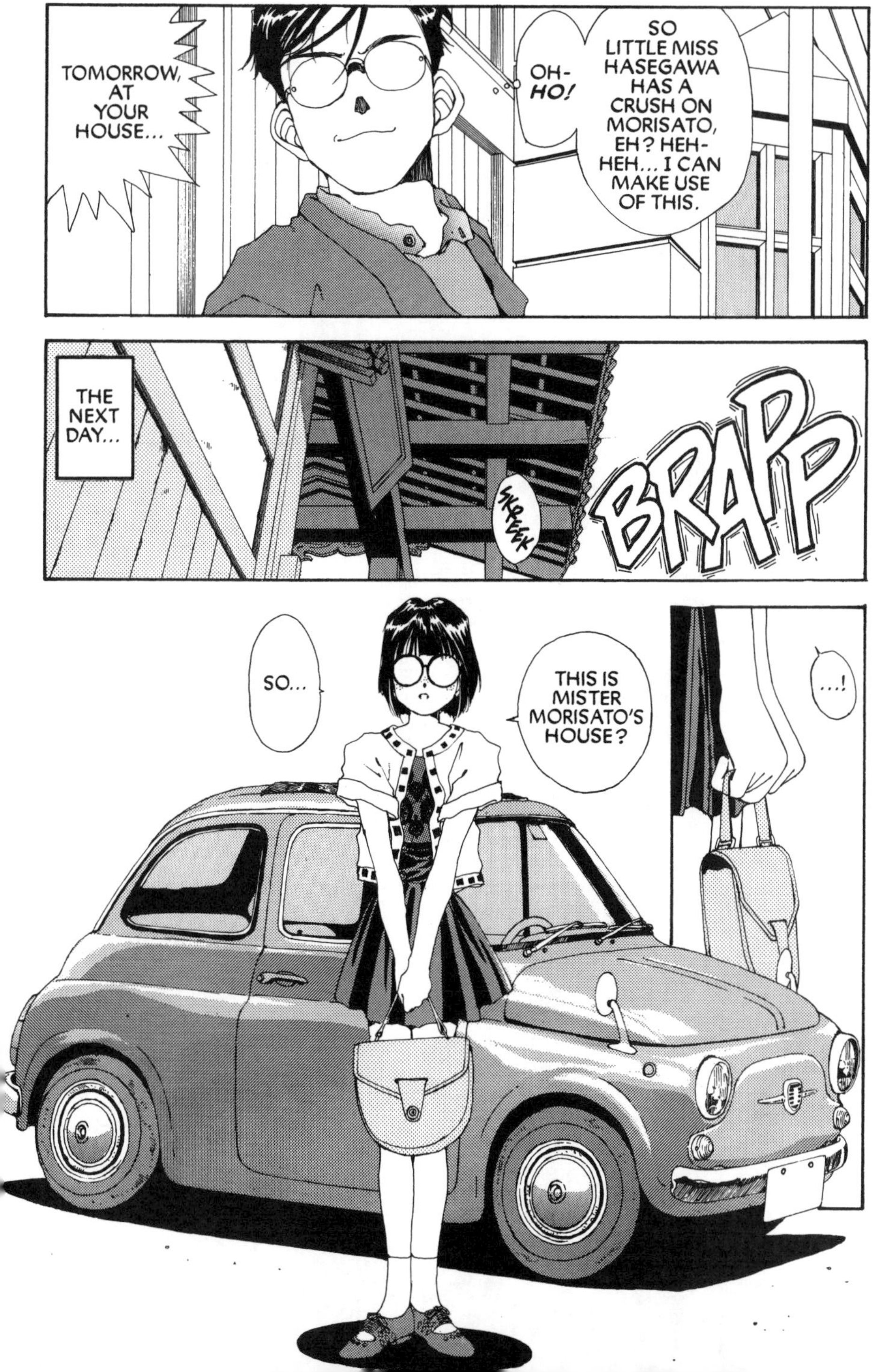
TOMORROW, AT YOUR HOUSE...
OH-HO!
SO LITTLE MISS HASEGAWA HAS A CRUSH ON MORISATO, EH? HEH-HEH... I CAN MAKE USE OF THIS.
THE NEXT DAY...
SKREEK
BRAPP
SO...
THIS IS MISTER MORISATO'S HOUSE?
...!

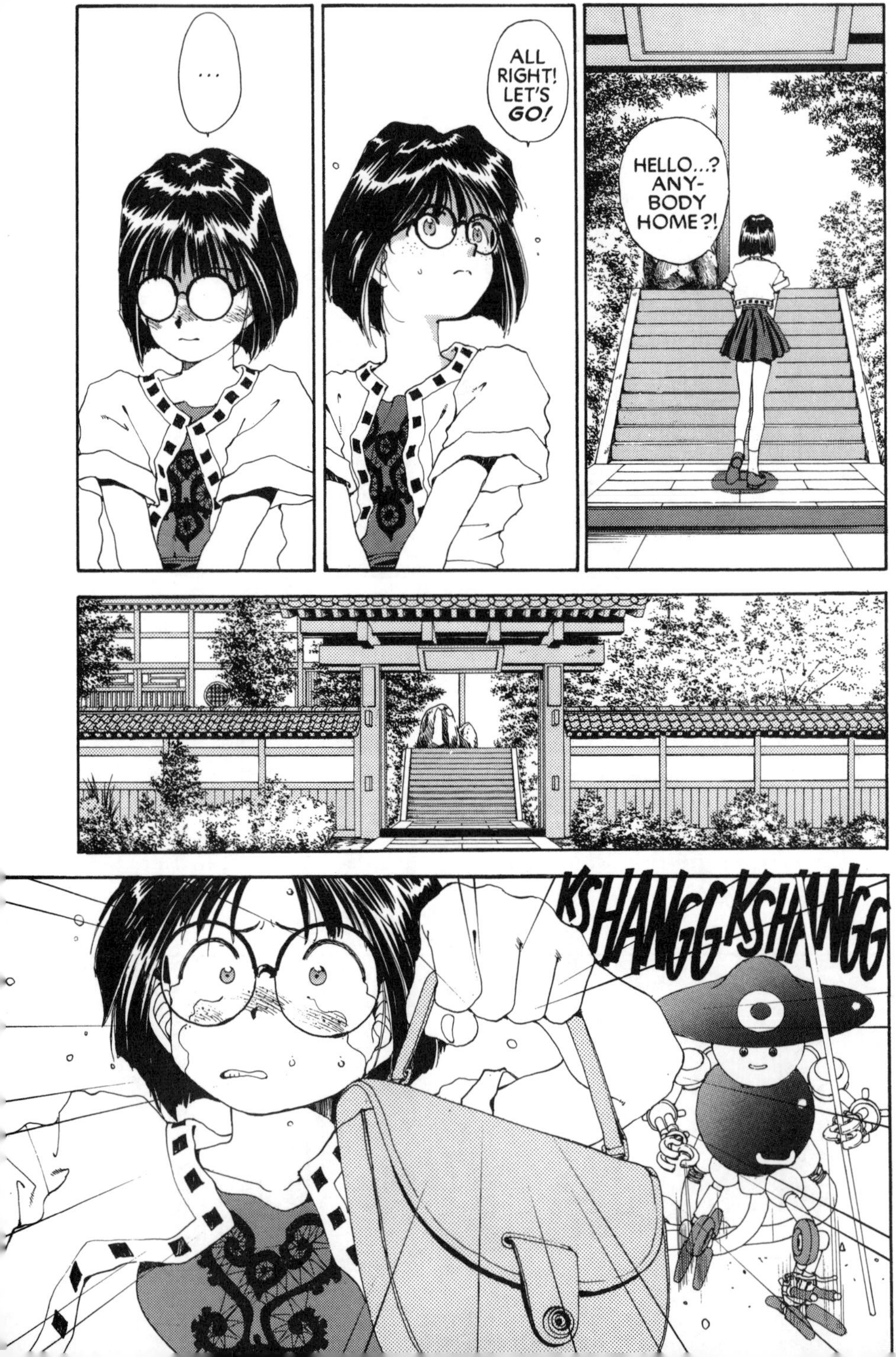
...
ALL RIGHT! LET'S *GO!*
HELLO...? ANY-BODY HOME?!
KSHANGG KSHANGG

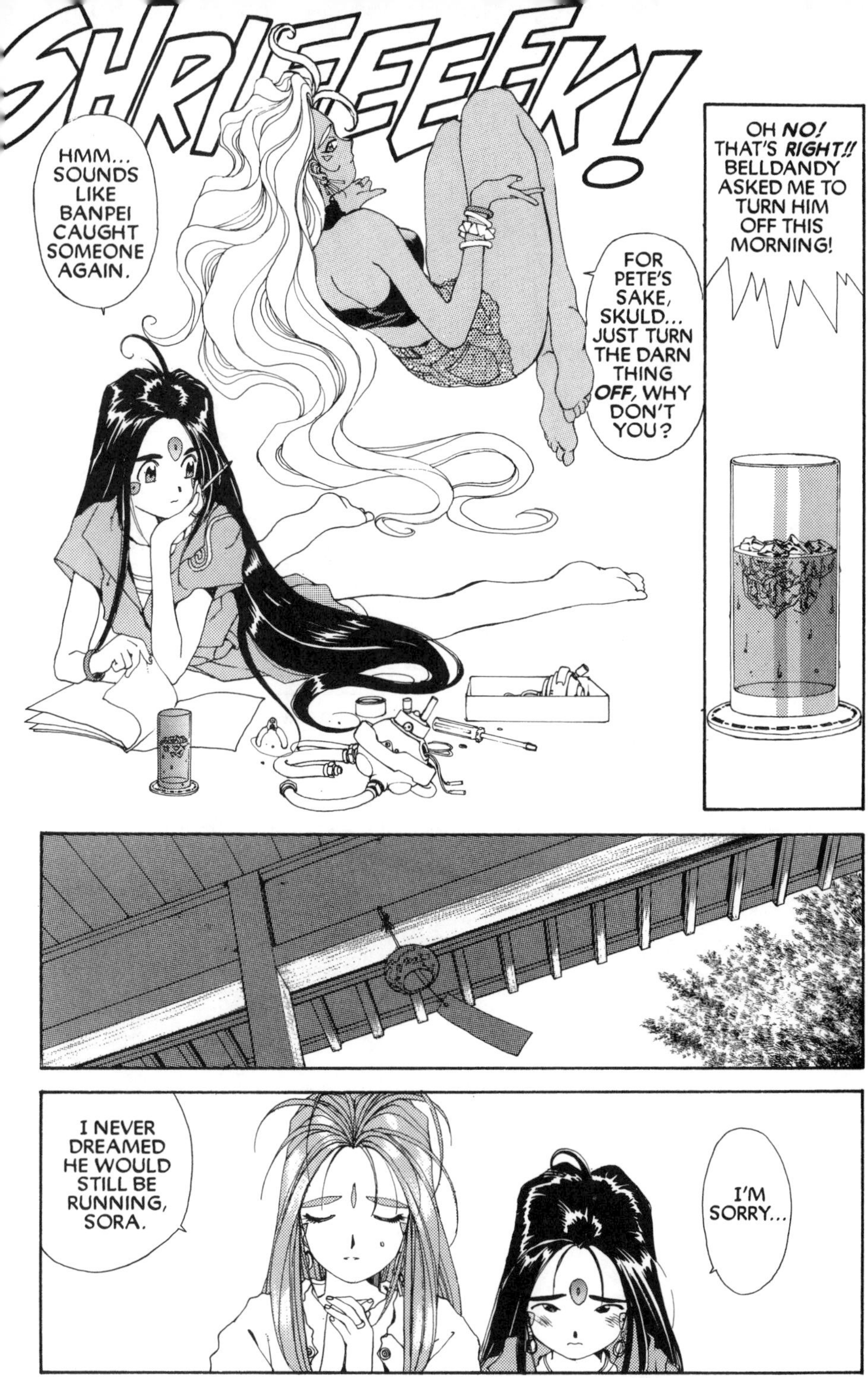
SHRIEEEEK!
HMM... SOUNDS LIKE BANPEI CAUGHT SOMEONE AGAIN.
FOR PETE'S SAKE, SKULD... JUST TURN THE DARN THING *OFF,* WHY DON'T YOU?
OH *NO!* THAT'S *RIGHT!!* BELLDANDY ASKED ME TO TURN HIM OFF THIS MORNING!
I NEVER DREAMED HE WOULD STILL BE RUNNING, SORA.
I'M SORRY...

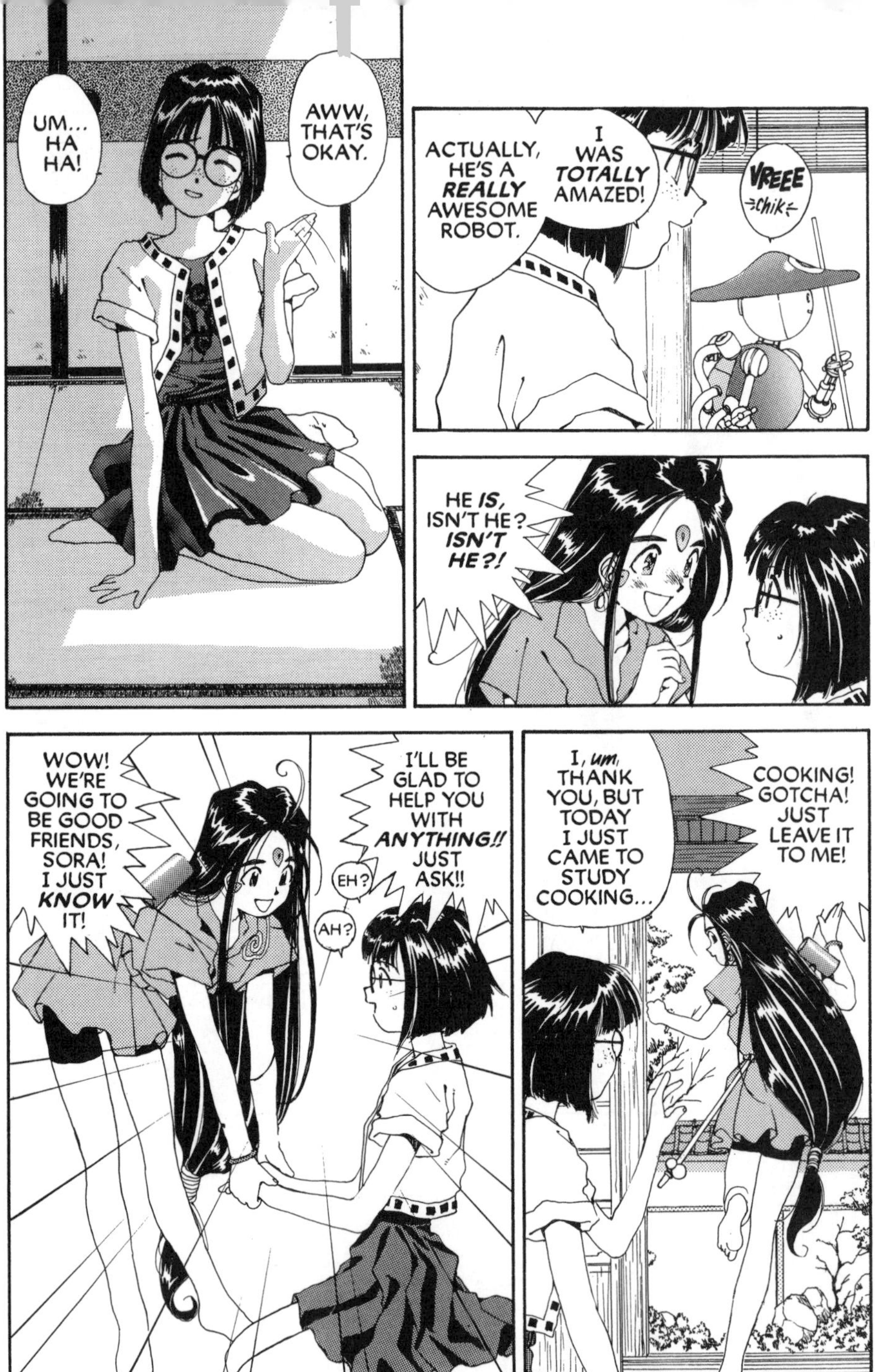
UM... HA HA!
AWW, THAT'S OKAY.
ACTUALLY, HE'S A REALLY AWESOME ROBOT.
I WAS TOTALLY AMAZED!
VREEE
chik
HE IS, ISN'T HE? ISN'T HE?!
WOW! WE'RE GOING TO BE GOOD FRIENDS, SORA! I JUST KNOW IT!
I'LL BE GLAD TO HELP YOU WITH ANYTHING!! JUST ASK!!
EH?
AH?
I, um, THANK YOU, BUT TODAY I JUST CAME TO STUDY COOKING...
COOKING! GOTCHA! JUST LEAVE IT TO ME!

DON'T YOU LEAVE BEFORE I'M FINISHED! PROMISE?!

SKULD, WAI--

....

WHAT DOES SHE MEAN, "LEAVE IT TO ME"...?

WELL, THEN-- SHALL WE GET STARTED?

AH? OH, YES. YES, PLEASE!

THAT'S GOOD! GO SLOWLY AT FIRST...

Y-YOU'RE SO LUCKY, MISS BELL-DANDY.

YOU'RE SUCH A GOOD COOK... SO BEAUTIFUL... EVERYONE LIKES YOU...

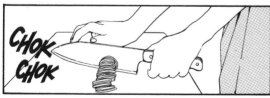

CHOK CHOK

OH, DEAR...

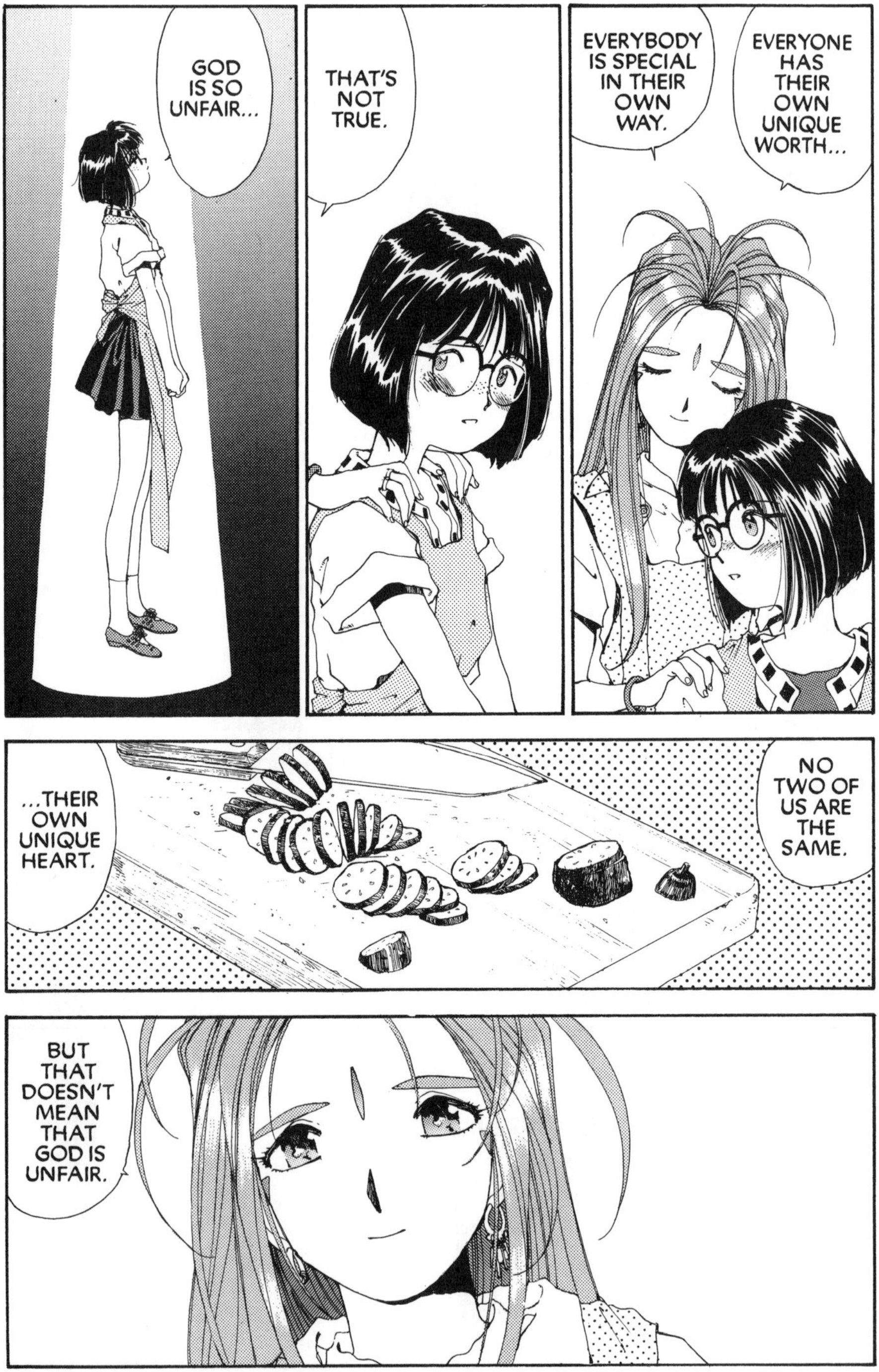
GOD IS SO UNFAIR...
THAT'S NOT TRUE.
EVERYBODY IS SPECIAL IN THEIR OWN WAY.
EVERYONE HAS THEIR OWN UNIQUE WORTH...
...THEIR OWN UNIQUE HEART.
NO TWO OF US ARE THE SAME.
BUT THAT DOESN'T MEAN THAT GOD IS UNFAIR.

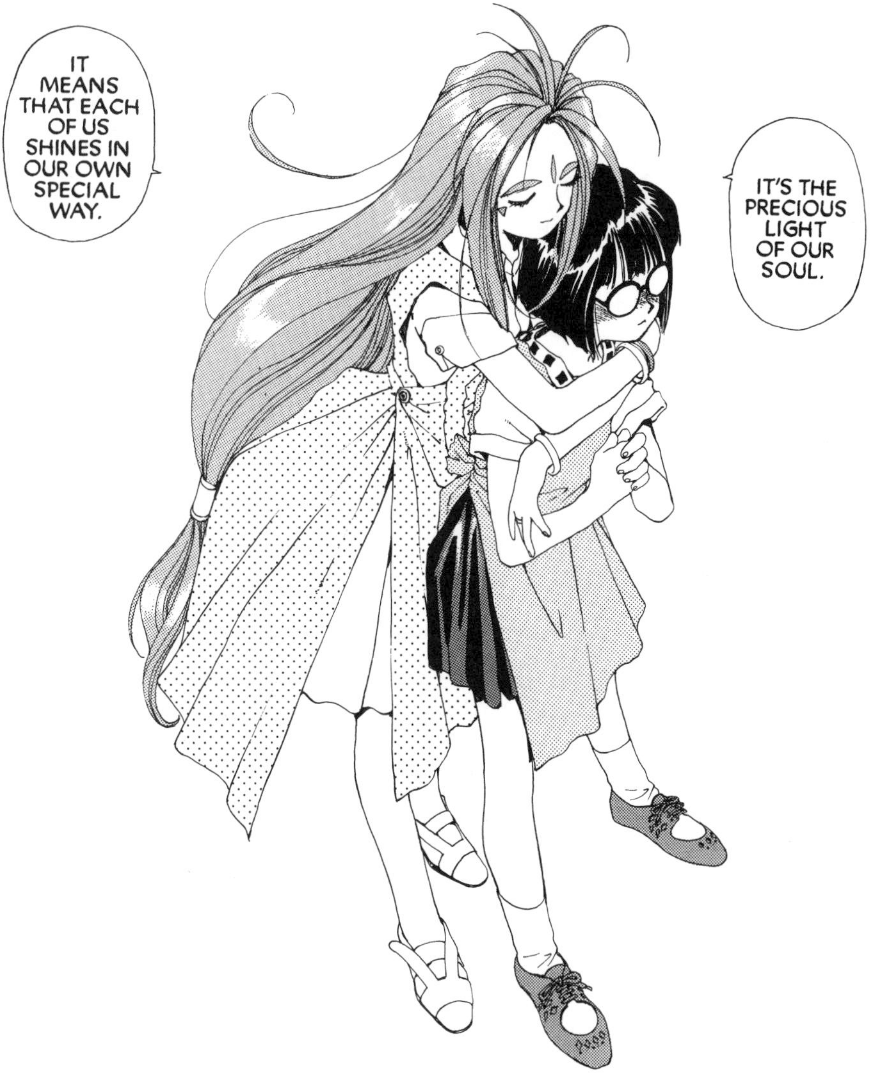
IT MEANS THAT EACH OF US SHINES IN OUR OWN SPECIAL WAY.
IT'S THE PRECIOUS LIGHT OF OUR SOUL.

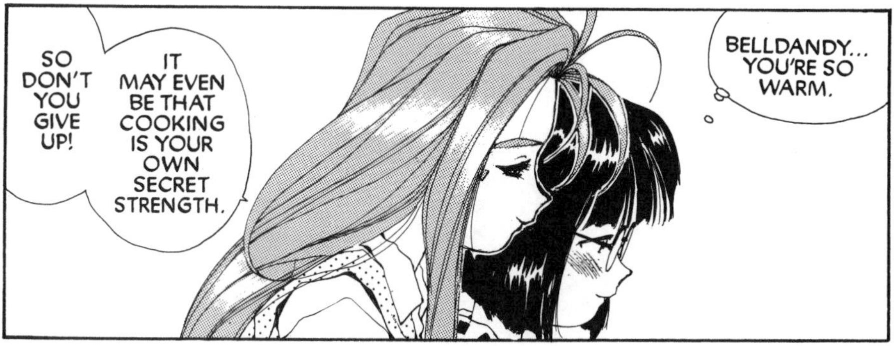
SO DON'T YOU GIVE UP!
IT MAY EVEN BE THAT COOKING IS YOUR OWN SECRET STRENGTH.
BELLDANDY... YOU'RE SO WARM.

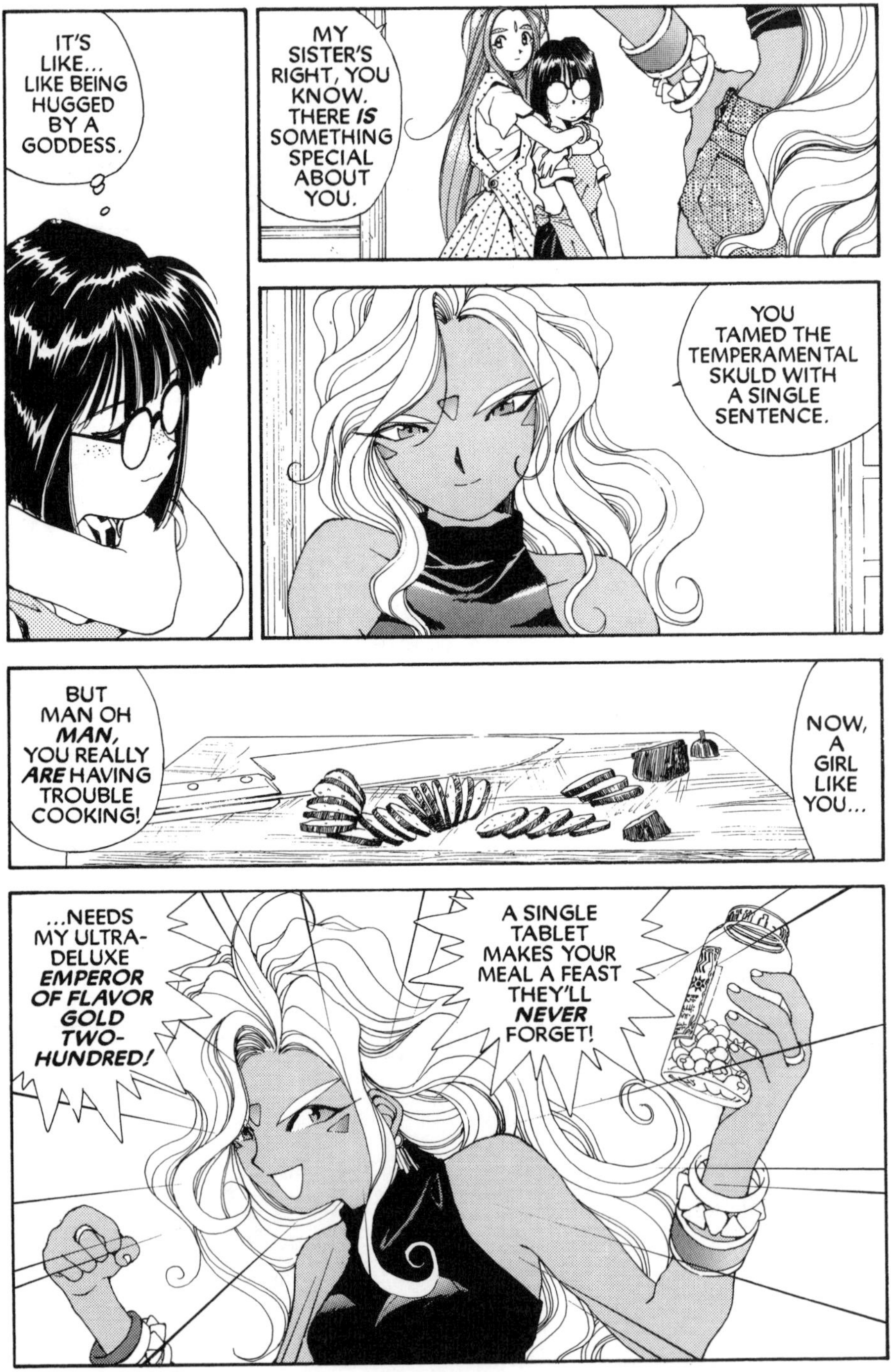
IT'S LIKE... LIKE BEING HUGGED BY A GODDESS.
MY SISTER'S RIGHT, YOU KNOW. THERE *IS* SOMETHING SPECIAL ABOUT YOU.
YOU TAMED THE TEMPERAMENTAL SKULD WITH A SINGLE SENTENCE.
BUT MAN OH *MAN*, YOU REALLY *ARE* HAVING TROUBLE COOKING!
NOW, A GIRL LIKE YOU...
...NEEDS MY ULTRA-DELUXE *EMPEROR OF FLAVOR GOLD TWO-HUNDRED!*
A SINGLE TABLET MAKES YOUR MEAL A FEAST THEY'LL *NEVER* FORGET!

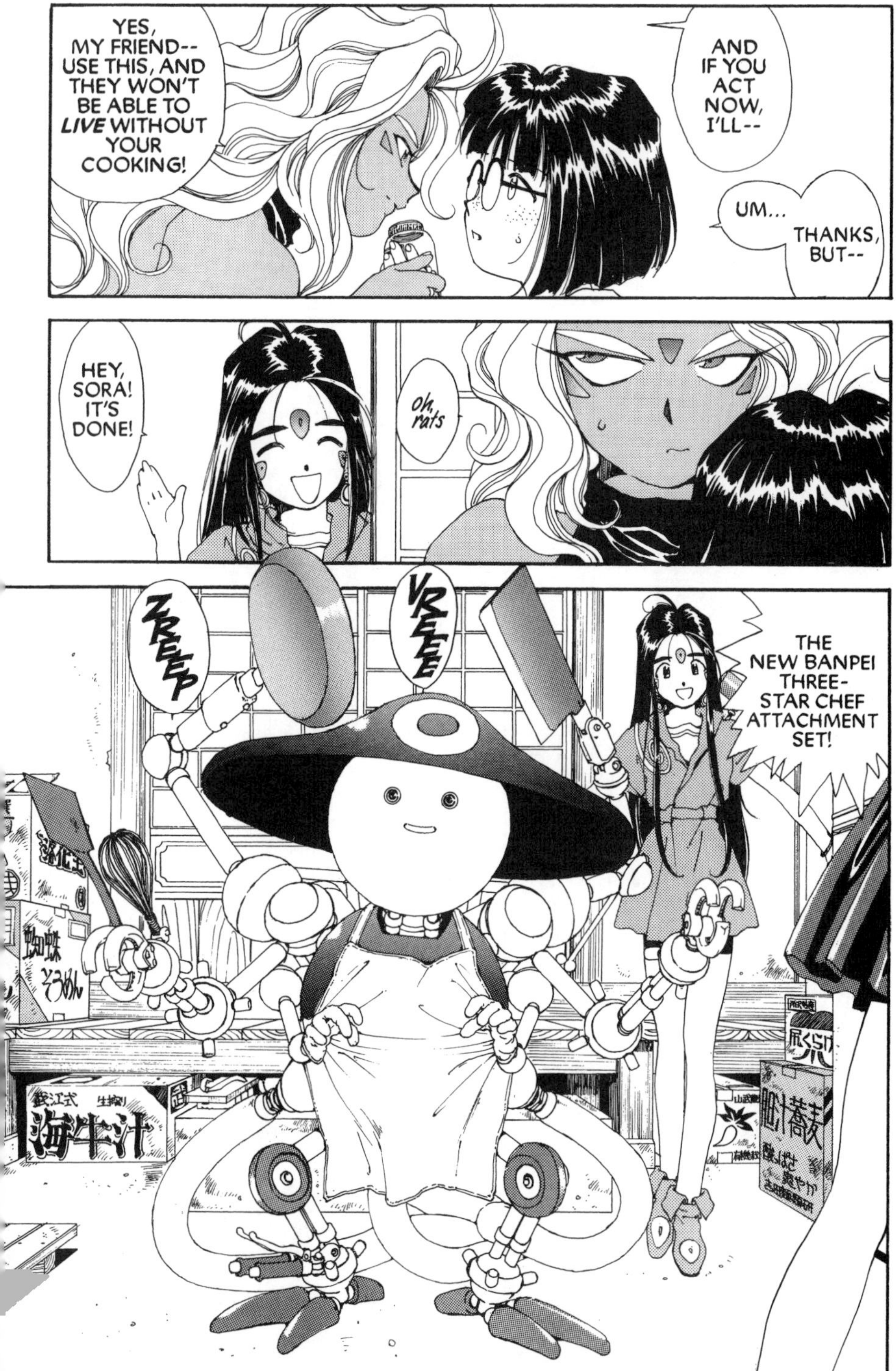
YES, MY FRIEND-- USE THIS, AND THEY WON'T BE ABLE TO *LIVE* WITHOUT YOUR COOKING!
AND IF YOU ACT NOW, I'LL--
UM... THANKS, BUT--
HEY, SORA! IT'S DONE!
oh, rats
ZREEP
VREEE
THE NEW BANPEI THREE-STAR CHEF ATTACHMENT SET!
海牛汁

GOSH... THANK YOU, SKULD... AND URD. FOR EVERYTHING.

BUT...

I WANT TO DO IT BY MYSELF, WITH MY OWN HANDS.

I'M SORRY...

AW, GEEZ.

WHAT A DRAG...

CAN'T YOU FEEL THAT POWER...?

SHE'S GOT SOMETHING POWERFUL INSIDE... SOMETHING INTENSE IS DRIVING HER.

SEE ...?

I WAS JUST TRYING TO HELP...

HEY, SKULD! CHECK IT OUT!

AND THAT'S WHY YOU SHOULDN'T INTERFERE.

THAT'S *SO* *LIKE YOU,* URD! AS IF YOU'RE *MISS* *PERFECT* OR SOMETHING!

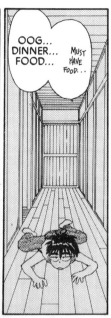

OOG... DINNER... FOOD...

MUST HAVE FOOD...

I SHOULDN'T INTERFERE?! AND WHAT ABOUT *YOU?!* YOU GAVE HER SOMETHING, TOO!

OOPS... YOU SAW ME? CLEVER LITTLE THING, AREN'T YOU...

THANK YOU *SO MUCH,* MISS BELL-DANDY!

I'M SORRY I KEPT YOU UP SO LATE.

BUT NOW I FEEL LIKE... MAYBE...

...MAYBE EVEN *I* CAN MAKE A DELICIOUS LUNCH-BOX.

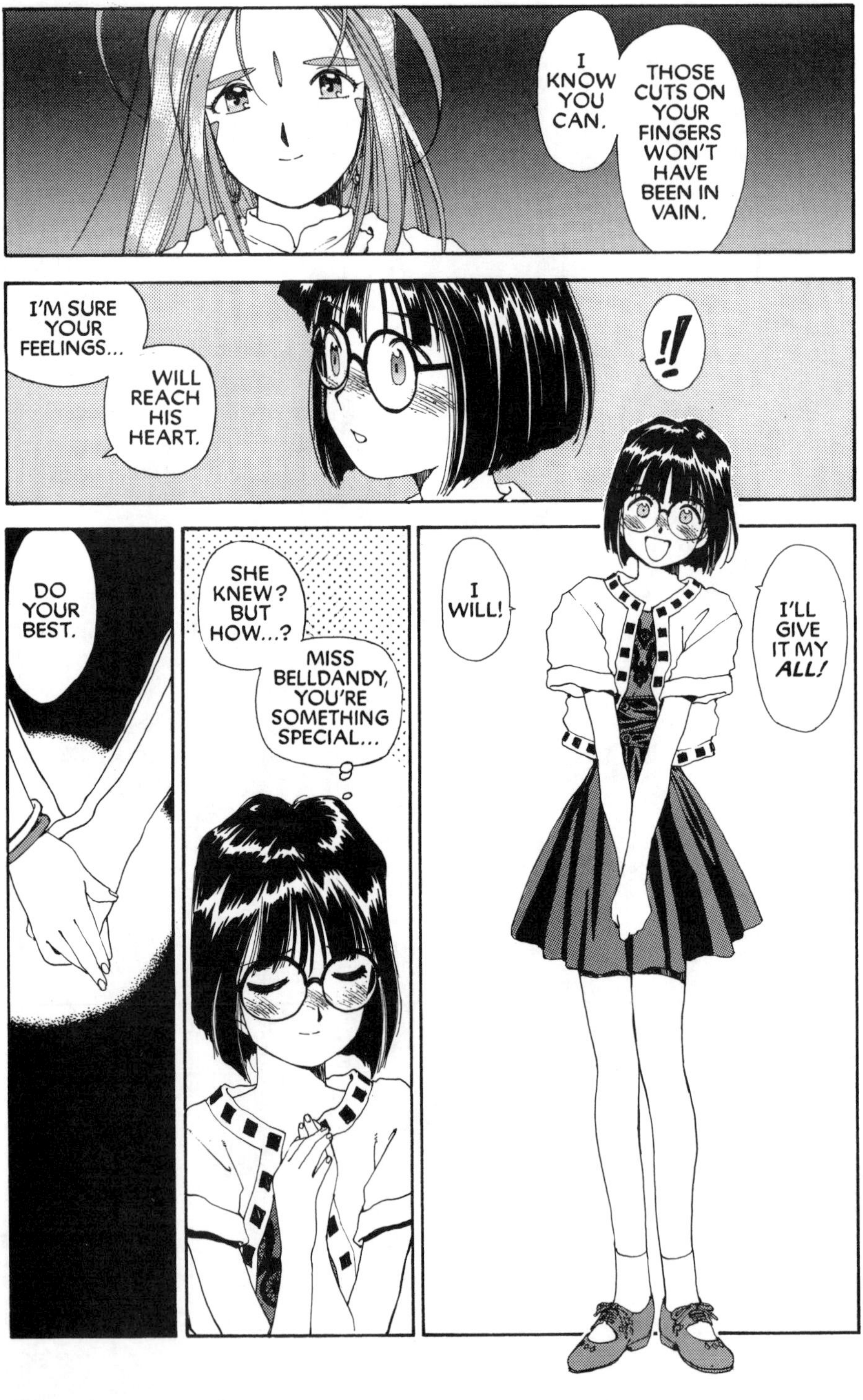
I KNOW YOU CAN.
THOSE CUTS ON YOUR FINGERS WON'T HAVE BEEN IN VAIN.
I'M SURE YOUR FEELINGS...
WILL REACH HIS HEART.
!!
DO YOUR BEST.
SHE KNEW? BUT HOW...?
MISS BELLDANDY, YOU'RE SOMETHING SPECIAL...
I WILL!
I'LL GIVE IT MY *ALL!*

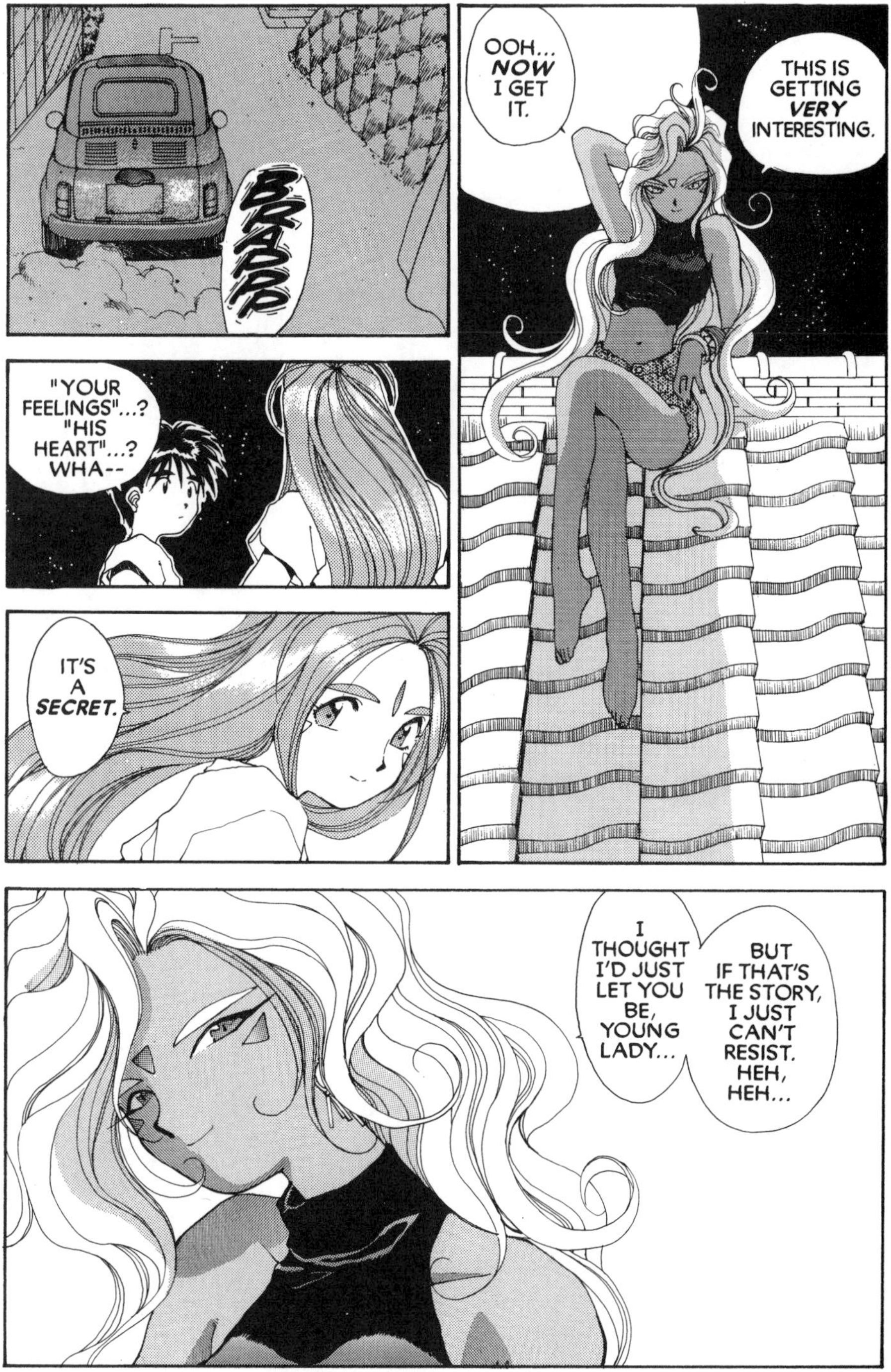
BRAPPP
"YOUR FEELINGS"...? "HIS HEART"...? WHA--
IT'S A *SECRET.*
OOH... *NOW* I GET IT.
THIS IS GETTING *VERY* INTERESTING.
I THOUGHT I'D JUST LET YOU BE, YOUNG LADY...
BUT IF THAT'S THE STORY, I JUST CAN'T RESIST. HEH, HEH...

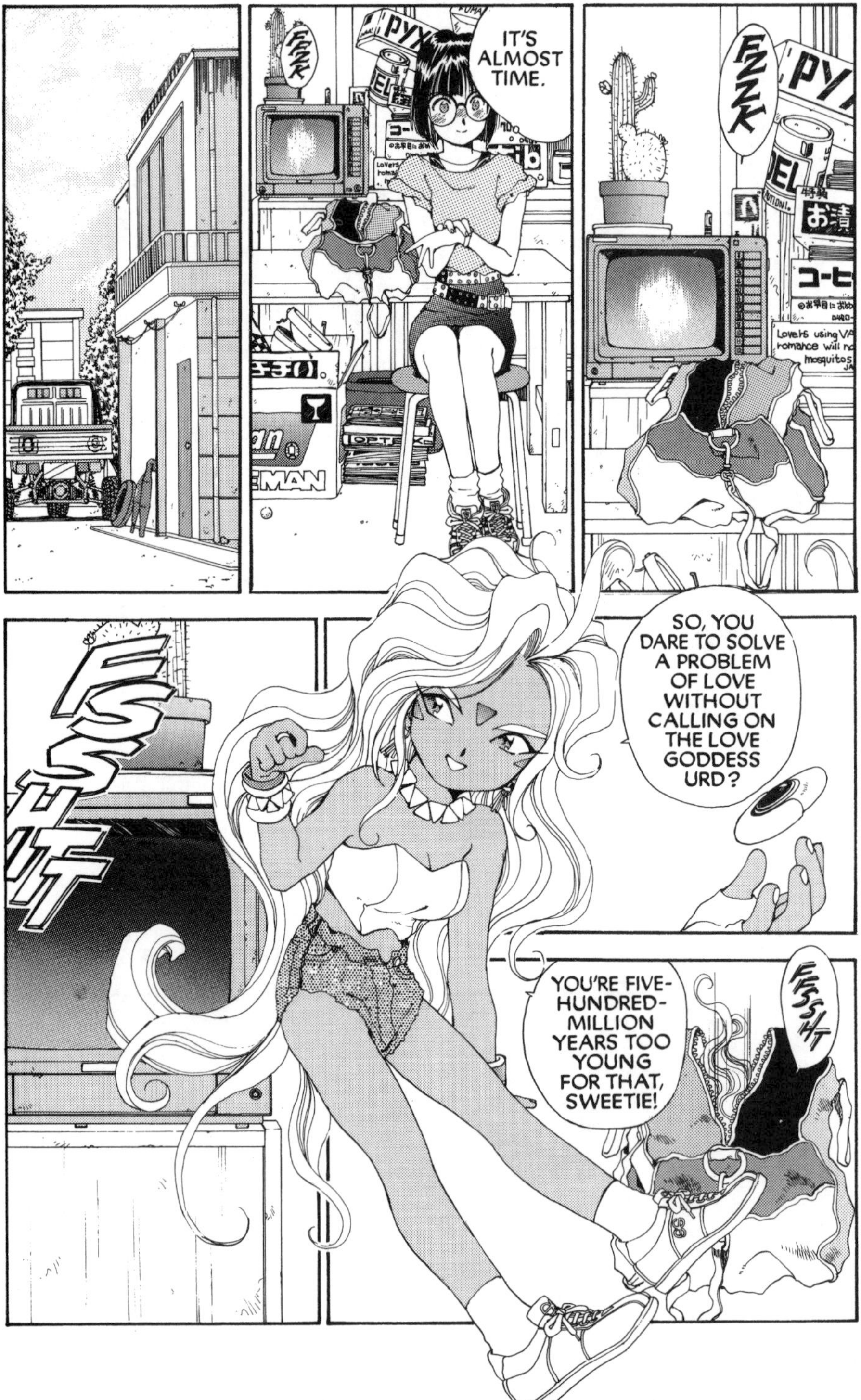
FZZK
PYX
IT'S ALMOST TIME.
FZZK
PYX
FSSHT
SO, YOU DARE TO SOLVE A PROBLEM OF LOVE WITHOUT CALLING ON THE LOVE GODDESS URD?
YOU'RE FIVE-HUNDRED-MILLION YEARS TOO YOUNG FOR THAT, SWEETIE!
FSSHT

HEH, HEH...

I PRAY FOR YOUR SUCCESS.

AS IF IT'S NOT A DONE DEAL!

OH, HI!

YO! SORRY WE'RE SO LATE!

AND NOW... THE RESULTS OF ALL MY PRACTICE!

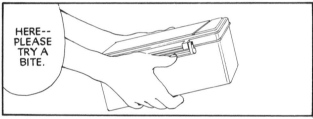

HERE-- PLEASE TRY A BITE.

WHATCHA LOOKING FOR, BELL-DANDY?

I THOUGHT I REMEM-BERED SEEING SOME TEA HERE BEFORE...

GEE... I DON'T REMEMBER SEEING IT. ARE YOU SURE?

I'LL POP DOWN TO THE CORNER STORE AND GET SOME, OKAY?

BUT WE DON'T REALLY...

AH, WELL... THAT'S OKAY. SO-- LET ME AT THIS LUNCHBOX!

YES, SIR!

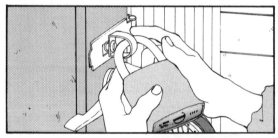

LOCKED! WE'RE LOCKED IN!

HEY!! WHO DID THAT?!

K-CHAK

?!

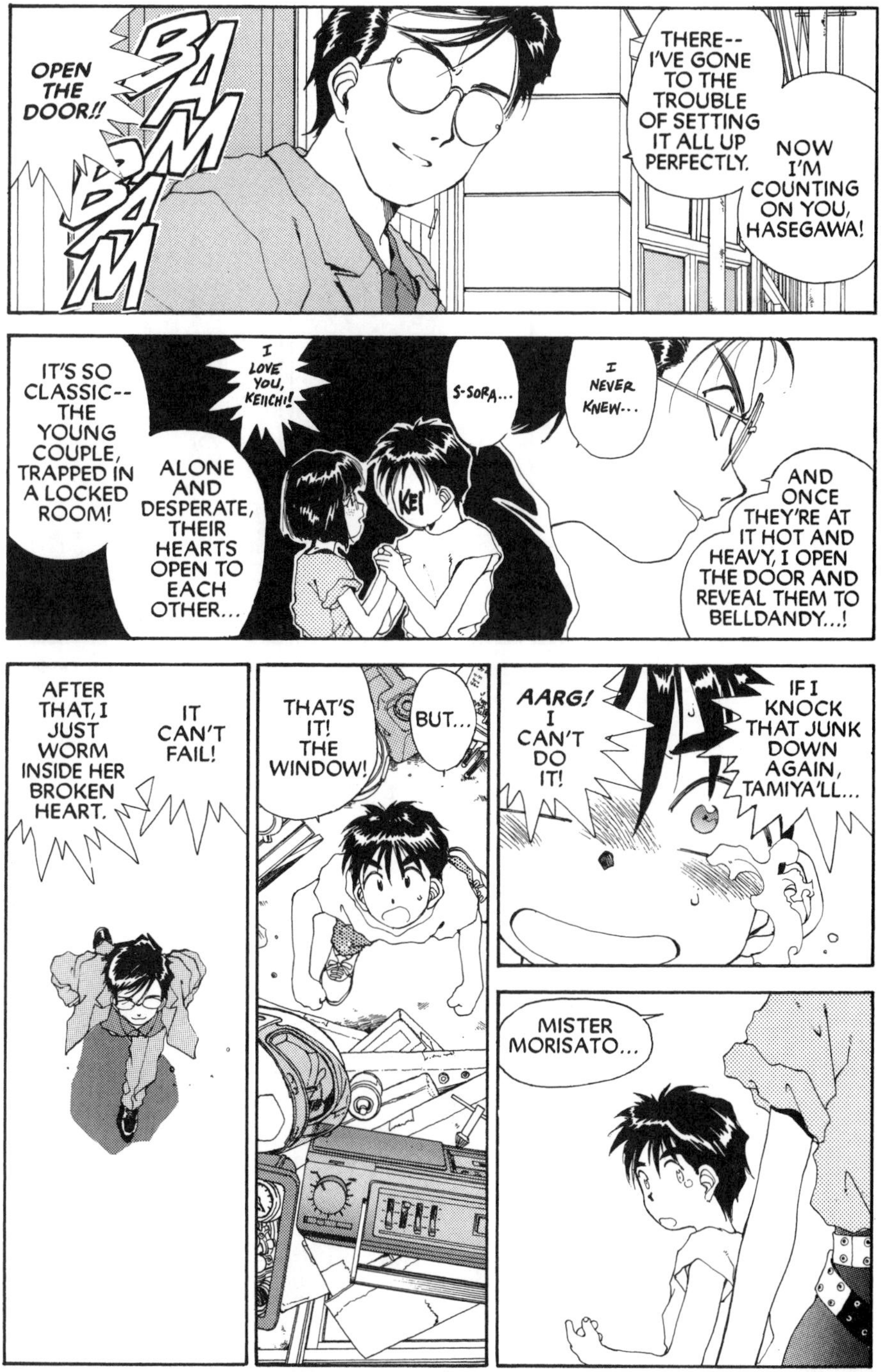
OPEN THE DOOR!!
BAM BAM BAM
THERE-- I'VE GONE TO THE TROUBLE OF SETTING IT ALL UP PERFECTLY.
NOW I'M COUNTING ON YOU, HASEGAWA!
IT'S SO CLASSIC-- THE YOUNG COUPLE, TRAPPED IN A LOCKED ROOM!
ALONE AND DESPERATE, THEIR HEARTS OPEN TO EACH OTHER...
I LOVE YOU, KEIICHI!
KEI
S-SORA...
I NEVER KNEW...
AND ONCE THEY'RE AT IT HOT AND HEAVY, I OPEN THE DOOR AND REVEAL THEM TO BELLDANDY...!
AFTER THAT, I JUST WORM INSIDE HER BROKEN HEART.
IT CAN'T FAIL!
THAT'S IT! THE WINDOW!
BUT...
AARG! I CAN'T DO IT!
IF I KNOCK THAT JUNK DOWN AGAIN, TAMIYA'LL...
MISTER MORISATO...

...DON'T WORRY. MISS BELLDANDY WILL BE BACK SOON.

WHY DON'T WE JUST HAVE LUNCH?

I THOUGHT I FELT SOMETHING... A TRACE OF POWER...

!

URD ...?!

HEH HEH

HELPING OUT THE HELPLESS...

MAKES ME FEEL *SO GOOD!*

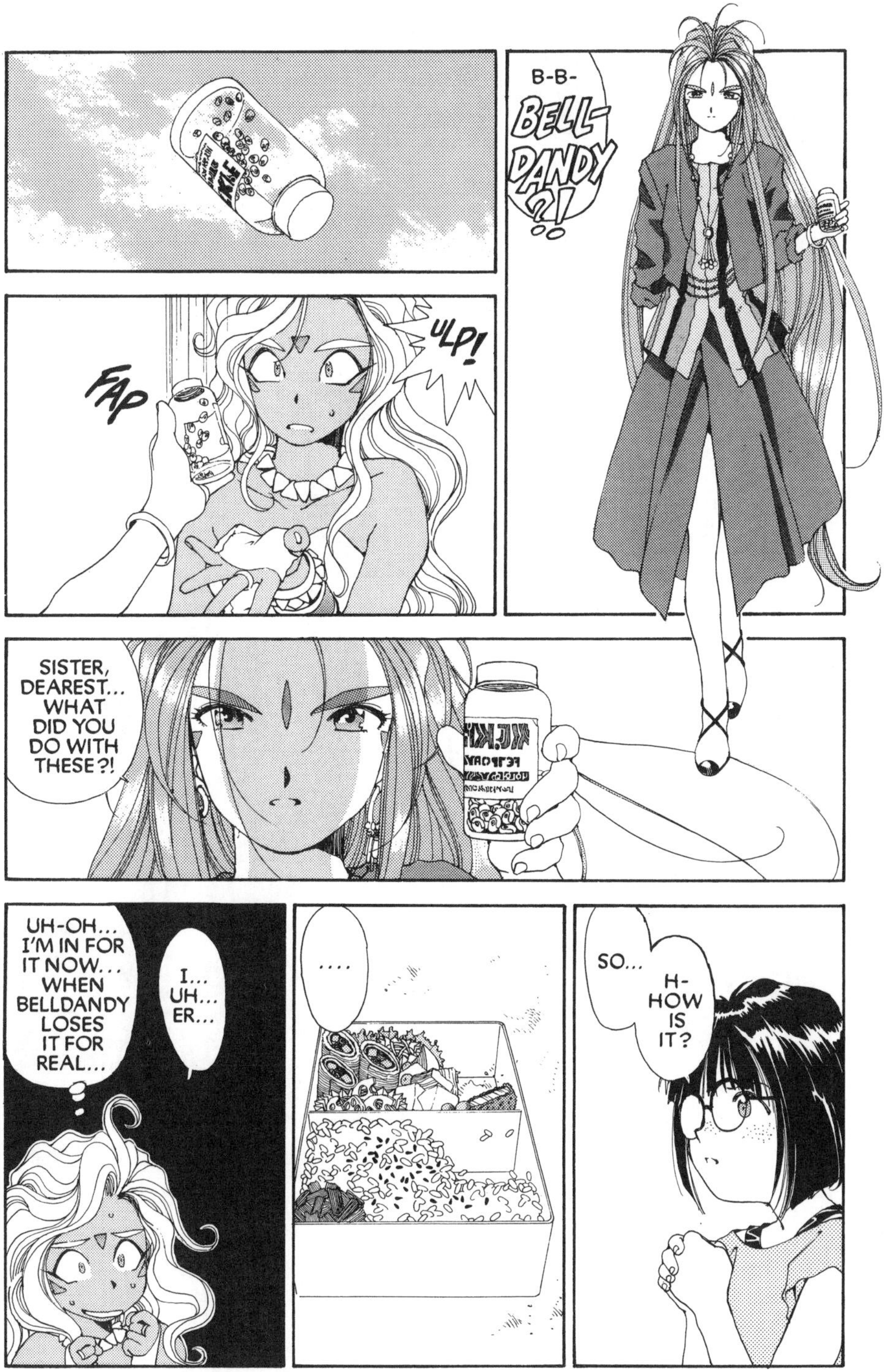
FAP
ULP!
B-B-
BELL-DANDY?!
SISTER, DEAREST... WHAT DID YOU DO WITH THESE?!
UH-OH... I'M IN FOR IT NOW... WHEN BELLDANDY LOSES IT FOR REAL...
I... UH... ER...
....
SO...
H-HOW IS IT?

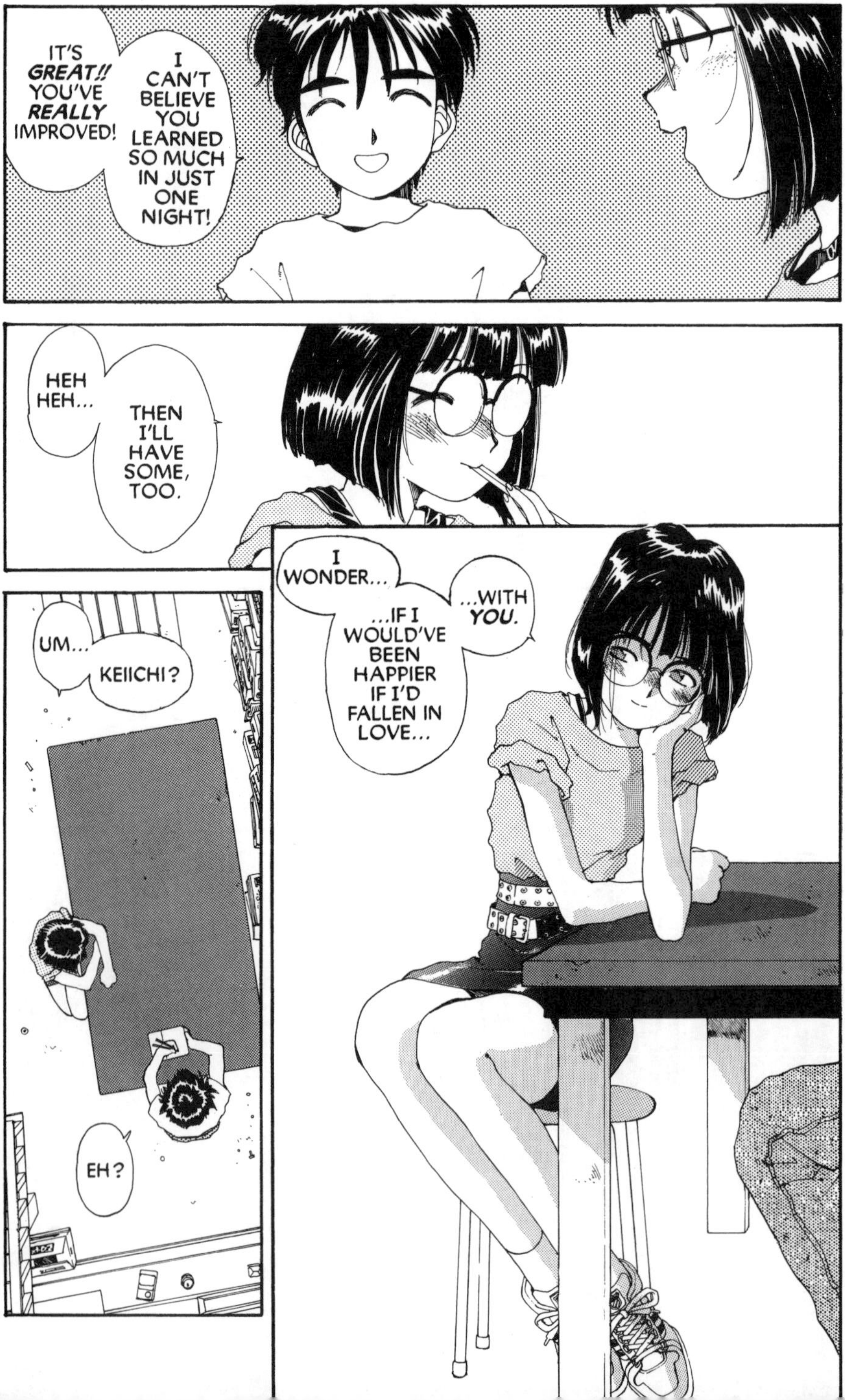
IT'S GREAT!! YOU'VE REALLY IMPROVED!
I CAN'T BELIEVE YOU LEARNED SO MUCH IN JUST ONE NIGHT!
HEH HEH...
THEN I'LL HAVE SOME, TOO.
UM...
KEIICHI?
EH?
I WONDER...
...IF I WOULD'VE BEEN HAPPIER IF I'D FALLEN IN LOVE...
...WITH YOU.

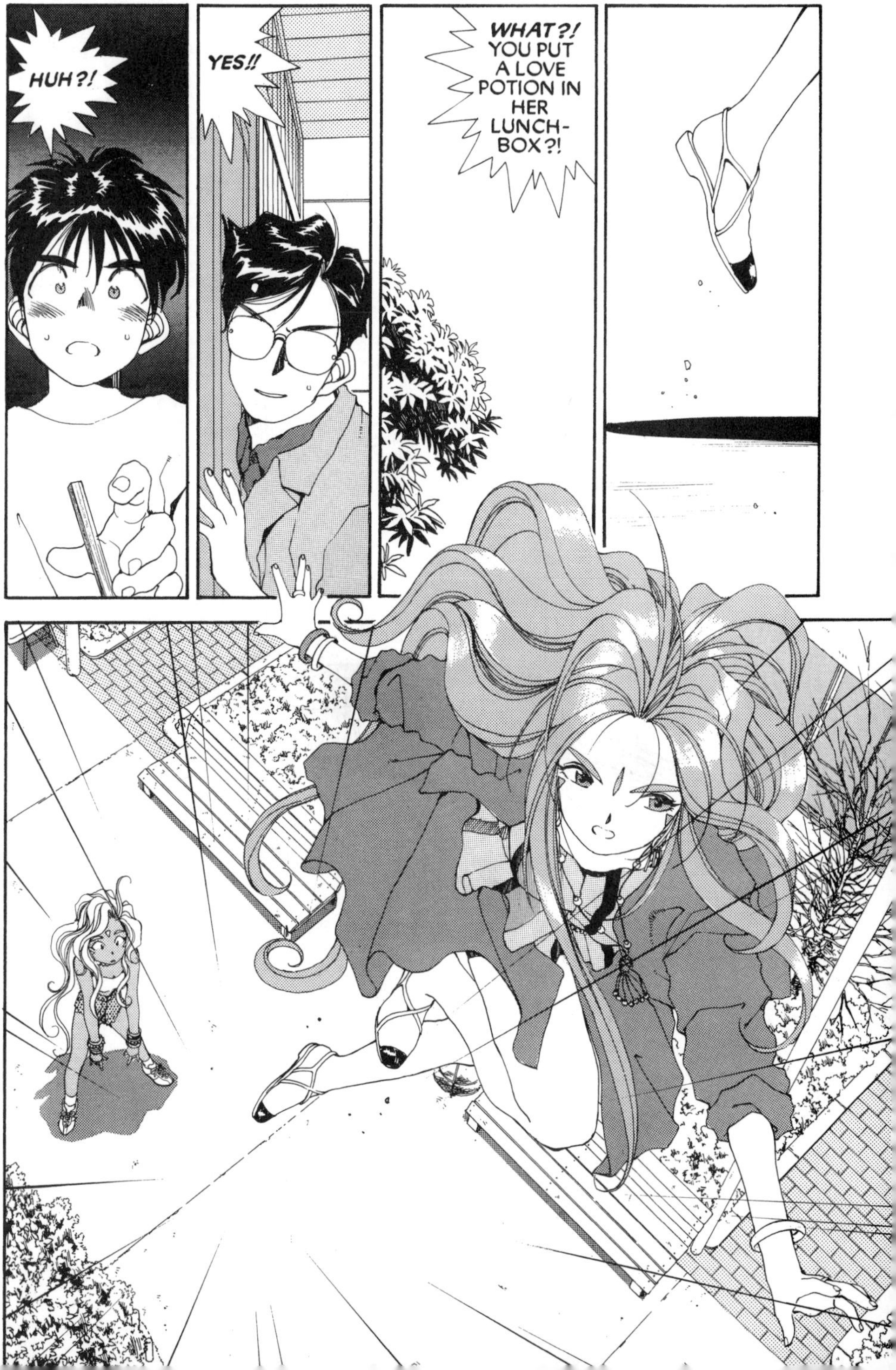
HUH?!
YES!!
WHAT?! YOU PUT A LOVE POTION IN HER LUNCH-BOX?!

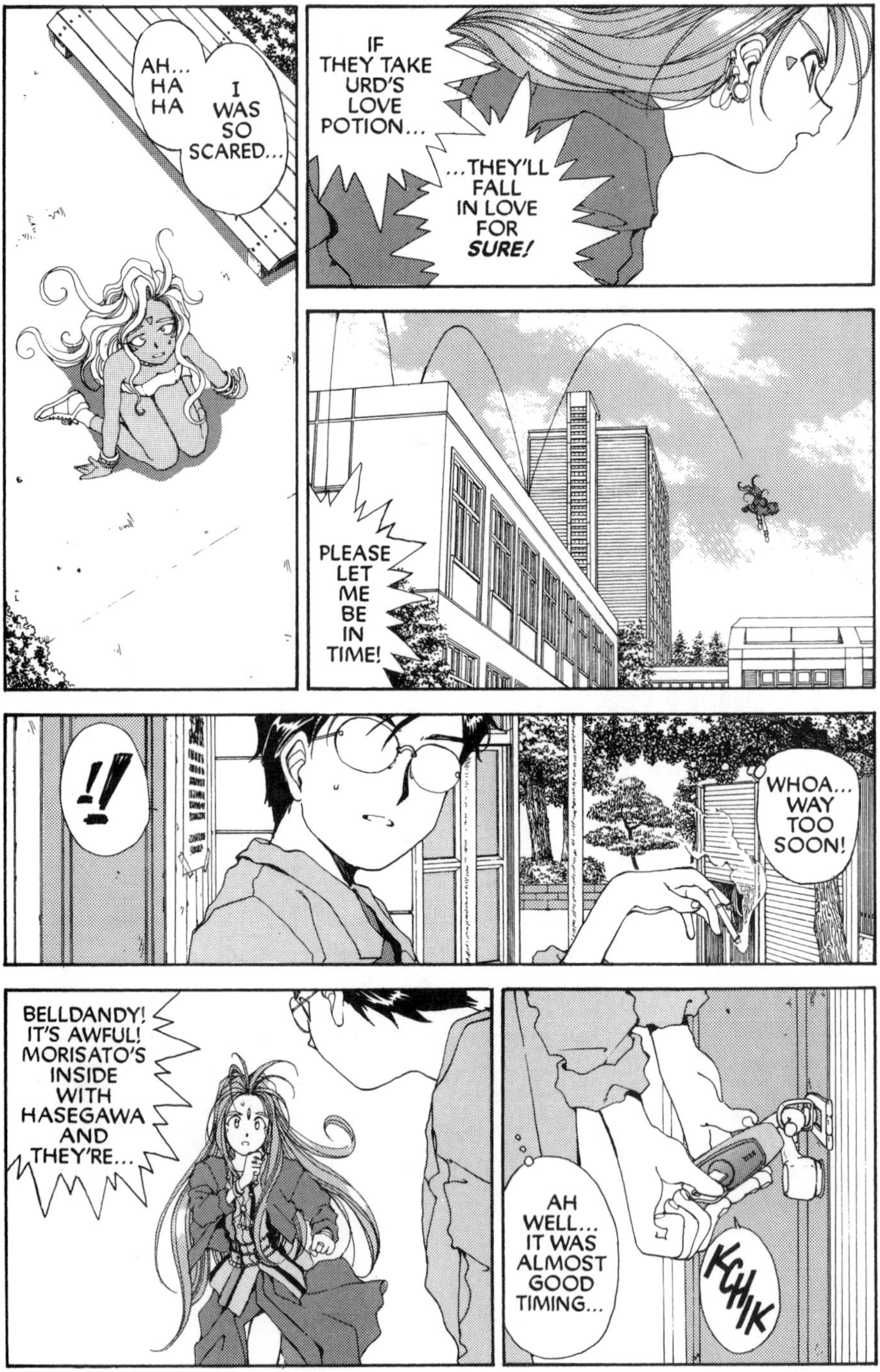
AH... HA HA
I WAS SO SCARED...
IF THEY TAKE URD'S LOVE POTION...
...THEY'LL FALL IN LOVE FOR SURE!
PLEASE LET ME BE IN TIME!
!!
WHOA... WAY TOO SOON!
BELLDANDY! IT'S AWFUL! MORISATO'S INSIDE WITH HASEGAWA AND THEY'RE...
AH WELL... IT WAS ALMOST GOOD TIMING...
KCHIK

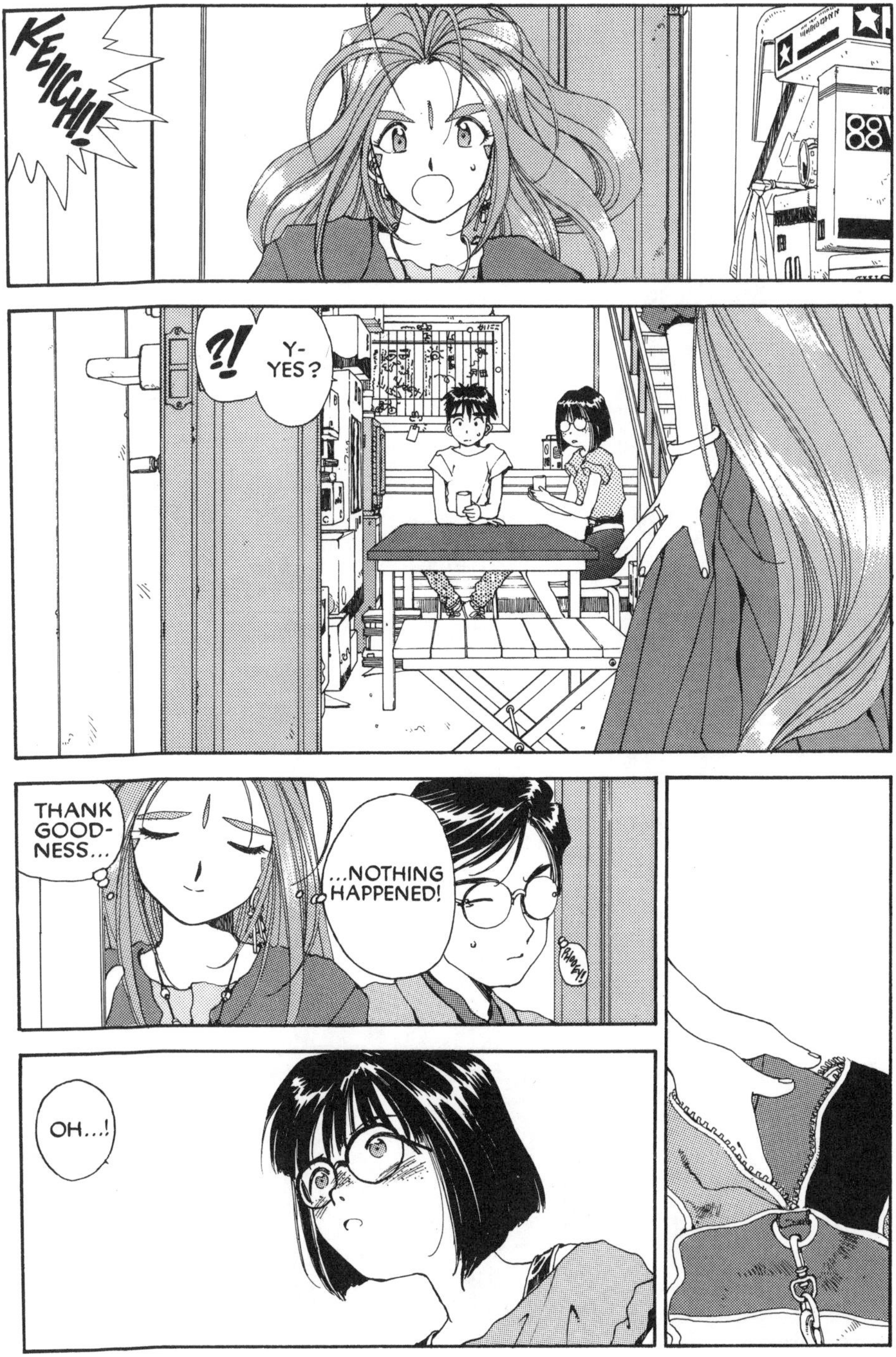
KEICHI!
?!
Y-YES?
THANK GOODNESS...
...NOTHING HAPPENED!
OH...!

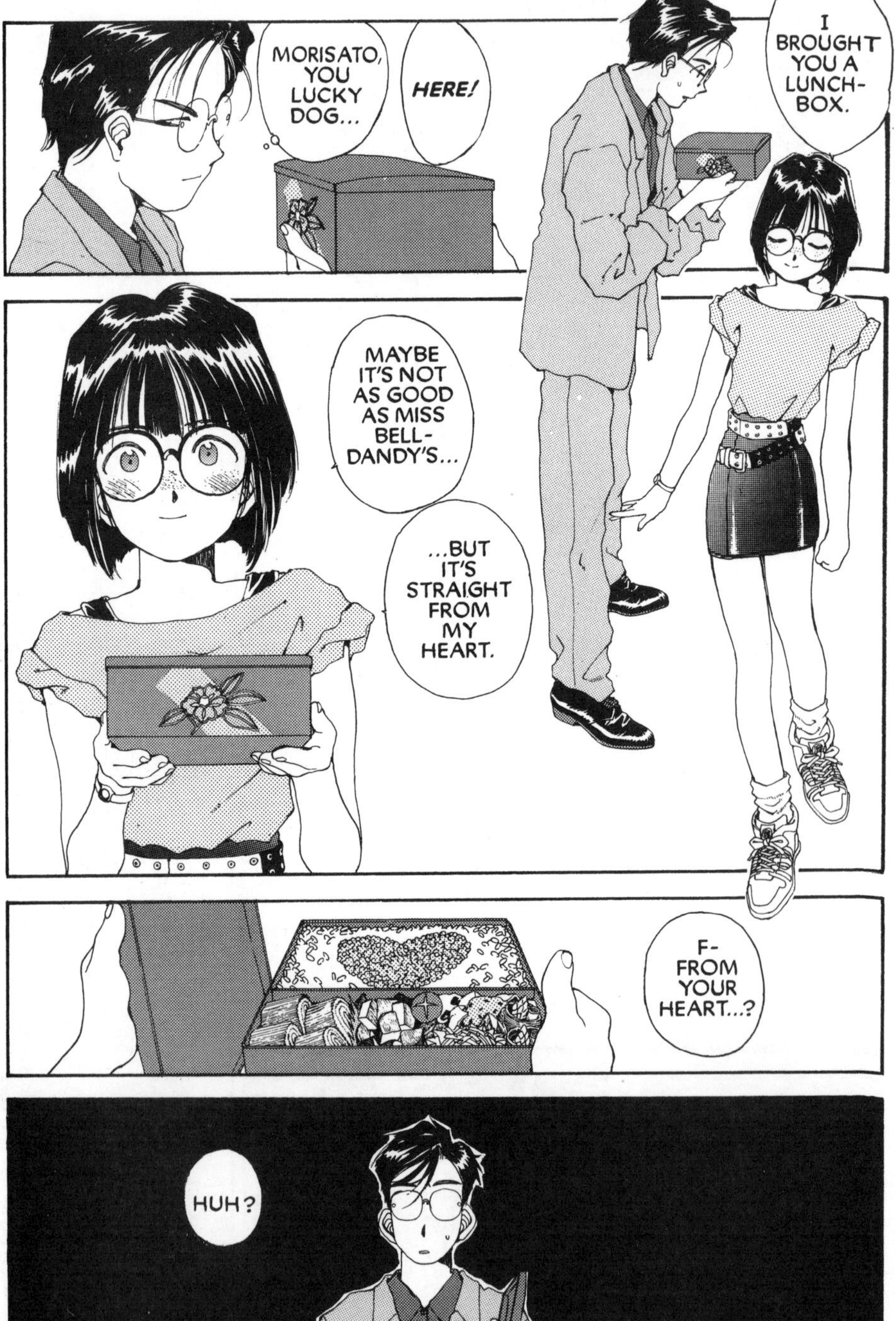
MORISATO, YOU LUCKY DOG...
HERE!
I BROUGHT YOU A LUNCH-BOX.
MAYBE IT'S NOT AS GOOD AS MISS BELL-DANDY'S...
...BUT IT'S STRAIGHT FROM MY HEART.
F-FROM YOUR HEART...?
HUH?

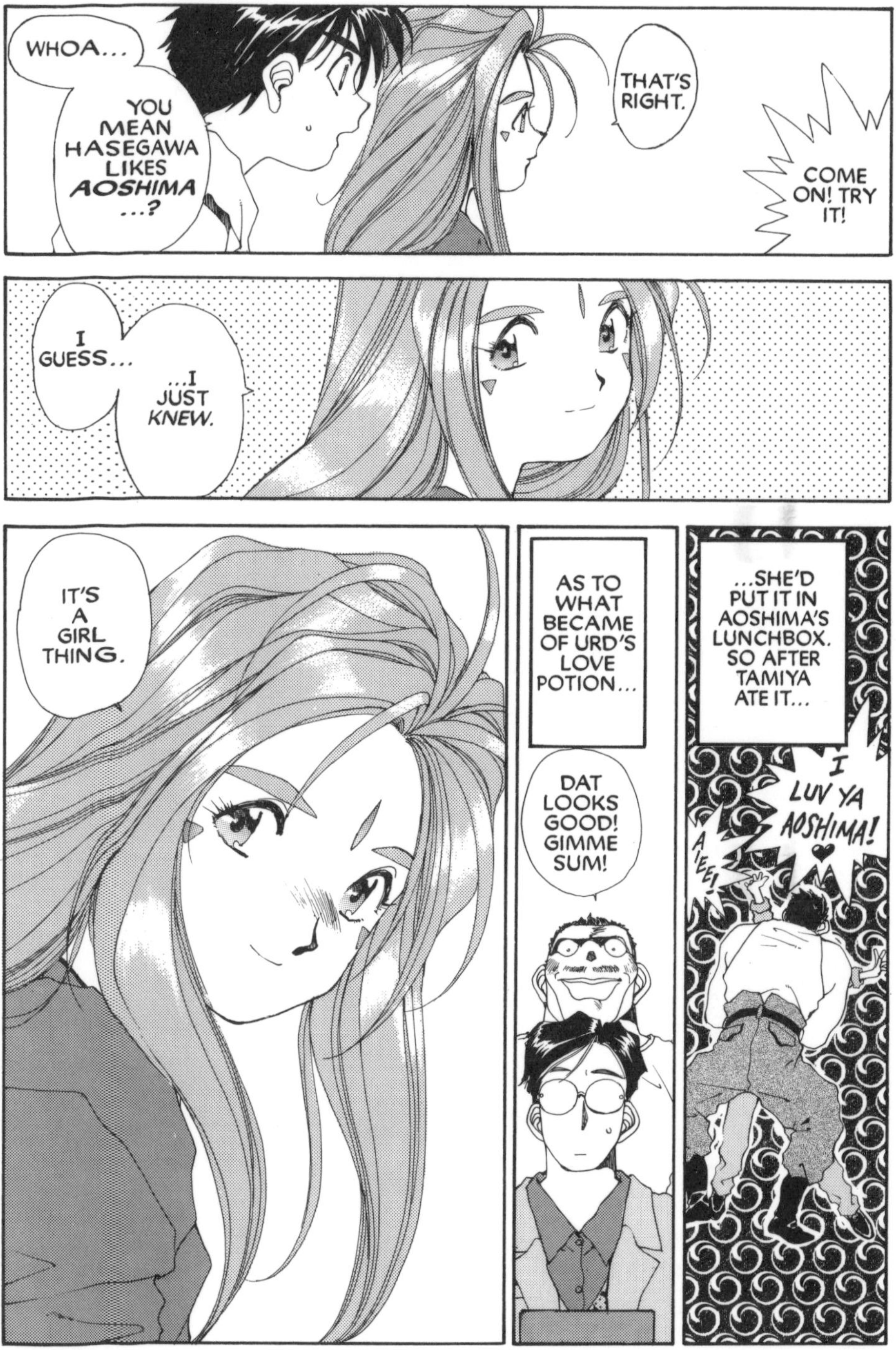
WHOA...
YOU MEAN HASEGAWA LIKES AOSHIMA...?
THAT'S RIGHT.
COME ON! TRY IT!
I GUESS...
...I JUST KNEW.
IT'S A GIRL THING.
AS TO WHAT BECAME OF URD'S LOVE POTION...
DAT LOOKS GOOD! GIMME SUM!
...SHE'D PUT IT IN AOSHIMA'S LUNCHBOX. SO AFTER TAMIYA ATE IT...
I LUV YA AOSHIMA!
AIEE!

KOSUKE FUJISHIMA

Oh My Goddess!

ああっ女神さまっ **Mara Strikes Back!**

While phoning a friend, college student Keiichi Morisato dialed a fateful wrong number and instead received a trio of beautiful sister goddesses. But what looked like the fulfillment of a young man's dreams quickly turned into a roller-coaster ride of magic, mayhem, and madness! This time out, Demon First Class Mara has healed from her defeat at the hands of the Lord of Terror and is ready to unleash a full-scale vendetta against goddess Belldandy and her sisters, and "cat fight" doesn't begin to describe the fury with which the fur will fly! *Oh My Goddess!* is quintessential manga — wild action, screwball laughs, and good, clean, sexy fun!

$14.95 U.S., $22.95 CANADA

DARK · HORSE COMICS ®

www.darkhorse.com